Word Work

Word Work

Surviving and Thriving as a Writer

BRUCE HOLLAND ROGERS

INVISIBLE CITIES PRESS
MONTPELIER, VERMONT

Invisible Cities Press
50 State Street
Montpelier, VT 05602
www.invisiblecitiespress.com

LIBRARY OF CONGRESS CATALOGING-IN-PUBLICATION DATA

Rogers, Bruce Holland.
Word work : surviving and thriving as a writer / by Bruce Holland Rogers.
p.   cm.
Includes bibliographical references.
ISBN 1-931229-17-1 (pbk. : alk. paper)
1. Authorship. 2. Authorship—Psychological aspects. I. Title.

PN 147 .R599 2002
808.2—dc21
2001051671

Book design by Peter Holm, Sterling Hill Productions

SECOND PRINTING

For Eric Witchey, because he'll take it to heart

acknowledgments

If Kent Brewster had not said yes to my harebrained scheme for a column to complement his harebrained scheme for a magazine, these chapters would not have been written. Who would have thought that "Staying Alive" and *Speculations* would continue for so many years? At various times, the columns were edited by Sasha Miller, Kent Brewster, Denise Lee, and Susan Fry, for whose contributions I am grateful. My students at the University of Illinois and in the Flatiron Writer's Workshop asked questions that became chapters, especially Edwina Mayer, Paul Wood, and Philip Brewer. I've learned a lot about writing from my colleagues in the Northern Colorado Writers Workshop, the Eugene Professional Writers' Workshop (www.wordos.com), Kate Wilhelm and Damon Knight's monthly Eugene workshops, and Bovine Smoke West. The Friday Poetry Lunch Circle writes poetry about as often as the ladies of Poker Night actually played poker, but we do eat lunch and talk and the other members—Holly Arrow, Leslie What, Nina Kiriki Hoffman, Martha Bayless, and Ray Vukcevich—help me end my workweek on a high note. At about the same time that I started writing my "Staying Alive" columns, Wil McCarthy founded a group for writers who were at a similar early stage in their careers. The Edge Group has been a continuing source of information, encouragement, and sorority. (I want to say *fraternity,* but the women outnumber the men.) Many thanks to Wil and to Sean Stewart, Sage Walker, Kathy Goonan, Linda Nagata, Valerie Freireich, and Maureen McHugh. Other writers whom I pestered for insight (sometimes without them even knowing it) include Jerry Oltion, Kathy Oltion, Kristine Kathryn Rusch, Dean Wesley Smith, David Bischoff, Billie Sue Mosiman, Beverly Suarez-Beard, K. D. Wentworth, Kevin J. Anderson, Alan Rodgers, Mark Anthony, Jean Auel, M. Shayne Bell, Susan Kroupa, Rick Wilber, Laurel Winter, Mark Rich, Martha Soukup, Amy Sterling Casil, Jane Yolen, Gregory Feeley, David Dvorkin, Alis Rasmussen, Harry Turtledove, Owl Goingback, ElizaBeth

Gilligan, George Guthridge, Howard Hendrix, James Patrick Kelly, Bruce Taylor, Michael Swanwick, Kay Kenyon, Pete D. Manison, Teri McLaren, Carla Montgomery, John W. Randal, Meg Turville-Heitz, Cynthia Ward, M. K. Wren, and Lois Tilton. There are others whose conversational contributions I am failing to acknowledge by name, but I am no less grateful to them. Janet Asimov kindly helped me to track down a most elusive citation. Dr. Sara Hodges is my emergency backup social psychologist. A special thank-you to Alan M. Clark, who is always just a phone call away and doesn't seem to mind when I call for no good reason and whose dining room table is my writing desk of last resort. Damon Knight read the book manuscript and made helpful suggestions. My agent Shawna McCarthy found an excellent publisher in Invisible Cities Press, and Joel Bernstein exhibited the perfect balance between a demanding editorial nature and an agreeable one. Thanks also to Rowan Jacobsen, Peter Holm, and Emily Webb. I owe much to the books listed in the bibliography, most especially to *Wishcraft*, the star I have steered by for twenty years.

contents

Part Two: *Writing As If It Mattered*

Part Three: *Step-by-Step*

Part Six: *Other People*

Writing as Passion and Path

"Do you know why I'd like to do what you do?" The woman addressing me at the party was a scientist. She was happy with her work, with the rewards of her career, but she had just confessed this secret longing. "I'd like to write fiction," she said, "because I can't think of anything that could be a more intimate expression of who I am. What you write is like a lover's whisper to the world. And the world listens."

Actually, the world doesn't listen to my stories with the rapt attention I crave, but this woman at least had the right metaphor: a lover's whisper. She understood writing as passion. When it comes to pleasure, writers are selfish and generous at the same time, the way a lover often is. Probably this woman could guess at the aches, the nights of sleepless obsession, the wild flings that are the writing life.

Sometimes when I'm reading my work aloud to an audience, my hands shake and my voice quavers. People who don't know me well may think that I'm trembling with stage fright. I'm not. What I'm feeling as I look from my manuscript to my audience isn't fear. In those first moments of a public reading, if I had the courage to speak what was in my heart, I would say to my listeners, men and women, young and old, "Now, with these words, I am going to make love to you all."

Right now, writing those words for this introduction, I feel embarrassed to make such an admission. Embarrassment, too, is part of the flush of excitement and fear that comes with a public reading. Being a writer means risking self-exposure, means daring to be embarrassed by what I find myself sharing with a room full of strangers, with the world.

It may be embarrassing, but it's true: Reading my work aloud is intimate and a bit erotic. When my audience laughs in the story's funny places, or when I feel the whole room go still during a poignant scene, all the people touched by my words are touching me in return.

But it isn't only in these public moments that I feel such passion. Alone in my study, thinking of exactly the right word for exactly the right sentence, I cry out loud, with a lover's exultation, "Yes! Yes! Yes!"

Or writing a loose and sloppy draft to discover what I have to say, I find myself surprised by what emerges from my words. Some idea, some startling image, some character arrests my attention and I find myself staring at what I've just done, fascinated. In love.

Writing is my passion.

Writing is also my discipline, my path. Like meditation, it absorbs my attention. Immersed in the problem of the next sentence, I lose track of my anxieties and fears. I am here now. And when the writing is not so absorbing, when I am distracted and troubled, the demands of the path at least keep me in motion and give a shape to my hours. Every day, I write.

Someone once asked Charlie Parker if he had religion. "Yes," he said. "I am a devout musician." As for me, I am a devout writer. Writing reminds me that I'm alive and must pay attention to living. The practice of making stories wakes me up to my own experience because wherever I'm stuck or having trouble, the next thing I see, the next person I talk to, the next book I read may contain the answer to my difficulty. Writing is as big as the world, and writing demands that I open wide to let that world in.

All of this makes the writer's lot sound pretty blissful. It can be. But passion, like any emotion, is delicate. It can be crushed. Like a lover, a writer can be spurned. "What you write is like a lover's whisper to the world," said the scientist. But what if the world turns away? What if the work of your heart brings rejections from editors, harsh criticism from your peers? What if the work you finally manage to publish is savaged by the critics? Or ignored?

Some writers will say, "You've just got to get tough. Harden your heart. This is a business." But if you're like me, a hard heart denies everything that gave you passion in the first place.

Even if your passion never faltered, there would still be other obstacles on your path. Writing takes time, and our lives are full of other demands. We may dream of making a living with our writing, but the rent needs paying whether the next book sells or not. Our romantic partners may not understand our priorities or a writer's odd habits. We doubt ourselves, are paralyzed with procrastination, feel blocked or at a loss for ideas. Sometimes we just get tired.

I've been there. I have felt the flame of my passion go out. I have fallen or been knocked off the path. I have stopped writing. And I have always started again.

The chapters in this book were originally published as columns in the writing magazine *Speculations*. From falling down frequently, I knew a lot about getting back up, and I was happy to share what I knew with the magazine's readers. But *Speculations*, devoted mostly to writers of fantasy, science fiction, and horror, has a small circulation. I wanted the columns to give advice and comfort to writers of other kinds of fiction as well as poetry and nonfiction. For all writers, the emotional, spiritual, and logistical struggles are much the same.

Sometimes in this book I will seem to contradict myself. But as Walt Whitman wrote, "Do I contradict myself? Very well, I contradict myself. I am large. I contain multitudes." The writing life is large, and it contains multitudes of truths that are sometimes at odds with one another. Mere inconsistency doesn't make something untrue.

You won't find anything in these pages about marketing your work. The only chapters about technique address not what you put on the page but *how* you get anything onto the page at all. There's very little here that will show you how to write better. Instead, this is a book about how you can more thoroughly, more happily, more productively *be* a writer.

Word Work is not, in the end, a book about the work you produce. It's a book about you. It's a book about how you can be more of what you want to be.

1. *a further introduction*
Hunters and Farmers

I'm having a hard time getting this chapter started. When I was jotting notes, I noticed that the plastic laminate on my lapboard needed gluing. It's needed gluing for a long time, but I only think about it when I'm *using* the lapboard. Today I set aside my notebook and got out the glue.

After I got back to work, my wife asked if I had some big envelopes. I got up to look, and after I had found her an envelope I noticed that the Kleenex box on my desk was empty. I went into the other room to get a new box, and there I noticed . . .

Well, it doesn't matter what I noticed next. I'm always noticing something. Sometimes it's something in my external world, like the lapboard, but it can also be a compelling thought or daydream. I'm spacey. I read slowly because I often have to reread; some word in the text starts me thinking about something else, and I'm off in my own ideas while my eyes keep scanning the page. In conversation I may actually hear only half of what the other person says. In high school I got really sick of hearing my friends say, "Earth to Bruce, come in Bruce."

Drifting attention is something that everyone has to some degree. But for those of us with attention deficit disorder, this distractibility is a key feature of our personalities. Indeed, I prefer to think of ADD as a personality type rather than a "disorder." ADD creates some problems, but it provides benefits as well.

In *ADD: A Different Perception,* Thom Hartmann refers to people with ADD as Hunters and those without as Farmers. He suggests that people with ADD may have actually had a competitive advantage in hunting societies where a "flash of motion at the periphery of [the hunter's] vision might be either the rabbit that he needed for lunch or the tiger or bear hoping to make lunch of him. If he were to focus too heavily on the trail, for example, and therefore miss the other details of his environment, he would either starve or be eaten."

But in the more recently evolved farming societies, a distractable mind became a disadvantage. When the conditions were right for

4

planting, "a farmer couldn't waste his day wandering off into the forest to check out something unusual he had noticed: he must keep his attention focused on that task at hand, and not be distracted from it."[1]

Thus, those of us with ADD are easily distracted Hunters in a world of steady Farmers.

Actually, a mix of people with Hunter and Farmer traits would be useful in any culture, so I find Hartmann's theory oversimple. But I like his terminology. Not only does it relieve us of the judgmental "disorder," but it also gets rid of the misleading "attention deficit." As any Hunter can tell you, the problem for us isn't that we can't pay attention. It's that we pay attention to *everything*.

Writing is the sort of occupation that's likely to attract Hunters, so I'm writing this chapter in part to say to my readers, "Is this you?" For me, finding out I have ADD helped me see a meaningful pattern in lifelong frustrations.

But there's more to the Hunter/Farmer metaphor than giving a deeper meaning to a medical diagnosis. I know quite a few people who don't fit the whole diagnostic profile of ADD, but who are clearly more Hunter than Farmer. Furthermore, writers need to be both Hunters and Farmers. Just as there are techniques that Hunters can use to thrive in a world dominated by Farmers, so can Farmers learn to hunt. It pays to develop the useful Farmer or Hunter traits that didn't come naturally to you.

What follows is a description of ADD, but it's also an inventory of traits that will help you see if you're mostly Hunter or mostly Farmer.

In general, people with ADD—the Hunters—are distractable, risk-taking, and restless. We may be impulsive or irritable. Our moods shift often and (to others and ourselves) mysteriously. We likely have many projects going at once, but we may finish only the ones that someone *makes* us finish. We change our plans all the time. What we were enthusiastic about last week isn't so interesting now because we're onto something better.

We doodle, but that doesn't mean we're not paying attention. Paradoxically, doodling (or twiddling our thumbs, or having music running in our heads) makes it easier for us to pay attention and not daydream ourselves out of the room altogether.

School was a challenge. Either we were too jumpy to sit still or too dreamy to pay attention. The pace of the classroom seemed painfully slow. If we did well in school, it was probably because we had teachers who let us learn in our own way but gave us real deadlines for projects, with frequent reminders.

We are easily bored but we don't get bored often. That's because the moment something fails to absorb us, we're gone. We channel-surf, and not just when we're watching TV. If we can't find something to think about, we'll find something to worry about. Hunters can be great worriers, weaving complicated tapestries of unlikely consequences out of the most innocuous materials. Meanwhile, we're forgetting to take care of details that have real and painful consequences attached.

When I started to sell stories, I probably signed three or four contracts before I read one. I looked at the seven-page contract for an anthology not too long ago and rationalized that I really didn't need to dither about all those unlikely-to-be-exercised subrights. Some bad contracts have bitten me, but I remain antsy and impatient about reading new ones. I have to force myself to sit down and read, clause by clause, all the way through.

We Hunters are often creative. Creativity is practically a diagnostic (though only one of many) for ADD, but we have more ideas than follow-through. And we're either disorganized or have had to work really hard to achieve some organization in our lives. We procrastinate, though we may not be aware that we're procrastinating while we're doing it. It's just that the day gets away from us one little thing at a time and bedtime comes and the project hasn't materialized. Again.

On the other hand, we can concentrate powerfully on something that intrigues us, something that offers continual challenges. I am easily distracted as I feel my way into writing the beginning of a short story, but once the draft is under way, just *try* calling me to dinner. This creates problems of another sort. We're often late because we were doing something else before the appointment and we had a hard time shifting gears. But we might also be late because once we started on our way to the meeting there were all these fascinating distractions along the way.

All in all, we show great promise and have shown it for years. If only we could "get it together."

Farmers, on the other hand, have it together. They find it easy to do one thing at a time. From kindergarten, Farmers fit right in to the social structure of school, and that easier fit has continued into adult institutions. They can easily stand to wait their turn to see the bureaucrat behind the counter without being antsy or escaping into a daydream. Some Farmers enjoy *being* the bureaucrat behind the counter.

Farmers know right where their tools are. They plan a project, take it step by step, and clean up when they're done. Farmer emotions have a lot to do with what's going on right in front of them at the moment. When you have a conversation with a Farmer, she is right there with you, hearing every word you say.

Creative Farmers are probably as good at generating ideas as creative Hunters are, but that's not where they spend their time. A few ideas are enough if you're busy bringing all of them to fruition. Creative Hunters, meanwhile, generate lots of ideas and turn only a small number of them (if any) into finished work.

Farmers are more likely to get work done. I think they are also more likely to get into a creative rut, doing essentially the same work over and over again.

All of this is oversimplification. Not all Hunters manifest ADD in the same way, so what I've written above shouldn't be taken as diagnostic. For those who want a good set of diagnostic criteria, there's one in *Driven to Distraction* by Edward Hallowell and John Ratey.[2] (The last criterion in their list is "Situation not explained by other medical or psychiatric condition," a reminder that diagnosis has to come in consultation with a professional who may see signs that something else entirely is responsible for what seems to you like ADD.)

If you can't know by reading this chapter or even a whole book whether or not you have ADD, you *can* at least determine whether you are more Hunter-like or more Farmer-like. Knowing that, you can change the way you work to put more Farmer steadiness or more Hunter flexibility into your life.

The suggestions I make below will make sense for some Hunters or Farmers, but not for all of them. One successful writer who read this chapter and suspected that he was a Hunter told me that he rarely met a deadline, ever. Deadlines did not spur him to work. He also said that he never made lists and found the whole notion of list-making to be stultifying and icky. In short, try what looks interesting or helpful, but don't take these suggestions as a prescription.

Some suggestions, then, for Hunters:

1. **Have deadlines.** Hunters need deadlines with real consequences to keep them focused. For me, a deadline
   that has an editor standing behind it always does the
   trick, because I'm afraid of damaging my career.
   However, invented consequences can work as well as
   natural ones. Attach a social or financial consequence
   to your deadline so that failing to meet it would cost
   you something you don't want to lose. Fear helps keep
   Hunters on track.

2. **Make lists.** Prioritize. Do the things with the highest
   priority first. When you're distracted by something
   that you think you need to do right now, look at your
   list. Is this really a higher priority? Probably not. Add it
   to the bottom of the list and get back to your priority
   work. Make a permanent list for things you need to do
   routinely like mailing out manuscripts that have been
   returned.

3. During work time, **use environmental cues** to remind
   you of your focus. When my third-grade teacher sent
   home the umpteenth note about my daydreaming, my
   father sent me back to school equipped with a muted
   kitchen timer. He had packed cotton balls around the
   bell. I was to reset the timer every five minutes, and
   whenever it went off, it reminded me to return my wandering attention to the classroom. Instead of a timer,
   you can use visual cues in your work area to draw your
   attention and remind you to stay on task. I often light
   a candle when I start to work. Every time I look at it, it
   reminds me that I'm supposed to be writing.

4. **Have a buddy.** Chapter 23 covers this in some detail. In
   addition to setting goals and coaching your progress—
   a buddy's primary duties—he or she can also screen
   your business decisions. Talk over your contract with
   your buddy, for example. Pick a buddy who's got some
   solid Farmer qualities.

5. **Let go of low-priority projects.** You have more ideas than you can bring to fruition. Select the best ones and drop the rest. Do it often. New ideas will keep appearing like kudzu.

6. **Ritualize. Schedule.** Let go of that fear that you're killing your spontaneity if you force yourself into a routine. You have spontaneity to spare. Scheduling part of the day won't kill that, so get to the desk at the same time every day.

7. **Consider medication.** This last one is only for the Hunters who are actually diagnosed with ADD. I've been prescribed very small doses of Ritalin, a stimulant that, paradoxically, slows down my racing mind. I take the drug only when I need to concentrate, and its effect on me is subtle but very helpful. It doesn't interfere with my creativity. However, some Hunters who have learned to be productive with multitrack minds actually feel dulled by a drug that narrows their focus, so medication isn't for everyone who has ADD.

Advice to Farmers is harder for me to offer. I've spent my life trying to figure out how to survive as a Hunter, and Farmers seem to me to live a charmed life. However, my life has more surprises in it than does the typical Farmer's, and my guess is that what Farmers may need is more of the unexpected. If you want to cultivate the Hunter in you, here are some suggestions:

1. The next time you're working on a story, do some **random research.** With the story half-written, go to the library, wander around, and pull two random volumes from the shelves. Read a page or two from the middle of each, taking notes. Now finish the story incorporating in some way something from the pages you selected. What you use might be tone, technique, or subject matter.

2. Try **reading and writing in some new genres.** If you write SF, read the fiction in the *New Yorker* and try

writing a *New Yorker* story. Or write poetry or a play, not because you're likely to find a ready audience or success in an area that's new to you, but because trying something new can open you up to new possibilities in your usual genre.

3. **Procrastinate.** Experiment with what it feels like to finish something at the last possible minute. If that feels too dangerous and unnatural, then try writing something much more quickly than you would ordinarily write it. Or much more slowly.

4. If you ordinarily plan your writing, try writing something with **no plan at all.** What you end up with may be garbage. That's worth risking now and then as an exercise in flexibility.

5. If you write one thing at a time, **try writing two at once,** alternating between them more frequently than seems wise. The more different the kinds of writing, the better. Splitting your focus can produce an interesting perspective on both projects.

Finally, as you work to balance your Farmer nature with your Hunter nature, consider collaborating with a writer of the other type. An externalized collaboration may help you to integrate internally. You may each gain a deeper understanding of your work habits by seeing how much they contrast with someone else's. Collaboration is tricky, and working with a writer whose method is very different may not yield a finished work that either of you is happy with, but you may return to your solo efforts with an expanded notion of the possible tools and procedures for writing.

My original ending for this chapter went like this:

"I've been sitting here for five minutes trying to think of a good close for the chapter. I'm only thinking about the problem off and on because there's an interesting bird in the backyard. I think it's a scrub jay. Where did Holly put those binoculars? I'll find them if it takes me the rest of the day."

This is literally true. (If you must know, it took me twenty minutes to find the binoculars.) But as my editor pointed out, this ending implied that having ADD is an excuse for doing things half-assed. Whether you're a Hunter or a Farmer, what matters is that you exploit your supposed weaknesses in a way that makes them as useful as your strengths.

The scrub jays that distracted me as I wrote this chapter eventually made their way into a short story called "With His Own Wings." It appeared in an anthology, *Elf Magic*.[3] If I weren't part Hunter, I might not have noticed those birds at all. If I weren't part Farmer, I might never have finished the story in which they appear.

Part One
Getting Started

2

The Difficulty of Beginning

I'm an anxious writer in any case, but no part of the writing process makes me sweat like the moment when I sit down to write the first sentences of a novel or story . . . or a chapter like this one, for that matter. I may have stacks of notes and a complete outline—a detailed map of the literary territory I intend to cross. Yet when it's time to set out on the journey, I freeze up. I brood, sometimes about the first sentence but more often about the state of my career, the condition of my bank account, or the countless more interesting projects I could be working on instead.

Faced with the need for a first sentence, I find all of my worst habits getting the upper hand. I review my notes, turn on the computer, and check my e-mail. I call up the word processor and stare at the screen while worrying about the cat. Is she getting enough exercise? I find her sleeping on the couch and coax her into playing with a string. I go back to look at my notes again. Then I check my e-mail. I have a snack. I have another snack. I see a spider, catch it in a drinking glass, and set it free outside. Finally, I sit down at my desk, roll up my sleeves, look over my notes one last time, and check to see if anyone's sent me e-mail.

This difficulty with beginnings is persistent, even during times when I'm generally not succumbing to procrastination. What is it that makes first sentences so hard?

According to some writers, the problem is one of inertia. When you go from note-taking to composition, you're shifting from analytical thinking to imaginal thinking. You stall because you have to stop and change jobs. When you were outlining, you were working with general ideas and vague representations. Now you have to start moving specific words into sentences and concrete images into scenes. A resting body tends to remain at rest, and the same may be true for a resting imagination. In this view, the imagination for creating a scene is different from the imagination you used to outline. It takes great effort to move words and images when up to now you've been moving only ideas.

This is a reasonable explanation, to some extent. Indeed, inertia helps to explain how much easier things get after the first sentences. A moving body tends to stay in motion. Once I've got the action moving a little bit, I'm out of my worst agony. (Being able to discriminate between degrees of agony is an asset to writers. "How did the writing go today?" "It was a little less agonizing than yesterday.")

If we go back one step earlier in the writing process, however, we'll see a flaw in this inertia model. Long before I outline a story, I daydream parts of it. I imagine the characters, the situations, the scenes. At some point I shift from such imaginal daydreaming to some analytical note-taking. That transition is always easy. In fact, as I develop a story idea I'm often switching rapidly between analytical and imaginal thinking. Since the transition between modes is so easy in this earlier stage, why should it be so much harder to leap into the imaginal thinking of actual composition?

I don't think that the shift between modes of thought is the problem. Inertia is a decent metaphor for explaining a small part of why it's hard to begin drafting, but the more powerful force at work is something more basic. The more powerful force is . . . terror.

Every phase of creation prior to the first sentences, whether daydreaming or cataloging character traits or outlining, is provisional. But the first sentences are momentous. Even though we know we can change them later, there's still a seeming fixity to them. Before, we were just fooling around. We were preparing to write. Now we are finally engaged in what most people would consider to be the real work of Actually Writing. We have *begun*.

It's as if writing were a high dive, and during the earlier stages we were just climbing the ladder. Now we're up there on the platform, curling our toes over the edge and looking at the water far below and all the people who are watching to see whether we execute a perfect one-and-a-half triple twist or break our ribs with a belly flop. All the fears common to writers seem to focus on this moment. It's show time.

I am extraordinarily gifted with neuroses, even for a writer, so my list of fears at such moments is a long one, especially when I'm facing a novel. I worry that this work I'm about to begin won't sell, that I'll slide deeper into debt. I worry that I'm not going to be able to keep track of all the details of the story and characters. It's all going to end up as a confused mess.

Or maybe not. Maybe the book will be good enough to be published, which is worse, of course, because my enemies will read it and find all its flaws. Or my family will read it and be wounded by it. Or readers will find a subtext that reveals my secret self, or allows them to invent one. "Every line of this book stinks of the author's racism and misogyny."

The fears that get to me the most are akin to dissertation fears. Students facing the necessary first sentence of a dissertation know that the limitless potential they've had as students is now going to be reduced to the limited reality of what they actually write. It's the desire to prolong the feeling of potential magnificence that keeps them from committing the first inadequate, disillusioning line.

Similarly, whatever novel I finish now is likely to become my "first" novel under my own name. Yes, I have finished three unpublished novels. I have sold three novels written under a pseudonym. But whatever novel I finish next is likely to be my "first novel" from the marketplace's perspective, and like the dissertation writer whose dreams of genius will be limited by the actual dissertation, my identity as a novelist will in some sense be fixed by the first book published under my own name. What if I've chosen the wrong book? What if this book is the beginning of a marketing dead end? Will I have to publish future work under a pseudonym, hit the *reset* button of my career?

If you think this is all terribly silly, you're right. Writers make choices about what to include, what to leave out, how to solve thousands of little technical challenges, and which book to write next. With hindsight, some of those choices will come to look like bad decisions. But the worse decision by far is to keep delaying, to avoid the anxiety of deciding by climbing back down the ladder of the high-dive platform.

I know this, and I have known it for a long time. But knowing that a fear is foolish isn't always enough to keep it from shaping our behavior. I have backed down the ladder on several occasions, thinking that I'd go find one that wasn't quite so high. One result, a positive one, is that I've written a lot of short stories. A less positive result is that I have filled notebooks and file folders with notes and research for novels that I decided were less intimidating than the one I'd been just about to start drafting.

Obviously, part of what a writer like me has to do is make a commitment to choose a project and see it through, no matter what. But that still leaves the question: How do those first difficult sentences get written? How do we get past the fear of beginning?

One thing we can do is attack the fear directly. Writing out all the things you're afraid of, cataloging your fears, allows you to see them clearly and sometimes refute them. It can also help to spend a few minutes scribbling down whatever's on your mind, clearing out emotional garbage.

The problem with these steps, though, is that they often become just another delaying tactic. There are days when I haven't written anything but pages of self-analysis confronting my fears.

Better to just jump in, and the way to do that is by Atomizing.

Atomizing a writing project means breaking it down into pieces that are too small to trigger your fear. Instead of jumping off the hundred-foot high dive, you're going to jump from a six-inch block. A writing project can be atomized in terms of time, attention, and ambition.

Atomizing Time. I usually write for about six hours a day. Sometimes, as I'll note in later chapters, I break that time into four ninety-minute sessions. Sometimes I divide the hours between two or three projects.

When I'm facing a first page, though, I often break my work session down to fifteen-minute commitments. I set a timer and tell myself that I'll work on this beginning for just fifteen minutes. At the end of that time, I'll be free to work on a task that makes me less anxious, or I can set the timer again. If I'm so anxious that even fifteen minutes seems like a long time, I'll commit to just five minutes, or even three.

Often, I'll lose myself in the writing once I get started and forget all about the timer. But if not, if the fifteen minutes are a continuous struggle, at least I'm not faced with the prospect of five more frustrated hours. I just have to decide whether or not to continue for another fifteen minutes. Usually I do, but sometimes I switch to a different project.

Atomizing Attention. A novel is like an enormous mosaic. If you confront yourself with the task of cementing ten thousand bits of colored tile to the wall, you're likely to feel overwhelmed. But a mosaic is made by fitting one tile at a time, just as the ten thousand sentences of a novel are written one by one.

You can try to atomize your attention by just *saying* to yourself that you're only going to think about the very first sentence. For some writers, that's enough. But some of us are helped by cues that remind us to think small. Novelists have written first sentences on the backs of envelopes. I've started stories by writing first sentences on sticky notes or in a tiny notebook. Lately, I compose a lot on my little palmtop computer. If I set the font size big enough, the screen shows only forty words at a time, which feels like writing on a small scrap of paper even though the machine has memory enough for a novel or two.

Atomizing Ambition. You have high hopes for this project, and eventually they may be realized. But in the beginning, don't think about writing a flawless novel. Aim for a draft of any quality. For at least the first few chapters, but perhaps for the whole first draft, set aside your notes and research. What you have in your head isn't enough, but it's enough for now because all you're trying to do is get a rough, inadequate version down on the page.

Calvin Trillin starts writing his essays with a draft that he "vomits out" before reviewing his notes. He destroys these drafts as soon as he has proceeded to a second draft. My guess is that knowing that the draft will be destroyed gives him the freedom to write it badly, and knowing that it's bad gives him the motivation to quickly produce the second draft that will let him destroy the first one. In neither of these first two drafts does he have to focus on his ultimate ambition.

(If you try Trillin's trick, you get a Free Bonus Neurotic Fear. What if you die between the first and second drafts? Everyone will conclude on the basis of your horrid draft that someone else must have written the books that you passed off as your own.)

You can also lower your sights by writing not *the* beginning, but *a* beginning. Try to open the first page of your story in four different ways. As you work on any one of the four versions, you'll know that you will probably throw away this version in favor of one of the other versions. The sentences that you're writing right now don't have to carry the full freight of your ambitions. You probably won't use them. At the moment, you're just practicing. Only later will you decide whether any of these practice efforts is worth keeping.

Try to start drafting when you know you haven't done enough research or planning. Many novelists write scenes that they ultimately can't use. So set out to write some of those.

Just as small pieces of paper can remind you that you're focusing your attention on only a few words, the quality or type of materials can limit your ambition. If you're writing with a cheap pencil on crummy paper, how ambitious can you be? If you're dictating your first draft (which is becoming ever more feasible with speech-recognition software), you can't expect the transcript to be deathless prose.

You might find that the opposite trick works, too. I have composed fairy tales using a font and layout that made my first draft look like pages in an expensive book, and I know writers who compose with expensive pens on expensive paper. Both tricks let you ignore questions about the quality of the prose. You're busy writing a page that looks good superficially as pretty marks on nice paper.

By atomizing time, attention, and ambition, you'll work on tasks too small and insignificant to be worthy of your fear. Eventually, you'll have your draft started. You'll have jumped from the high dive. The rest of the job isn't quite as simple as letting gravity take over, but you are finished with what is, for many of us, the most daunting step.

3

Discipline and the Mythical Beast

Writer's Block is a mythical beast.

How do you feel, reading those words? Such a statement is bound to generate an emotional response because most readers will assume that I'm using the word *mythical* to mean "untrue." It looks like I'm taking sides in the old debate about whether Writer's Block is a very real and debilitating psychological monster or simply an excuse for the lazy. But I'm not. I'm using *mythical* in the original sense.

A myth is a richly symbolic story that explains something, and it isn't subject to rational verification like a theory is. If someone hears a myth speak to her, then for her it's a true myth whether there's a shred of verifiable fact in it or not.

What's more, myths support a wide range of competing truths. This is what Claude Lévi-Strauss, the social anthropologist, was getting at when he wrote that all versions of a myth are the "true" version. There's a reason that people tell conflicting stories about the volcano god—did he marry the sea goddess, or did he marry the rain goddess? Both versions were told and retold because the listeners sensed a truth in each.

Writer's Block is a myth with zealous adherents. One group of true believers insists that Writer's Block does not exist. If you feel stymied, they say, you can just put your head down and do the work anyway, and the block will go away. The other true believers are sure that Writer's Block does exist, and that determination and hard work only make the block worse.

They are both right.

Here's some great news: The former camp is right more often. For most of us, most of the time, feeling stymied in our writing has a simple cause. It may be plain and simple inertia—starting *anything* can be hard, whether it's an exercise plan or a short story. It may be a matter of appropriate awe—a novel is so enormous when viewed from the first blank page. It may be a matter of conflicting priorities—you can't start writing because of the long list of *other* things you have to do today, or because you think your spouse is feeling neglected. Maybe the voices of the naysayers (the small-press editor who wrote that insulting rejection, for example) or your own internal voices of doubt are louder than usual today.

Alternatively, you may have sold yourself on the romantic side of Writer's Block. It's so noble to suffer (well, to be *seen* suffering). When you suffer in a very public way, you get some of the glamor of art without all the work.

In any of these cases, you can successfully work your way through the problem. Discipline will get you going again, and a jump start is all you need. Altering your emotional state (see part 5 of this book) can even make the discipline easier to muster.

But there are some versions of Writer's Block that are a bit more serious and don't respond as well to discipline. One is the result of *willpower* coming smack against *won't power*. This is what happens for some writers (some—certainly not all) when they try to force their way across a blank page without much idea of where they're going or how they should proceed. They push themselves to come up with something then and there, and they're miserable the whole while.

Soon, such writers become habituated to misery. That is, every time they sit down at the writing desk, they remember what a miserable time they had during their last writing session, and a part of them quite reasonably refuses to go on. The urge to escape the dreadful Desk of Exsanguination is at least as powerful as their drive to keep working.

Even here, there's some pretty simple advice to apply, and it comes from *A Writer's Time* by Kenneth Atchity: *Never sit down to write until you know what you're going to write.*[1] A corollary to this came from one of my psychology professors, who told me that whenever I was stuck for a next sentence, I should stand up and face away from my writing desk and not sit back down until I had the next sentence in mind.

This is, in fact, an altered-state strategy: You sit down at the desk only when you're in a resourceful state (having a good idea for the next sentence). Soon, the desk becomes the place where your good ideas get poured out, and sitting down at it to write the first sentence makes the next sentence easier.

(This is probably a good time to remind you that we're talking myths here. I think the above is good advice for writers who find that discipline is so painful that it becomes counterproductive. For my part, I prefer Raymond Chandler's myth: One writes by sitting at one's desk for six hours, either writing or staring at the wall. In this version of reality, you write because *not* writing bores you silly.)

The most serious Writer's Blocks, the ones that most defy discipline as a cure, are the blocks that arise from real and important conflicts.

Several paragraphs ago, I dismissed "conflicting priorities" (your spouse feels neglected) as ephemeral blocks you could break through with discipline. But that's not always so. Just how neglected does your spouse feel? Are suitcases piled beside the door, and are the Yellow Pages opened to the section listing ATTORNEYS—MARITAL AND FAMILY LAW? If so, then putting your shoulder to the wheel and getting your four pages written anyway is hardly a wise move. If you try to do just that, is it surprising that you encounter more and more internal resistance?

Some writers are able to put their writing first no matter what else is going on in their lives. No compassion, concern, or responsibility ever touches them—the work is all that matters. They may believe that they have to live this way in order to be successful artists. *Be careful what myths you choose.*

For most of us, lives without our loved ones, without a roof over our heads, without some sense of integrity and fellow-feeling would be miserable indeed. What makes us writers is the need for writing in our lives, but it's not the only need we have.

Sometimes you're blocked because your energies really should be going somewhere else at the moment. At other times the conflicts that seem urgent are only fear or inertia masquerading as something important. This is a tricky call to make, and every writer needs to sort it out for herself again and again. Most days when I have a mania for cleaning out my closet, my best move is to write. But if my whole life feels dreadfully cluttered and it's making me crazy, cleaning out the closet may actually make the writing go much better later on.

Finally, there are blocks that arise from conflicts about your writing itself. This is what happened to me a few years ago when I was collaborating with other writers on an anthology of detective stories set in a fictional city that we had imagined together. I had been with the project from the beginning, helping to map the setting and develop the story arc that all of our stories would contribute to.

I was supposed to write the lead story for the collection . . . and I couldn't. It was as if I were a car with a broken driveshaft. I could rev my engine, talk to the other writers on the project and feel fired up. I could even go through the motions of getting into gear by writing sentences. I altered my state, and I concentrated. I made myself stay at the desk and write. But I couldn't get the wheels to turn. The sentences just wouldn't come together into anything that felt like a story.

This happened at the end of a very productive year of writing stories, including some other detective fiction. I wasn't trying anything I hadn't done successfully before. Why was I stuck?

I spent some time writing about the problem, and I began to see my resistance to writing the story as a signal. For the past two years I had been intending to get to my second novel, but had managed to fill my writing days with short stories instead. That second novel was, in fact, an easy thing to avoid. Every story I had written recently had sold. One of my short stories had even brought me an Edgar Allan Poe Award nomination. My first novel, on the other hand, still languished in slush piles. So I kept writing short stories, staying with what was successful.

To understand why success can go stale, it's useful to think of Abraham Maslow's hierarchy of needs. Some needs are more basic than others, Maslow explained, and we have to satisfy the more basic needs before we feel comfortable pursuing the next ones.

What we all want, ultimately, is self-actualization, the achievement of our full potential. But there are needs that are far more basic, and wherever a basic need isn't fulfilled, the higher-order needs are quickly forgotten. If I'm thirsting for water and someone deprives me of my more basic need for air, I'll forget all about my thirst until I find a way to breathe.

Conversely, once my basic needs are met, I start craving fulfillment of my higher needs. I first want to fulfill my physiological needs, then my needs for safety, then my needs for social interaction and love, then my needs for esteem and prestige, and finally, when I feel secure in these, I will seek actualization of my full creative potential.

Writers have their own hierarchies of needs. For example, I have always wanted to be a novelist *someday*, but in the meantime I have wanted to know that I could get published, that I could make money from my writing, that I could get my byline before a national audience, that I could achieve a measure of recognition in my genre. When I was unpublished, publishing anything, anywhere, was terribly important to me. Only after I had started to feel some confidence that I could publish repeatedly did I think about other achievements.

As my needs for money and recognition have changed, I've taken on and abandoned different kinds of writing, from poetry to erotic letters to *Woman's World* mini mysteries. It hasn't been a tidy progression, but in general I have moved from one kind of writing to another according to what needs I needed to fulfill, going from the most basic drive to publish anything anywhere to higher needs such as publishing in a prestigious national magazine.

The reason I was blocked on the detective story was that I had already satisfied the needs that writing it would satisfy. In fact, short stories had been feeling rather unsatisfying to me for about a year. But I wouldn't quit, because I was good at them. The block was a signal that I had ignored my inner voices too long.

Ultimately, I gave in to this block. I took its message seriously, dropped out of the detective story project, and notified anthology editors that I wasn't interested in entertaining any invitations. These were hard decisions, but they felt right. I got to work on a novel.

After a while my needs changed again. I needed money, and short stories promised a quicker, more reliable sale than continued work on the novel. So I went back to stories. The fact that I changed direction again does not mean that the block was illusory or that my decision to drop stories was the wrong decision. Dropping short stories and picking them up again were both decisions made on the basis of which needs were the most compelling ones at the time.

Some writers get their security, social, and esteem needs met in other ways, and the very first fiction they write is a product of self-actualization. The rest of us work our way to our true calling only one small step at a time, with what may look like steps back as well as steps forward.

Writer's Block may be a signal about a writer's choice of projects, subject matter, or even work habits. If all the writers around you work piecemeal on six projects at once, you may try to work that way yourself.

But if you're a one-thing-at-a-time kind of person, you may only discover the routine that suits you when a six-things-at-once approach leaves you feeling unable to write.

In general, it's a good practice to treat all blocks as emotional noise. Work under the assumption that Writer's Block is an imaginary beast. But when writing through the block doesn't make it go away, pay attention. The rare work stoppages that you can't defeat with enthusiasm and discipline are almost certainly signals that something's amiss in your life, your work habits, or your goals. In that case, work under the assumption that Writer's Block is a real live monster that you ignore at your peril.

4

Procrastination as War

I was still working on this procrastination chapter two days after the deadline. Good thing, too. Would you want procrastination advice from someone who had no firsthand experience? Or from someone who had procrastinated years ago, but could hardly remember the details? I have procrastinated masterfully since childhood. I procrastinated yesterday, and I put off getting to work today. Chances are good that I will procrastinate tomorrow. My credentials are excellent and up to date.

Anyone with my expertise knows that there aren't any cures for procrastination, at least not for genuinely heroic cases like mine. But there are treatments for it, ways to manage the problem so that things, more often than not, get done on time.

Some of my readers, a blessed few of you, won't know what I'm talking about in this chapter. The key to writing for you is, well, just sitting down and writing. You always write exactly what you want to, because . . . whatever else would you write? You've never had to discipline yourself to write. You represent the ideal the rest of us are trying to attain, and I invite you to take a bow now and go away. Skip ahead to another chapter. And wipe that smirk off your face.

In this chapter I'm going to talk about procrastination as a war. In the chapter that follows this one, I'll look at procrastination as a kind of emotional armor. For explaining either model, it helps to introduce two pigs.

Richard Scarry wrote and illustrated a children's book about Pig Will and Pig Won't. Pig Will was helpful and polite and tidy. Pig Won't wasn't. Superficially, these two characters resembled the *Highlights for Children* characters of Gallant and Goofus, a tidy boy and a messy boy who gave etiquette lessons by example, good and bad. But the tone of the "Goofus and Gallant" feature was judgmental—Goofus's misbehavior was supposed to be *shocking*. In the Richard Scarry story, as I remember it, Pig Won't wasn't condemned or reformed. He was still Pig

Won't in the end, Pig Will's equal, and that makes him a better archetype than Goofus.[1]

One way of seeing Pig Will and Pig Won't is as expressions of the superego and the id. Pig Will loves rules and wants to please others. Pig Won't hates rules and wants to please only himself. But I think we can leave Freud out of the equation and see the pigs more simply as expressions of willpower and won't power. Pig Will seeks the benefits in any proposed activity, and Pig Won't avoids the drawbacks.

So the pigs represent dynamic forces, urging us to act or to hesitate. They often struggle, and that struggle is expressed as procrastination.

Procrastination patterns evolve. It happens like this: Writing is an opportunity to succeed, to fail, to change our social standing, to expose our hidden selves. It's risky. So in the beginning, Pig Won't is likely to have the upper hand. We have stated our intention to write, but the force of hesitation is stronger than the force of action.

In this stage procrastination is expressed by long-term delays. External conditions aren't right. We'd like to write, we intend to, but the kids are too young. Free time comes in odd blocks of five minutes here, fifteen minutes there, or half an hour at nap time. That's not enough time to actually *do* anything, right? Or else the office is a mess, it's too small, it's too noisy, or the equipment is antiquated. There are other pressing demands. The writing will come after the move, after the vacation, after the car is fixed. Next year, next month, next week, things will be better.

For me, this stage has often taken the form of thinking that I needed more education. I was going to write after I finished my creative writing degree (which took so much of my time and energy that I didn't have much time for writing anything except for course assignments, or so I said). When I had enough education to be *teaching* the writing courses, then I was going to write as soon as I could afford a reduction in my teaching load. Then when the load was reduced, I was going to write as soon as I had finished absorbing the secrets of the latest how-to-write book.

At some point we're likely to say, "Hey, this is ridiculous! I'm procrastinating! I'm going to put a stop to it right now!" And by an exercise of willpower, we make a pronouncement, insisting, "I am absolutely going to start writing this month." And we move to the next procrastination stage.

Now the procrastination is short term. We've decided, say, to use a week of vacation time for getting the novel started. On the first day, we wake up feeling hopeful. We're going to get so much done, right after this load of urgently needed laundry. And who can write while the dryer's running? It's a beautiful day for January, and fresh air always helps us think. And so on, until we're getting ready for bed, full of resolve that tomorrow will be better.

We've made some progress. The distant future in which we were going to write has come at last. But Pig Will and Pig Won't are skirmishing. Pig Will's intention to write seems more serious now, so Pig Won't puts up some serious resistance to match.

We get through this stage by another act of will and perhaps a rule such as "I write every weekday." Monday comes, and now the advantage tips toward Pig Will. But Pig Won't isn't out of the game. Monday morning, we research. Monday afternoon, too. And Tuesday. The next weekend, we go to a writers' conference and meet some editors and agents. We're finally doing things that look a lot like work and look *almost* like writing. Reading magazines for market analysis, talking to other writers, mailing manuscripts, networking . . . these are all professional activities. But they aren't writing.

When I wrote tie-in fiction for Wizards of the Coast, I sometimes counted hours reading their magazine, *The Duelist*, as writing time. Got to keep up with new-product development, after all! When I saw how unproductive I was as a result of such thinking, I made strict rules for what I could and couldn't do with writing time.

However, the more we try to overcome Pig Won't with rules and strictures, the more Pig Won't resists. The war between the pigs escalates, making ever more stringent rules attractive. At one time, I liked to cite Dean Koontz's self-reported writing schedule, his assessment of how hard one should work early in one's career: "I used to work ten to twelve hours a day, seven days a week, with an occasional day off for some folly or other."[2] I thought my own practice should be as demanding. Now, there are people who write at long stretches like this for pleasure, because they are fully absorbed in their work, but Koontz meant writing with Marine Corps discipline. Hear the disdain for the "folly" of days off? Professionals are always saying to beginners that they must cultivate discipline.

When I was teaching, I liked to repeat the Koontz sentence to my students, perhaps hoping that it would generate in them the kind of despair it generated in me. Certainly it helped to maintain my superiority as the man who was trying to apply this iron discipline to himself, and it might humble them enough to keep them from asking, "So what time did *you* start writing today, Bruce?"

I *did* attempt twelve-hour days. I berated myself for failing to stay at the desk that long even once.

But I kept at it. Even without twelve-hour days, I made enough rules and cultivated enough discipline to make Pig Will overcome Pig Won't. I gritted my teeth and ground out my pages.

When we get that far, is that victory? We write. But the progression has been one of forcing the other side into silence. The victorious Pig Will oppresses Pig Won't. Pig Won't still wants to be heard, so he fights back with guerrilla tactics. We are writing, but there's enough hesitation still to keep us from writing what we dream of writing. We pursue any paying opportunity that comes along. We earn money, but don't advance our own writing. I've done this in a variety of ways—by writing erotica, *Woman's World* mysteries, or tie-in fiction. For a writer called to such projects, this wouldn't be procrastination. In fact, all through this process, the one way that we know we're procrastinating is by a certain creepy feeling. We aren't satisfied. We're working hard, but this isn't *it*.

At this last stage, I have sometimes tried to push my way through with one last act of will. But Pig Won't and Pig Will are always roughly equal in power. If we're at war with ourselves, victories will be brief. So by an act of will and lots of rules, I could get myself to do my true work for a while. But eventually, Pig Won't would dig in his hooves and I would stop, emotionally stymied, unable to get myself to just do it. Blocked.

If you recognize yourself in this progression, wherever you are in it, I hope you'll give yourself credit for coming as far as you have. Writing the wrong work is much better than never beginning to write at all. Trying to write and experiencing a block is also better than endlessly researching the marketplace. It's possible to get enough work done in the midst of this war to have a decent career.

More satisfying, though, is to arrange a cease-fire between pigs.

Here's an exercise that I've done with some of my students. We did it to identify Heart-Sufficient Goals. As I'll discuss further in chapter 31, Heart-Sufficient Goals are goals that are driven by love and that depend on outcomes you alone control.

Step One: Write down in a sentence or two what would constitute Success As a Writer for you. What accomplishment or action would satisfy you?

Step Two: Assume that you can't have the outcome of Step One. It's unavailable. So what could you have instead that would constitute success? Write that down.

Step Three: Assume that you can't have what you've just written in Step Two. *Now* what would constitute success?

By the third step, all of my students have written down a Heart-Sufficient Goal. A few of them, actually, have written a Heart-Sufficient Goal in the first or second step and have thus had a hard time coming up with a replacement goal. Heart-Sufficient Goals are foundations, and it's difficult to go much deeper than the foundation.

But there is a step beneath the Heart-Sufficient Goal. It's a step that leads not to willpower or to won't power, but to *willingness* power.

Step Four: Assume that you can't have your Heart-Sufficient Goal. Now finish the sentence, "I am willing to be happy anyway, because . . ."

Willingness power is the ability to accept what comes in the absence of discipline or fear, and the first step to exercising it is to identify your most cherished outcome and let it go.

There are other steps. Willingness power is also the power to examine the urges of both pigs, to accept those urges, and, again, to release them.

I said earlier that Pig Will seeks benefits and Pig Won't guards against drawbacks. So on a big sheet of paper, try writing down all the benefits that Pig Will wants to claim by getting you to write your most authentic work. (You can draw your pig, too.) It doesn't matter what you think of the benefits—whether you think they're likely or honorable. List everything that Pig Will hopes might come your way as a result of your writing. My list, for instance, includes groupies. Hey, I can dream, can't I?

On another sheet, write out everything that Pig Won't wants to protect you from. What are the awful things that could happen as a result of your writing, especially if you just did exactly the kind of writing you really want to do? Some of the things on Pig Will's list will appear on this list as well. Pig Won't knows the downside of fame and fortune, the lost privacy and alienated friends. Write it all down. My list includes the consequences of groupies.

Now go through both lists. Read each item aloud and say after it, "I'm willing to have this. I'm willing to do without it. With or without it, I am willing to be happy anyway because . . ."

Some things on your list will make you laugh when you announce your willingness to have them (groupies, for instance) or to do without them (social diseases). Others will make you uncomfortable. Those are the Pig Will/Pig Won't ammunition dumps. You may have to repeat the words a few times, or repeatedly change your reason for being happy anyway, to disarm them. Eventually, though, you'll have given Pig Will and Pig Won't smaller stakes to fight over.

If you do these exercises instead of just reading about them, you can use the pig lists as a treatment the next time you catch yourself procrastinating. Read the items aloud again, stating your willingness to do with or without. Your pigs may be worried or excited about things you hadn't thought of before, so you can add these to the list. After a few minutes of willingness to receive or do without various consequences of writing, you should find it much easier to set everything else aside and spend at least a little time doing your most important work.

5

Procrastination as Armor

Procrastination is a *good* thing. It must be. If it didn't provide some benefits, why would we cling to it so devotedly?

I see procrastination as a sort of emotional armor, protecting me from certain fears. For me, then, a first step in overcoming procrastination is *having less to be afraid of.*

I've identified five styles for my own procrastination, and I have a name for each one: the Perfectionist, the Hedonist, the Accommodator, the Tactician, and the Crisis Manager. There are, I'm sure, other styles for other people, but I won't pretend to understand those well. Instead, I hope that a look at my own patterns will help you to reveal the hidden payoff in your own delaying tactics, whether yours are just like mine or not. What follows is a description of each style, an analysis of what it protects us from, and some suggestions for making that kind of procrastination less necessary.

The Perfectionist

The Perfectionist uses procrastination in two ways. In the worst case, that of the *puer aeternus* (eternal child), the Perfectionist never does much of anything. He spends time thinking about what wonderful things he's going to accomplish one day, but he hardly ever gets started on an actual project and certainly never finishes anything. The *puer* puts off trying forever.

Another kind of Perfectionist is able to make the effort and get things done, but the work comes only after a long period of procrastination that changes the working conditions. Ideally, the procrastination sets up some kind of disaster. The most common disaster is a deadline disaster: The work needs to be done *now,* when there isn't enough time to do it well. But other disasters will also serve—breaking up a supportive relationship, say.

After the disaster, there's no way the Perfectionist can produce perfect work. "I'll just do it anyway," he says, "even if these conditions force me to lower my standards." Lowered standards let the Perfectionist excuse any problems in the finished work, because the work was done under hopeless conditions. And if the work does turn out to be pretty good, why, just imagine what the Perfectionist could have achieved under ideal circumstances!

The Perfectionist is afraid of being judged unworthy. His self-worth is tied to his accomplishments. It's as if he were constantly being graded by his friends, his family, his God (which may in this case be named Literary Posterity). *In fact, he's relentlessly and severely grading himself.* The grade he longs for is impossible to achieve. Even if the Perfectionist spent years creating one work of art that was universally proclaimed as perfect (Ha!), he would fault himself for producing such a small body of work.

Procrastination lets the Perfectionist grade himself on the curve. It guarantees that his work will never be the best it could be.

The cure for this is to surrender the whole idea of "the best it could be" and begin settling for what *is*.

Suggestions for Protecting the Perfectionist: Try finishing in thirty different ways the sentence, "I'll never be perfect because . . ." Whining is allowed. In addition to writing wise things like "I'll never be perfect because my standards for perfection conflict with one another," it's fine to write things like, "I'll never be perfect because we moved house too many times when I was a child." The thirty sentences aren't designed to teach you maturity but to help you see why you should *always* be graded on a curve. You already have plenty of reasons to be imperfect. There's no need to manufacture new ones.

Along the same lines, compose a written excuse from God. "Please excuse Bruce from being perfect today for the following reasons."

It also helps to express goals in terms that make for an easy A. Make your aims modest, rather than grandiose.

The bigger project for us perfectionists is to separate our self-worth from our outward accomplishments.

The Hedonist

The Hedonist's procrastination strategy relies on pleasure. She avoids work by saying, "I don't really feel like doing this right now. It's such a beautiful day that I'd really love to take a walk." Or else she'd like to go shopping, or watch television, or eat ice cream.

(Writing that sentence just now made me wonder what sort of ice cream we have in the freezer right now. Vanilla and two sorbets, as it turns out. But my wife was in the kitchen, and I never eat ice cream before noon. If there's a witness.)

Sometimes instead of eating ice cream the Hedonist will look productive. She'll avoid the uncomfortable phases of creation by endlessly repeating the phases that she enjoys. Revisions are hard work, so every time she undertakes one she soon puts it aside in favor of drafting a new story. Or revisions might be the part she finds pleasure in, so two sentences into a first draft she abandons it in favor of an endlessly reworked story from her files.

The Hedonist is afraid of a joyless, unpleasant life. The inclination of some is to tell her to just grow up, to recognize that later pleasures are bought with some current discipline and discomfort. But she knows all that. Not only does such advice not help, it ignores the legitimacy of the Hedonist's fear. Often the threat of a joyless life is tangible to the Hedonist because it describes the life she is already living. She's not happy.

Suggestions for Protecting the Hedonist: It's possible that the Hedonist needs a new mate, new climate, and new religion to be happy. Those are often the things that will occur to her first. But probably her lack is something much simpler and downright physiological. Our brains and our bodies hunger for pleasure. If we aren't getting enough of it, we crave it all the time. If the Hedonist is having more fun, she won't feel the need to resist every stretch of uncomfortable or challenging work.

Make a list of things you like to do. Emphasize things that make you laugh, moan with pleasure, or bliss out. Include activities that take some advance effort and planning, but also things that you can do spontaneously. Then start doing the things on the list, not during your writing time, but regularly. Plan for some pleasure, preferably the bone-deep buzz of ecstatic pleasure, every day.

Pleasure outside of your writing life is the key here, but there's some good, too, in making your writing area more pleasurable. Turn on music. Hang a painting. Bring in some flowers. And if your chair really is uncomfortable, find a better one.

The Accommodator

The Accommodator is solicited to write a novel for a game based on the life of Johnny Appleseed. The project isn't really right for the Accommodator, but it's so nice to be asked, and saying yes to this project might lead to something more appropriate later on—you never know. Then there's an invitation to write a story for an original anthology. The anthology's topic doesn't really interest the writer, but again, it's so nice to be asked. And a local writing contest needs a judge to pick out and write a little something about the winning story. The contest can't pay anything but it's publicity, sort of, and once again, it's so nice to be asked . . .

The Accommodator's writing time is limited by nonwriting projects he has said yes to. He's baking cookies for the PTA, even though he doesn't have children of his own. The cause is a worthy one, and it's so hard to say no. Then there's the political campaign he's helping with, the volunteer hours at the library. He's helping out with a dozen other worthy causes or friends in need. Only now, with so many projects in which he has a minimal stake (except for a little money here or there and the fact that it was *so* nice to be asked or *so* nice to be needed), the Accommodator somehow isn't getting to any of the things that would top his list of personal goals. He may be busy, but he's busy doing things for other people.

If he writes at all, the Accommodator writes to please others, not to create the things he first dreamed of writing, things that would first and foremost please *him*.

The problem for the Accommodator isn't really that he volunteers, but that he sets no boundaries. He says yes to everything. The result is that he burns up the time that could be used for saying yes to the most important things.

The Accommodator is afraid of being unloved. He is praised for his many hours of volunteering, for being an unfailing friend, for being so easy to work with. All of this translates into feeling wanted and needed and *loved*. Actually, the Accommodator doesn't have to fit this picture of voluntary community service at all. The activities he uses to squeeze out time for his own work might be a lot of small domestic ones—making the kids' lunches when they're old enough to do it themselves. Whatever the activity, the Accommodator is likely to feel that saying no to it will seem selfish. And selfish people, the Accommodator thinks, are unworthy of love.

When the Accommodator does get around to some of his own true work, he feels a little guilty doing it, a little less lovable. So he procrastinates with more things that are done for other people.

Suggestions for Protecting the Accommodator: Notice, first of all, that I'm not saying that selfless service to others is a bad thing. But it needs to be balanced with doing what you must do for yourself. There's a problem only when doing things for others overwhelms you *and you're unhappy about it.*

In that case, you need to learn to say the things that the Accommodator has a very hard time saying:

"I am going to deny someone else some time or effort that they would appreciate and take this time for myself."

"My own work is important."

"Someone else can do this thing I'm being asked to do, but only I can write my own work."

More to the point, since the Accommodator procrastinates with activities that will help him feel loved, he needs to feel securely that he *is* loved apart from his good works. Feeling such unconditional love is a project of religion, therapy, or your closest relationships. As a small step, you might try a few minutes daily of thinking tenderly about people you love and set aside some time in the day for a few *small* loving gestures.

Then the next step is to sometimes, when appropriate, say *No.*

The Tactician

The Tactician delays the battle by positioning and repositioning her troops before the assault. She won't attack a problem if her plan isn't perfect, if the supply lines aren't fully protected, if she doesn't have complete intelligence about the enemy.

Another way of thinking of her is as a cook who is always moving projects to the back burners to simmer.

She is right to think that many things improve with time, that writing is often improved with some research. But troops who are endlessly repositioned drain their energy with marching. Things left on the back burner can burn up or boil off entirely.

The Tactician is afraid of starting too soon, of spoiling a project by committing to it before the best ideas have emerged. What she's really afraid of, then, is making errors. And errors are part of the creative process. There's no way around them.

Suggestions for Protecting the Tactician: Since the Tactician is right that some waiting will often improve a work, it helps to make sure that she does get the time she needs for simmering, for moving the toy soldiers around on the map before the real ones are committed in the field. Try setting time aside for "prewriting" a project. And go ahead and put some things on the back burner.

But keep track of what's on that back burner, and have a limit. Simmer no more than, say, three pots at a time. If you think of a fourth idea, you have to either write it or let it simmer while one of the other "pots" comes to the front burner and gets written. Or set a timer for each pot that simmers. By what date will you move that project to a front burner and begin to write?

It also helps to keep track of simmering projects by posting a list of them. Seeing how much is on the back burner can reassure the Tactician that there is already plenty of simmering going on; that she isn't rushing things if she presses ahead with one project now.

The Crisis Manager

The Crisis Manager loves deadlines, and he loves taking on more work than he can probably handle. Like the Perfectionist, if he has plenty of time to do something, he procrastinates until the last minute, but not because he has to be forced to lower his standards. No, the Crisis Manager delays because the last-minute crisis, the uncertainty about making the deadline, will give him a great adrenaline jolt. It makes him feel important to be enervatingly busy. If he's an Accommodator, being in Crisis Manager mode lets him tell people that he'd love to be doing more to meet their needs, but he's so overcommitted with other deadlines that he can't—he's utterly powerless and shouldn't be blamed.

The Crisis Manager also gets protection from having to make decisions, since in a crisis it's clear what his priorities have to be. This saves him from some of the Tactician's stalling.

But the main thing that motivates the Crisis Manager is *thrills*. Barely getting things done is exciting!

The Crisis Manager is afraid of boredom. And crisis management of deadlines is safer than the things that some people do to stave off boredom—bungee jumping, say. If the Crisis Manager enjoys the thrills and isn't too often hurt, then this kind of procrastination may be worth keeping, since my **Suggestions for Protecting the Crisis Manager** boil down to: Have a more exciting life outside of writing. If that means driving fast, trying daredevil sports, or sleeping with strangers, maybe it's better to get your galley proofs in at the last possible second.

You might consider, though, the possibility that the Crisis Manager is just generally understimulated, in which case the Hedonist's cure of daily planned pleasure might protect the Crisis Manager from the boredom he fears.

Also, learning to do new things can provoke a mild form of the anxiety that the Crisis Manager craves, so you might try lessons in ballroom dance, tennis, conversational Japanese, or something else you know nothing about and have no reason to think you have any talent for.

Your armor probably looks a bit different from mine. You may need protection from different emotional dragons. The main thing is to understand that it will be hard to take off the armor of procrastination before you have tamed the dragons.

6
The Rite Stuff

In the second chapter, we looked at the difficulty of beginning a project, but it's not just beginning the *beginning* that can be difficult. The transition from doing anything else to starting the day's writing has given lots of writers trouble. Just look at all the different ways they tried to deal with it. Kingsley Amis, J. G. Ballard, and Norman Mailer are among the writers who have started their writing sessions with alcohol.[1] Bottled courage, I suppose. Thornton Wilder's habit was more healthy. He said, "My springboard has always been long walks."[2] James Jones would spend an hour and a half "fiddling around" to "get up the courage and nerve to get to work." This fiddling consisted of drinking coffee, smoking cigarettes, and looking at the previous day's work until "finally there's no further excuse."[3] May Sarton warmed up for writing poetry and fiction by first writing letters.[4]

Why is it so hard just to begin cold, to say, "The writing begins now," and begin it? As I noted in the second chapter, the answer for some of us is sheer terror. I'm afraid of exposure. What will people think of me if I write convincingly and sympathetically from a rapist's point of view? What if my writing reveals shortcomings in my education or character that I'm not even aware of? What if I write badly? Even if I'm not actually afraid on a given day, I may at least be dismayed. I'm discouraged over the size and complexity of my project. How will I ever get the pieces of this novel to work together? Or perhaps I'm anxious over the failure that's inherent in all ambitious writing: The words on the page will never stack up to the embryonic inner vision that inspired me. If my writing session is still hours away, then these negative feelings are remote, too. But the closer I come to facing the first word, the more anxious I'm likely to feel, and if I delay getting started, then guilt twines with the anxiety. These various bad feelings build like a force field around the writing desk. The closer I get, the worse I feel.

If I can just get to that first word, then the force field begins to fade and I'm too busy concentrating on the next word, the next thought, to worry. But simply knowing this does not make writing the first word any easier.

In addition to the emotional barriers, writing requires a shift from the urgencies of real life to the abstract problems of the page. Again, just knowing that I need to shift my thinking isn't enough. What I need is something to do, an action that carries me from whatever else I was doing to writing.

Some techniques for managing the transition are better than others. The ones I pointed to in the first paragraph would all be hazardous to me. Managing emotional difficulties with a drink is practically the definition of alcohol abuse, and writers who prime the pump with Scotch or beer are probably buying fluency at the price of quality. Kingsley Amis admitted as much when he said, "It could be that I could have written better without [alcohol] . . . but it could also be true that I'd have written far less without it."[5] I've tried taking long walks to get going. The walks got longer and longer while I started writing later and later in the day. Fiddling, too, can stretch into the third bowl of cereal and the careful perusal of yesterday's paper, right down to the want ads. While I'm not a very faithful letter writer, I have sometimes warmed up by writing e-mail, a task that can expand infinitely.

There are a few *little* tricks that help me get going. One of them is to write early in the day, making the transition into wakefulness a transition into writing, too. This helps me in a couple of ways, when I manage to do it. First, starting when I'm sleepy helps me over those initial barriers of fear and anxiety. Almost before I'm awake enough to know what I'm doing, I'm starting to write. (I suppose this is a little like beginning the session with a drink, though the numbness wears off a lot faster.) Second, writing first thing does away with any guilt I might feel about not having started yet. I don't anxiously wonder, during breakfast, exercise, and getting dressed, how long it's going to take me to get going today. I've already started. And because I've already started, those activities are a break from my writing, not avoidance behaviors. The emotional difference is vast. Third, having already dipped into my work increases the chance that my mind will drift back to it as I'm exercising or showering.

I also try to atomize the task so that when I get out of bed, it's not to "work on the novel" but, rather, to write the next paragraph. I may, in fact, get on a roll and write several pages before I take a break, but a paragraph is all I expect of myself at first.

Finally, I try to follow Hemingway's lead and end each day's work with a half-completed sentence, with a moment in the story where I know what happens next and know how to show it happening. It's easier to get up to finish a sentence than to start one. Beginnings come easiest at the end of a day, when I'm already in the swing of things.

All of these are helpful techniques for breaking through the resistance barrier, but there's one that's even more important to me: I have a ritual, one custom-made for my own emotional barriers and the difficulties I have in moving into writing from anything else.

Of course, all the behaviors I described in the first paragraph are rituals. They're akin to the behavior of Bill Swift, a baseball pitcher who listened to Frank Sinatra songs for twenty minutes before every game, or Jerry Rice, the star wide receiver of football's 49ers. Rice was always the first player to arrive in the locker room, where he would dress meticulously, trying on several pairs of socks and pants until he had selected the ones with the right feel.[6] These behaviors are different from the superstitions that some athletes have—there's nothing magical about a ritual; it isn't an attempt to control the outer world. A ritual is about the *inner* world, about getting into a particular mental state. In part, a good ritual lets athletes leave behind distractions—problems at home, disputes with management, disagreements with teammates—so that they can concentrate on the details of playing well. But it's also about entering the feeling of good performance. When Jerry Rice fiddled with his uniform until he felt right, he played right.

As I've already pointed out, the rituals of drinking, walking, fiddling, or writing something else don't suit me, because I tend to get lost in any of them.

There are briefer writing rituals. Hemingway used to sharpen twenty pencils before he got to work. Isabel Allende lights a candle for dead relatives. One writer undergoes a "cleansing ritual" before she works on her novel; to anyone else, it looks like a shower. These rituals are more like what I need, something that conveys me quickly and simply to where I need to go, something that I won't get lost in.

I've had several different prewriting ceremonies over the years, but here's what I do now. On top of my dresser, I keep a cat-shaped candle-holder that belonged to my mother, two candles that I burned when my mother died and I kept a vigil with her body, a pin promoting breast cancer awareness (also my mother's), some bells, some natural objects (bird feathers, stones), a tiny statue of Shiva/Nataraja, a one-inch picture frame, and my Writers of the Future trophy.

I hesitate to call the space a shrine because of that trophy. I'm afraid of creating the impression that I worship at the church of my ego. But shrine it is, and the trophy is there for good reasons.

The ritual begins when I light the candles. Then I ring the bells in a way that gets me to notice that I'm standing *right here,* that the moment is *right now.* A lot of my anxieties spring from not noticing that I'm here and now, and that I'm *always* here and now. So the first step is to ring the bells until I'm really present.

After that, I spend some time looking at the objects, appreciating them. There's a part of me that rebels at working indoors all day. The stones and feathers are a small consoling dose of what I'm afraid of missing. Several other objects remind me of my mother. There's a lot about her that I'm working to understand, and much of it relates to the challenges of a creative life—some challenges that she met, and some from which she retreated. The avatar of Shiva reminds me of reincarnation, which is my metaphor for storytelling as a multigenerational project, a flame that keeps burning in different lamps. The one-inch picture frame reminds me that I can only work on small things, one word or one thought at a time.[7] Finally, the trophy is there as an inoculation against the fear that I'm really no good. I could just as easily use something more prosaic like a photocopy of my first byline or words of praise from a mentor. But the trophy is beautiful.

After that, I spend a little time in communion with other people, dead and alive, who are present in my imagination. Finally, before I blow out the candles, I announce my willingness to write, to take the next step along the path, to serve.

All of this takes five minutes. At the end of that time, I go and write. Usually.

Exactly when I use the ritual varies, but it's either the first thing I do when I get up—even before the first paragraph of the day—or it's a way of getting back on task after breakfast or some other interruption.

Some days I still get knocked off track somewhere between the candles and the keyboard. Half an hour after the ritual, I find myself reading a magazine. That's when I go back for a second dose of candles, bells, and contemplation. Only on my most resistant days do I need to light the candles for a third time.

Most prewriting rituals grow organically out of the writer's anxiety, and we tend to hang on to the first one that works. Any ritual that does the job is worth keeping . . . unless there are aspects of it that you don't like. My earliest rituals were as much about avoidance as making a transition, so I typically spent two hours warming up to write. Worse, I know a lot of writers whose rituals involve cigarettes, which presents a problem when they want to quit smoking and keep writing.

If you want to experiment with inventing a new ritual, here are some suggestions:

1. Identify what makes the transition to writing difficult. What negative feelings do you need to combat on your way to the desk? Think of ways to counter these feelings with ritual. Perhaps you can use objects, as I do, for reminders. You might find it more effective to use music that reliably changes your mood, or to read something inspirational. Against the fear of writing badly, some writers have made a habit of starting the day with a reading from an inferior published writer. "I can do better than that!"

2. Think about other rituals that you like—sacred or secular, institutional rituals or the quirky rites of your family. Are there aspects that you could incorporate in a writing ritual?

3. What people, divinities, institutions, or principles support your writing? How can you symbolically remind yourself of that support, that alliance?

4. Appeal to the senses. A good ritual anchors you in physical experience. If there's a smell that would mean, "Ah, writing!" (the smell of freshly sharpened pencils, perhaps), try to incorporate it.

5. Make it yours. A ritual can be exactly as spiritual or sec-

ular as you are. It can be something that you have to do anyway, such as taking a shower, so long as you invest it with significant details—a different soap and shampoo for your prewriting showers, distinguishing them from ordinary showers.

Perhaps the most important aspect of a ritual is that it should be something you'll enjoy doing. My ritual works for me partly because even when it's hard to make myself go to the writing desk, it's easy to light my candles and ring the bells. The ritual is something I can approach in any mood, and then the ritual changes my mood to one conducive to writing.

One thing to watch out for, if you're like me, is getting *too* elaborate in the invention of rituals. Like trying to create the ideal office, inventing your ritual can become an excuse to delay writing until everything's perfect. Don't spend a week shopping for the perfect writing candle. The point, after all, is to get to work.

Part Two

Writing As If It Mattered

7

The Foam-White Bull

Here's a very old story that, like most myths, might mean many things. I want to examine what it says to writers and other artists.

This fellow called Minos wanted to rule the island of Crete just as badly as some people want to write. He prayed to the gods to send a sign confirming his divine right to be crowned king. Poseidon, the sea god, answered Minos's prayer. A white bull, white as sea foam, came from the waves. This was Poseidon's gift.

Minos knew the religious conventions of his time. When a god sends you a gift, it's not supposed to be yours to keep. Poseidon expected that King Minos would sacrifice the bull that had confirmed his special status.

But as soon as the crown was on his head, Minos started to think of being king as a solitary achievement, something he had done for himself. He lost sight of the true nature of kingship, forgetting that a king, like an artist, is an ordinary person acting out an extraordinary role.

Once a man becomes a king, he doesn't belong to himself anymore. He belongs to his people. Once a man or woman becomes an artist, he or she belongs to the art. Putting on the new clothes of an important role is called *investiture*. But you can't put these new clothes on over the old ones. You have to divest yourself of who you used to be. You have to take the extraordinary role seriously, leaving your old clothes and old possessions behind.

Minos refused to give up his former identity as a man of worldly property. He cheated the god. In the place of the divinely beautiful foam-white bull, he sacrificed another white bull—a very fine one, to be sure, but not the bull that his kingship demanded.

And because Minos held back the sacrifice that his role demanded, his queen, Pasiphaë, developed an unhealthy interest in the bull. She lusted for it, and who can blame her? The bull radiated divine power. If

Pasiphaë's desire was unnatural, it was only because the bull itself was unnaturally appealing.

The upshot of Minos's greed was that his queen gave birth to a monster that was half man and half bull, the Minotaur. The beast was a blemish on the family reputation for the rest of Minos's reign. It was kept in the royal basement, where it ate youths and maidens. That is, the monster devoured the future. Minos's dream of kingship ended in nightmare.

When I first started writing, I thought I was entering a glamorous career. I knew, because everyone was eager to tell me so, that there would be hard times along the way. Fine. I could handle some lean years on the way to fat ones. If I didn't appear on the *Tonight Show* until I was, say, thirty years old, I could handle that.

I had completely unrealistic notions of what it would cost me to be a writer, and I knew little about the true benefits of the profession.

I was equally naive about being a husband, a role I also took on early in life and in partnership with a young woman who, I would say, knew just as little about what it took to be a wife. In my early writing and in my failed marriage, I was willing to make sacrifices if I could be pretty certain of what I'd get in return, but I wasn't good at making those sacrifices that were a surrender of who I had been before I became a writer and a husband. I didn't embrace the sacrifices that were called for by my new identities.

The myth of Minos and his foam-white bull is useful for reminding us that we've got to relinquish some of our former lives if we're going to be kings or spouses or writers. But all this business about *sacrifice* can be misleading. It makes the whole business sound like a matter of economics: You pay your sacrifice on this side of the equation and get your new role, with its attendant benefits, on the other side.

In fact, it often turns out that the sacrifice *is* the benefit.

Writing about marriage, Joseph Campbell evoked the Taoist image of the interacting light and dark, yang and yin, male and female, creating a new unity. "Marriage is not a simple love affair," Campbell wrote, "it's an ordeal, and the ordeal is the sacrifice of ego to a relationship in which two have become one."[1]

Similarly, a proper king is no longer *himself*. Ancient kings lived in splendor as a sign of the people's prosperity, but being closely identified with the people and their fortunes meant that the remedy for plague or famine or other disasters was to sacrifice the king. He was expected to be just as willing to die as he was to adorn himself with jewels. Being king was an ordeal.

Art can also be an ordeal, one in which the personal ego is diminished for the sake of the art. Just as no king automatically gets a victorious or prosperous reign, no artist gets guaranteed results from sacrificing himself in the fires of becoming an artist. You take on the ordeal of being an artist, and your reward is . . . you get to be an artist. That's all. That's all that you can be sure of. The only other guarantee is that if you accept your gifts halfheartedly, you'll suffer. When the king forgets the balance of receiving and giving back, the land is blighted. In some stories, *everything* dies when the king forgets his proper place.

All right, so that's the mythic truth. The point of this story is that you must honor your gifts. If you don't, you'll end up with a Minotaur in your basement, devouring your own beautiful and promising children. But what do *gifts* and *sacrifices* mean in practical terms? What have the gods given you, and what do you owe in return?

I can't say. Even if I know you very well, I can't do more than guess about your gifts, because you have to recognize them as gifts before they have any potency. Someone may say to you, "What a gift you have for saying the right thing," but if you don't think that it's true or you don't think of that trait as important, then "saying the right thing" is not a gift of the sort I mean.

Important gifts, the gifts from the gods, are the flip side of our callings. What do you feel called to do? What is your purpose in life? The answers to these questions can help you to see what gifts you have that will help you fulfill that purpose. Or if you're not sure of your calling, you can consider what important gifts you seem to have. What traits are your truest expressions of yourself? What are your talents? If you used them fully, what would you be doing? Maybe that's what you're called to do.

I think that some of my own gifts include: the sensitivity to know musical writing from writing that plods along, a strong empathy for others, a knack for inventing interesting lies, great tolerance for ambiguity and contradiction, and the urge to have everyone in the room pay attention to me. These gifts are tightly wound with my calling to write.

And what do I owe for these gifts? I'm not always sure. In real life, the bargain isn't as explicit as Poseidon's. The gift isn't as specific as a bull from the sea, and the response expected from you isn't as simple as one ceremonial slaughter. The sacrifice of art is like the sacrifice of marriage. You give day by day, and what's required of you changes day by day. It often comes down to noticing how you feel about small decisions. Last Sunday, did you write for two hours and take a walk with your spouse, or did you watch football most of the day? How did you feel, once the hours had been irrevocably spent, one way or the other?

What the myth tells us is that if we don't make the sacrifices, whatever they are, we will be in pain. Worse, the gods will laugh at our folly. They offered their gifts, and look at how badly we received them! Don't expect further gifts when you've failed to respect the ones already offered. If Jehovah calls and we don't answer, then he promises: "I will laugh at your calamity; I will mock when your fear cometh."[2]

Let's say you take all of this very seriously and resolve that you will do better than Minos. You will accept the responsibilities that come with your gifts. You will answer your calling.

The gods still have reason to laugh. They like to set impossible tasks for us mortals, issuing more than one call at once and watching us break ourselves upon the contradictions. Up on Olympus, this is high comedy.

Most of us have to respond to two or more callings simultaneously. Often, those callings and the sacrifices they demand are in conflict. Being a devoted parent, for instance, may demand that you sacrifice writing time to be with your children. Being a devoted writer may demand that you sometimes close the door to your children in the afternoon, forbidding them to enter unless the house is on fire. Both sacrifices are demanded by the gods. Either action, closing the door or turning off the computer, may create Minotaurs.

The situation sounds hopeless, and for good reason. It *is* hopeless. If you try to understand your gifts and make the sacrifices necessary, your calculations may be off. You may give too little of yourself, or too much. If your multiple callings require conflicting sacrifices, you probably won't be able to balance them perfectly and will end up with at least one small Minotaur.

It's not easy being mortal. The laughter of the gods rings in our ears, and some days we are justifiably bitchy about it. You can't win. You just can't win.

But you can lose well. The story of Minos tells us about the consequences of one kind of failing, but there is a worse one that Minos avoided entirely. As I said in the beginning, Minos wanted to be king just as badly as some of us want to be writers, to be artists. And he did it. Minos paid dearly for hoarding part of his gift. But he didn't hoard all of it. *He was king.* He lived out the identity he had chosen. If Minos had been less than who he was, he would have been hollow by the time he was old.

The gods have stacked the deck in this game, and mortals can't completely win. But by taking up the vestments of writer, spouse, parent, or any heroic role, we can at least ensure that we don't completely lose. When the gods laugh at our struggles, at least their laughter will be light. At least they'll be laughing at men and women worthy of a foam-white bull.

8
How to Be Your Own Bad Agent

Your Aunt Peeny calls you up with a wonderful idea. She's just been reading the latest Danielle Steel novel. It's about this man and this woman, see, and these complications and an unknown identity and more complications and sorrow and revelation and true love victorious but bittersweet in the end. The book is just flying off the shelves. Aunt Peeny says to you, "You're a writer. Why don't you write a book like Danielle Steel and make a lot of money?"

If you're a big fan of Danielle Steel, if you've been working hard to finish a novel that you hope will be Steel's hottest competition, then you can say, "Thanks, Aunt Peeny. That is, in fact, exactly what I'm trying to do." You might feel some mild exasperation at how easy she makes it all sound, but you don't really mind.

On the other hand, most of us either aren't Danielle Steel fans or, even if we like her writing, don't have plans to ever write anything remotely like her novels. If you fall into this camp, then Aunt Peeny's call will reveal how completely clueless she is about you and your ambitions. This may amuse or irritate you, depending on how personally you take it. Above all, you don't take her suggestion at all seriously. After you hang up the phone, you don't give Danielle Steel another thought all day.

The next day, your phone rings again. This time, it's your Bad Agent on the line. He's just been reading the latest Danielle Steel novel. It's about this man and this woman, see, and these complications and an unknown identity and more complications and sorrow and revelation and true love victorious but bittersweet in the end. The book is just flying off the shelves. He knows that you've got what it takes to bang out a book like this, and he's meeting next week with an editor who is looking for books to keep Danielle Steel readers happy in the months when there aren't any new Danielle Steel novels. Why don't you hammer out three chapters and an outline over the weekend?

If it were your Good Agent calling to say the same thing, it would be because you were exactly the sort of writer who did actually want to do Danielle Steel one better. But this is your Bad Agent. In some ways, he knows less about you than Aunt Peeny does. He does at least know what you're capable of. He knows that with some prodding, you could write a book that he could sell to this editor. So he's calling to prod. But he doesn't know, or doesn't care, that Danielle Steel is not a writer you want to emulate.

If he's a very effective Bad Agent, you'll drop whatever you were working on when the phone rang and get right to work on the proposal. The result might be that you throw yourself into a project that goes nowhere, but if you're reasonably talented and flexible, the result might be that the proposal sells, and so do the four sequels. Maybe all five books are best-sellers. Your Bad Agent buys a Lexus on the commissions, and you sit by your swimming pool thinking about tax shelters and wondering why you're so unhappy.

Again, if your Good Agent landed you beside the same swimming pool, you'd be happy. That's the difference between the Good Agent and the Bad Agent.

Of course, what I'm really talking about here isn't agents, good or bad. It's about how we direct ourselves onto a path that leads to the right goal, or the wrong one. I've seen writers steered toward the wrong goal by family, friends, fellow writers, mentors . . . and agents. The Bad Agent does a good job of standing in for all the others because his motives are so easy to understand.

The Bad Agent is the sort of person who knows the price of everything and the value of nothing. He wants money. He wants to maximize his 15 percent by maximizing what you earn. He can be a shortsighted Bad Agent, focusing only on the near term, one book at a time, or he can be a wise Bad Agent, focusing on maximizing your income throughout your career. But money is his only focus.

Well, maybe not. It's also possible for a Bad Agent to interfere with your ultimate happiness in other ways. Maybe your Bad Agent thinks of you as a prestigious author, so he doesn't even consider you for a big-money novelization of a movie you adored and would *love* to flesh out into a book. Maybe prestige is the last thing you care about.

In short, a Bad Agent doesn't consider the totality of what you want. To be your own Bad Agent, emphasize one or two of your motivations to the diminishment of others. I can practically guarantee that you'll be unhappy.

On the other hand, if happiness is what you want . . . Well, I can't come as close to guaranteeing that. However, if you take an inventory of what motivates you to write and try to make career decisions based on *all* of your motivations, you'll do a better job of being your own Good Agent, or of training your agent to be your Good Agent.

So what motivates you? Here are some possibilities, things that motivate me.

Money. For some writers, this motivation isn't just at the top of the list, it *is* the list. They say to their agents, "I don't care what the book is. I don't care if I don't get a byline, or if they use my byline on bad writing I didn't actually do. I don't care if I can't ever tell anyone I wrote this book, or that I didn't. Maximize my income. I'll do whatever it takes. Just get me the contracts."

There's nothing wrong with writing for money and only for money. While it may be destructive to care about nothing *in life* except for money, writing is just one piece of your life. If you're in writing for the money, if you don't feel bad about what you're writing, and if you get your other satisfactions elsewhere, well and good.

As for me, I want at least enough money to keep writing full time.

I'd be astonished if you didn't care about money at all. Money is a terrific tool. Applied thoughtfully, it could help you to pursue any one of the motivators that follow.

Prestige. My writing brings me various kinds of prestige. Some people are impressed to learn that I write at all, or that I write full time. Others are impressed only by particular pieces that I've written, or by where stories or essays were published.

Of course, some people are thoroughly *un*impressed when they get an inkling of how much I earn from my writing, which is a good reminder that prestige isn't general. If you're writing to impress, *whom* are you writing to impress? The prestige of publishing in one place will earn you scorn from some quarters. Whose respect do you want?

Credentials. This is a specialized subcategory of prestige. The fiction and critical writing portions of my bibliography provide me with important credentials when I seek work as a teacher or speaker. My credentials were important in selling this book to my publisher and perhaps in convincing you to read it. Credentials allow me to keep doing what I love to do.

Celebrity. At writing conferences where I'm a paid speaker, I am a literary star. My meals and accommodations are complimentary, and participants appreciate the contents of my presentations and the energy and enthusiasm I bring to teaching and making keynote addresses. In my home, I'm just the guy who feeds the cats. At a conference or delivering a speech to a corporate or nonprofit audience, I'm a big fish, albeit in a small pond. I enjoy my celebrity status for the hour or for the weekend. This isn't the only reason I go to conferences or do public speaking, but it's a factor.

If someone reliable told me, "Write a story about X and I can promise you'll be invited to be Guest of Honor at a science fiction convention where you'll be wined and dined and broadly saluted," I would probably write a story about X.

Social Identity. My social identity is part of my persona, the mask I wear for my interactions with other people. When people say at a party, "And what do you do?" they are asking about status (which prestige contributes to), but they are also saying, "What sort of mask do you wear in the world?" I like the Writer mask. It allows me to excuse both my prying questions and my habit of watching silently on the periphery, collecting information.

My social identity also determines whom I hang out with. I like hanging out with other writers and artists.

Learning. Every time I write another story in the Cat Crimes anthology series, I set out to learn something about cats that I didn't know before, something I can build a story around. I have learned that deer will bolt in fear when a little house cat stalks them. I have learned that cats measure territory in four dimensions. For other stories, I have soaked up the history of the Battle of the Bulge, researched the life cycle of tapeworms, steeped myself in Lewis Carroll.

I love learning, whether about something outside of myself or about the machineries of my own emotions and beliefs. And I love to deepen what I learn by writing about it.

Sense of Purpose. I hope that I'm doing more than using up electricity as I sit here at my keyboard. There are certain gifts I want to give to my readers. Understanding. Solace. Joy. I want to pass along neat tidbits about cats. Certainly I have learned more compassion through my writing; I hope that I'm teaching it, too.

I also feel my purpose is fulfilled when I keep the faith and write every day, especially on the days when it's hard. Part of my purpose is to be an example to other writers. Look. Here's Bruce, struggling with his emotions, making and regretting wrong choices in his career, scraping by financially . . . or not. And still he goes on.

Authenticity. What I most want to write, and what I have lately come more and more to write, is the work that comes primarily out of what I want to express, not what the marketplace has proved eager to receive. And whether I'm writing to fill a market niche or have my own idiosyncratic say, I try to write with the words that no one else would choose, to celebrate my unique perspective.

I am making art out of my self. I am in the art I make. It's true that every artist creates from a unique perspective, but some kinds of work minimize the artist's particularity. There are some work-for-hire novels that a hundred other writers could write just as well as I would, and in roughly the same way I would do it. I prefer to let one of the hundred others do that work.

A Practice. I can't exactly meditate while I write. Writing is such an absorbing activity that it's hard to stay fully aware of my body and my breathing as I do it. But I do approach writing in the spirit of meditation.

My hours in this chair are my practice. This is the discipline that anchors my life. But if the word *discipline* conjures images of drill sergeants and deprivation, think again. My practice is gentler than that. For certain hours out of the day, I am here, engaged, concentrating . . . or gently bringing my attention back if it has wandered.

The previous motivations that I have examined may be about the life we make for ourselves with our accomplishments. A practice, on the other hand, is about the life we make moment by moment, regardless of whether we accomplish anything or not.

Fun. I saved this one for last because as adults, we do often think of it last, if we think of it at all. One of the things I do for fun is perform public readings of my work. Certain stories crack up my audiences. Sometimes, if I haven't rehearsed enough to keep this in check, those stories crack me up, too, and I'm like the guy who can barely get to the punch line, he's laughing so hard. And that's fun.

When you start getting serious about writing as a business, fun can be one of the first motivations you dismiss as distracting. Much work done in the spirit of fun turns out to need sober revision, but that's no reason to think that the more fun you have, the worse the product will be.

You may share some of my motivations. You may be driven by others I haven't mentioned. Try taking an inventory of all the reasons why you write.

As you review your motivations, remember that one project does not make a career. Everything you write does not have to feed your every desire. But if you find that you have to spend six months writing a novel for the money, and only for the money, then perhaps you can give yourself time for a little project—a short poem, say—that seeks to satisfy another of your motivations.

And if you know what you really want, you'll be able to recognize and resist the Bad Agent when he calls.

9
Dreaming of Pisgah

I am easily blown off course by my own self-doubts and second-guessing. There are so many decisions to make in this writing life. So many alternatives look attractive. Should I go on dividing my time among several projects, writing a bit of this and a bit of that every day? Or will I be happier if I choose one project and work on it exclusively? Is it time to concentrate on novel-writing and give up short stories for a while, or even for good? When I'm feeling poor, should I set aside my ultimate ambitions and spend a few weeks writing erotica for some quick cash?

If I make such decisions consciously, I'm likely to change my mind the next day. I don't entirely trust decisions that I arrive at by reason alone. Reason and practicality are important in decision-making, but by themselves they can lead me away from my authentic self. The practical choice is not always the right one.

Fortunately, I have a source of excellent advice, a way of discovering what it is that I *really* want. I let my dreams tell me what to do.

Looking to dreams for direction strikes some people as folly. They lump dream interpretation together with systems of supernatural divination and dismiss it as nonsense. After all, most people who tap their dreams for advice believe that dreams are signals from above or from below. That is, they either see dreams as messages from a celestial realm, from a higher power, from God, or else they see dreams as messages from our psychic depths, from id-ego-superego conflicts, from the collective unconscious.

In fact, say the skeptics, dreams don't come *from* anywhere at all. Some brain scientists dispute the notion that our dreams have any narrative content whatsoever. According to this view, the sleeping brain's synapses are firing in a very disorganized way, sort of like dumping out the day's sensory trash. When we're actually dreaming, we're not having a coherent experience at all. The dream stimulus, the sleeping experience, is a random assortment of dissociated sensations. We only create the dream story as we wake up and try to make sense out of this neuro-physiological noise.[1]

If this view is correct, then dreams don't come from anywhere. We don't actually *have* them. Rather, we *invent* dreams by "remembering" them.

And this view may very well be correct. It doesn't, however, debunk the whole notion of dream interpretation.

"But it does!" say the debunkers. "Dreams have about as much meaning as the shapes of clouds. If you see a cloud shaped like a horse, that doesn't mean that you've been sent a message about horses."

They're right, and they are wrong. If you see a horse cloud, that doesn't prove that you've been sent a horse message. But you have *received* a horse message. Indeed, the fact that you see a horse where your best friend sees a dragon tells you something about yourself. And self-knowledge is what dream interpretation is all about.

So it doesn't matter whether the source of dreams is divine, psy-chological, or accidental. What matters is the interpretive process that starts with dreams and ends with self-awareness.

Such awareness, for some of us, comes hard. We can see our true selves, know our deep preferences, only by seeing them indirectly, out of the corner of our eyes. Dreams, whatever their original source, are remembered as little narratives built from our personal symbol systems. Does it matter whether the interpretation of those narratives *discovers* wisdom that was delivered with the dream or *invents* wisdom from a dream that had none built into it? No. *Discovery* and *invention* name dif-ferent perspectives on the same process of pattern-making, whether we're talking about the interpretation of dreams, the evolution of phi-losophy, or the writing of a novel.

What matters isn't the origin of dreams, but the result of the dream interpretation. If, after interpreting our dreams, we feel that we know ourselves better, then the exercise is useful. We don't have to believe in the "validity" of dreams to use them as advisers. Our nocturnal Adviser doesn't have to be "real" to be wise. Messages don't have to come from anywhere to prove meaningful.

So if the power is all in the interpretation, how *do* you interpret dreams? Here are some things to try:

- Pay attention to how you feel about dream elements.
- Consider any object, person, or event as if it were a metaphor. If you dream about a dairy, what conventional expressions are there using the term *milk?* Then consider your private idiosyncratic meanings. If you are lactose intolerant, milk is something that doesn't like you, that your body rejects.
- Try thinking about each person in your dream as an aspect of yourself. But don't stop there. If you dream of a particular person, think about what lessons you learned from knowing him or her, what that person's "message" to you has been.
- If you dream of someone who is sort of two people at once, or who switches identities between two people you know, think about what those people have in common.
- Assume that the dream is a message from someone incapable of speech. The dream is like a game of charades. What message is being acted out for you?
- Dream associations may be universal (red is always the color of blood), specific to your culture (green is the color of money in the United States, but not in most places), or specific to you (when you were a child, you said your favorite colors were black and silver and your mother said that those weren't colors). Assume that the sender of this message knows all kinds of things about you and may pick details meaningful to you and not to anyone else.

These are suggestions. There are no hard-and-fast rules for dream interpretation, just as there are no absolutely universal symbols. Red may always be the color of blood, but that doesn't mean that red always stands for blood or things associated with blood.

Here are some of my own dreams, and what I made of them.

My Heart Transplant. Not long ago, I dreamed of a surgeon who showed me the heart that he planned to implant in me. The object he held didn't look like a heart at all. It looked like a cooked chicken breast, and I told him so.

"Oh, that's just the appearance it gets from the Teflon coating," he said. But whether the "heart" was a chicken breast or something coated in Teflon, I didn't want it. The heart I already had was the one for me, and I wasn't going to let him cut it out.

When I woke up and thought about this dream, I concluded that it was about authenticity and risk-taking. There were three ways to live my life, according to the dream. I could have a chicken heart and try to avoid all risks. I could have a nonstick heart with a protective coating and seem to take risks while not letting anything really touch me. Or I could have the vulnerable, sticky heart I already had; I could take risks and allow myself to be affected by the outcomes, both good and bad, in an unguarded fashion.

The sticky, risky, vulnerable heart—that's the one for me.

Killer in the House. This dream came in the midst of a conflict I was having with the directors of a writers' conference. Long after I had agreed to speak at the conference, long after the brochures were printed, the organizers sprang a little surprise on me. Because I was speaking at the conference, they informed me, I could purchase my conference registration at a "special discounted rate."

Charging the faculty to hang out with other faculty and students seemed absurd to me—the conference equivalent to vanity publishing. I'd never heard of any conference doing this, and I'd been to quite a few. I groused to my wife. Holly's advice: If I thought I was being treated badly, why put up with it? Quit!

It's hard for me to disappoint people. I am so eager to please that I sometimes let others walk all over me. As uncomfortable as I was with the conference's policy, it seemed important to keep my word, to be reliable, to be *nice*. But Holly convinced me, in the end, to stand up for myself. I told the conference that I wouldn't be coming after all. The conference's programming coordinator told me that my resignation distressed and disappointed her. I felt miserable, but I stuck to my decision.

That night, I dreamed that Holly had let a killer come live with us. I couldn't sleep (in the dream), and while I tossed and turned, I could hear the killer moving around in the house. When I went to the bathroom, there he was with a knife, sizing me up. But he wasn't going to kill me, I realized. As long as I was aware of him, keeping my guard up,

I was safe. Still leery of him, I realized that I could deal with having him in the house. He wasn't so bad, after all.

Dream characters are often aspects of self, and I often think of dream houses as symbols for my whole psyche. Holly had let a killer into the house. That is, she had introduced an aspect of self that I'd kept hidden before when she reminded me, in effect, that I didn't always have to be an eager-to-please puppy. Sometimes I could be a killer, a rottweiler. Sometimes I *should* be a rottweiler. After the dream, I felt better about my resolution to stand up for myself.

This story has a happy ending, by the way. The programming coordinator had always thought that charging speakers was a lousy policy, but no speaker had ever complained before. Armed with my resignation letter, she persuaded the conference committee to change the policy not just for me, but for all speakers. Then she asked me to reconsider. I did. It was a great conference, and I was glad to have gone . . . on terms I could live with, thanks to my inner killer.

Dreaming of Pisgah. In the spring of 1996 I stopped writing short fiction, planning to write only novels instead. Daily, I wondered (well, *obsessed* is more like it) about whether I was doing the right thing. At this time, Holly and I lived in Champaign, Illinois, where I hadn't succeeded in connecting with many other writers. Before that, we'd lived in Boulder, Colorado, where I'd known dozens of writers, and we were about to move to Eugene, Oregon, a town crawling with writers.

I dreamed that I was in Boulder with Holly's brother, Phil, who in the dream sometimes became my father, who is also named Phil. I wanted to go to a town called Pisgah, near Eugene. Phil drove me there in his red pickup truck. He used a shortcut that reduced the distance between Pisgah and Boulder to just a few miles. When we got to Pisgah, I could see Eugene from there. It looked like a wonderful place.

Phil and I got into a green sports car to return to Boulder. A green car? That was the wrong car, we realized. We got out, grateful that no one had seen us get into a car that wasn't ours. Instead, we got into a *red* sports car for the drive back.

Why was "Phil" in this dream sometimes my father and sometimes my brother-in-law? My dreams like to pun. I think the Phils changed because the sound of the name was more important than the identity of the person. The Greek combining form *philia* means "love," as in *philosophy, cryophilic,* and *Anglophile.*

Love drove the red (color of passion) vehicle a short distance from Boulder to Pisgah. Mount Pisgah is the place from which Moses looked down into the Promised Land. When I stood in Pisgah, I saw Eugene. So I should let love do the driving. If I did so, I'd like the journey. I'd go to places like Eugene and Boulder.

As if to underline the importance of passion, I was reminded that the green vehicle wasn't mine. Mine was the red one. But the vehicle itself changed from a truck to a sports car. The driver remained constant, the color was the same, but the vehicle was a different one.

The vehicle of passion may change, the dream told me. Sometimes I'll want the pickup, sometimes the sports car. Sometimes a novel, sometimes a short story. I can't know in advance. What matters is picking the red one.

Maybe the debunkers are right. Maybe dreams don't come from anywhere at all. Reflecting on them is still a good exercise in understanding ourselves.

But I can't close without admitting that I am a believer. I do think my dreams come from somewhere, that they aren't just the detritus left by my brain's janitorial crew. Few of my dreams are as memorable or as elegant as the ones above, but when I do have such a powerful dream, I try to do something to act it out symbolically. Wearing a red shirt for the Pisgah dream, for example, serves as a reminder to myself to heed the dream, to remember what I've learned from it.

Occasionally, some little synchronicity reinforces my belief that some dreams do have a Sender. When I had my Pisgah dream, I hadn't been to Eugene yet. I hadn't seen any detailed maps of the area. When Holly and I arrived in town and I unfolded the first such map, one of the things I saw was the mountain park overlooking Eugene. Mount Pisgah.

Every time I hike there and look down on my new home, I think of the operating instructions I received from that dream. I think about what I'm supposed to be doing here and how I'm supposed to do it. A voice from above, from below, or from somewhere not yet imagined once whispered *Pisgah* to my sleeping brain. That whisper helps me remember where I am and what course I must set from here.

10
Dreaming of Jelly Beans

When I was eleven years old, I dreamed that I held in my arms an enormous basket of treasure: purple, orange, red, green, and yellow jelly beans. I could barely get my arms around the basket, it was so big. And it was mine. All mine.

I awoke from that dream so slowly that when I opened my eyes, I thought I would see the jelly beans next to me in the bed. Of course, they weren't there. The more I woke up, the more I knew that I couldn't have those jelly beans. They couldn't make the crossing from the dream world to the waking one. That didn't stop me from wanting them, however. Even when I was fully awake, I ached with disappointment.

It wasn't just the jelly beans that I wanted. The whole idea of bringing back something from my dreams, of waking up to a magical gift or transformation, appealed as much as the jelly beans themselves. One of my favorite fairy tales was the one about the shoemaker and the brownies. While the shoemaker slept, kindly brownies did all of his shoemaking for him. I wanted brownies to do something like that for me.

As I discovered much later, even if we can't get jelly beans from our dreams, a lot of writers do get gifts from the dream world. Some gifts come in the form of advice—not about a particular story, but about how we're living our lives as writers. I've already addressed this use of dreams in the preceding chapter.

Here I want to cover the sort of gift that I craved and for a long time thought I was never getting—the gift of collaborative dreams that *do* contribute to the writing of a particular story. Such dream gifts are of four types: Raw Ideas, Solutions to Problems, Deeper Connections, and Actual Words.

1. Raw Ideas. This gift comes when you dream of an incident or an image that you then turn into a story. Clive Barker did this with a dream about rotting berries.

The day before his dream, Barker walked through a London market where fruit vendors were sorting rotten strawberries from the good ones. The stench of fermenting fruit permeated the market. Barker's dreams that night were rich with the same smell, but with a difference. In the dream, the scent was not revolting, but erotic. Everything about the marketplace was sexualized by it. Lust was in the air, in every object. Doors and windows were enormous . . . well, you get the idea.

Barker saw the dark side of such generalized eroticism, and he wrote "The Age of Desire" about an aphrodisiac that sexualizes every experience. The man who is given the drug wastes away, consumed by lust. He dies happy, though. Even death is irresistibly sexy to him.[1]

2. Solutions to Problems. You're stuck with some aspect of your story. There's a plot wrinkle you just can't iron out, a character you can't connect with, a passage that you rewrite endlessly and still can't get right. Sometimes a dream will give you the solution.

Isabel Allende had rewritten the last fifteen pages of *The House of the Spirits* ten times. Something was wrong with the voice, and she didn't know how to fix it. Then she had a dream about talking to her grandfather as he lay in bed. In the dream, she was telling him about the book. When she woke up, she realized that she'd been narrating the whole book to him all along. The natural ending, she concluded, was for the narrator to tell the epilogue as if the grandfather were now dead and she were sitting next to the body, telling the last of the story very simply. Thinking of the epilogue in this way, Allende was finally able to write it to her satisfaction.[2]

3. Deeper Connections. Some writers dream about their works in progress. Anne Rice has dreamed of being her vampire character Lestat.[3] Allan Gurganus's characters appear in his dreams.[4] Reynolds Price doesn't dream about his characters, but he sometimes has dreams that he thinks are appropriate to the characters he's currently writing about. He dreams their dreams.[5]

This sort of dream can be an intensification of your conscious work of invention. At the very least, it's confirmation that you're immersed in the work, but such dreams can be much more than just a sign that you're absorbed day and night. Maya Angelou points out that writers can be timid about their own characters, can be "hesitant to get to a depth of a character, to admit that this fictional character does this, thinks this or has acted this way."[6] In a dream, the character may reveal parts of herself that need to be played out on the page if the story is to have its full impact, its authentic truth. A deepening dream can force you to look at things your conscious mind doesn't want you to consider because they're disturbing. Maybe your story needs just such a disturbance.

4. Actual Words. The *New York Review of Science Fiction* published a series of short-shorts that Michael Swanwick wrote when he was dreaming. No, I don't mean that he had a dream, wrote down a report of it, and called the result a story. He actually dreamed that he was writing and was able to wake up and transcribe the text that his sleeping brain had already composed. Talk about coming back with the jelly beans![7]

As far as I know, no one but Michael Swanwick has had lucid dreams of writing a story, word for word. But I do know writers who have been given story titles or exchanges of dialogue that they were able to write into a story.

For a long time I wanted to collaborate with my dreaming self in one of these four ways. It didn't happen. Once or twice I successfully wrote a story from the germ of someone else's dream, but stories inspired by my own dream images never came to anything. I never had a dream that helped me over a plot problem. I didn't dream of my characters. No nocturnal muse whispered story titles into my ear.

As other writers told me about the treasures their dreams had given them, ranging from small details for one book to "the whole thematic thrust" of another, I started to feel like the only shoemaker in town whose brownies were on strike. Everybody else seemed to be waking up to piles of finished shoes.

That's an exaggeration. Even at my most envious, I didn't think that others were waking up to piles of *finished* stories. Dreams provided tantalizing images, compelling scenes, or intriguing moods, and the writers who remembered those dreams went on to do the usual hard work of turning those initiating fragments into stories. Only Swanwick actually came back from dreamland with finished work, and his sleep-written stories were only a few dozen words long; even the most generous brownies had their limits.

Acknowledging the limits of what dreams could contribute to my writing, I still wanted them to contribute *something*. So I kept a notebook next to my bed, tried various alarm clocks in search of one that would wake me gently without tearing the delicate fabric of dream memory, and got into the habit of telling my dreams to Holly every morning after she told me hers.

And still I didn't get the gifts I was expecting. Of my eighty or ninety published stories, I couldn't point to any that had come to me, in any way, through a dream. All my ideas arrived when I was awake. I may have been daydreaming, or I may even have been drifting off to sleep when an idea came. More often, I was wrestling ideas out of the air quite deliberately while I sat in front of the keyboard. My dreaming self just didn't collaborate with me in any of the four ways I've listed.

As a result, I frequently wavered in my devotion to remembering my dreams. Most of the time, I don't remember my dreams without effort, and periodically, I'd stop trying. Holly would still tell me her dreams and ask about mine, but I'd have nothing to report. Eventually, I'd try again to track my dreams. After a while, I'd again stop.

Finally, I noticed an interesting and purely subjective correlation: When I tracked my dreams, my writing went better.

I don't want to exaggerate the difference. It was subtle. I've written well during the times when I wasn't remembering my dreams, and I've sometimes struggled to write during a period of good dream recall. But I tend to have more productive days when I'm remembering my dreams, and I tend to have a harder time getting stories written when I'm not paying my dreams any attention.

One possible explanation for this is that, as I noted in the "Dreaming of Pisgah" chapter, I do get good advice from some dreams. When I'm recalling my dreams, I'm more likely to feel centered and on track, or else to notice that I'm off track and to get some reminders about what to do about it.

I have another theory, though. I think that I've been getting some jelly beans all along. Dreams may put me on better terms with what some call "the unconscious" and the writer Damon Knight calls "Fred." All this time that I was mad at Fred because he wasn't collaborating with me in my sleep, he was. So to my list of four collaborative gifts from dreaming, I have added a fifth.

5. Fred's Goodwill. To understand this gift, I had to reflect on why Fred sometimes becomes reluctant to collaborate with me when I'm

awake. There was a time in my life when we never failed to work beautifully together. In grade school, Fred and I used to spin endless yarns together about smoky flying-saucer battles and space monsters. Fred told me the stories and I drew the illustrations. The two of us spent most of third grade collaborating this way, especially during math lessons.

My teachers and my parents thought Fred had gotten out of hand, so I had to learn to shut him up. It wasn't easy, but I managed to keep him stifled while I learned long division.

As I got older and developed an interest in telling Fred's stories to other people, I began to discover the ways in which Fred's stories could go wrong. He meandered. He didn't always have a point. He was inconsistent. So I learned to edit him while he worked. When I needed ideas, he'd send some up and I'd reject most of them. Once we had an idea, I'd prod him for elaborations, and I'd reject most of those, too.

Fred's experience with my waking self must be irritating. Ninety-nine percent of the time, I'm saying to him, *No! Not that! Something better!* I'm so good at striking down his suggestions, it's a wonder that he ever cooperates at all.

When I dream, however, Fred is uncensored. By recalling my dreams, I say *Yes* to my unconscious. I think Fred appreciates this.

On the other hand, if I don't make an effort to recall my dreams, if I don't honor Fred's nocturnal efforts, then is it so surprising that he should balk when, awake, I call on him for help? I can imagine Fred saying, "What, you want a story? All night I gave you stories. You didn't bother to remember even one!"

Maybe this is all a load of hooey. If so, it's the sort of hooey I will cling to tenaciously even after it's debunked. Why? Because it works for me. Recalling my dreams makes my writing day easier. Or I think it does. Perception can be everything.

Dream recall may smooth your relationship with Fred, too. If you don't recall your dreams now, but would like to, here are a few suggestions:

Wake Yourself Gently. Dream recall is often best if you're allowed to wake up gradually, without any sort of alarm clock. For most of us, this is impractical. In that case, try to find an alarm that will wake you gently, without overpowering your dream sensations with music or words. Ideally, you want to be able to lie in bed, unmoving, when the alarm first goes off. My current alarm turns on a soft light and a recording of ocean surf. My wife sleeps right through it, but it's enough of a signal to wake me. (I also have a much brighter light on a timer as a backup.)

Keep a Dream Journal. Write in it every morning, even if it's just to say, "I don't remember any dreams today." At first, you may remember nothing, but the daily reminder that you want to recall your dreams will eventually help you to do so. Put the notebook where you can find it in the dark. You may find yourself waking up during the night to record your dreams. I've found it helpful to use a pen with a built-in light. I can see what I'm writing, but the light won't wake Holly.

Remind Yourself at Bedtime. Going to sleep with the intention of recalling your dreams also helps. Before bed, I drink half a glass of water and tell myself that when I finish the water in the morning, I'll remember any dreams that slipped away.

Sweet dreams!

11
Death and the Day Job

One of the almost universal scraps of writing advice is, "Don't give up your day job." But for many writers who still have a day job, writing full time remains a potent goal or even the touchstone for being a "real" writer. Not everyone who says that he longs to write all day would actually be happy living the life of the full-time writer, but for those who burn to try it, "Don't give up your day job" can be dream-killing advice.

Those who offer the advice don't usually mean, "Don't give up your day job *ever*." More likely they mean, "Don't give up your day job until it's time, until you're ready, until you have some other way to get what your day job gives you now." So then the question becomes: How can you know when it's time? When will you be ready to jump in?

The answer is often stated in terms of money. I've heard it said that when your half-time work brings in half the money you need and has done so consistently for two years, then you can think about going full time. Or you can make the leap when you have a year's income in the bank. Such advice, while sound and practical, is not at all the first thing you should think of when you wonder whether or not to write full time.

Admittedly, money is the first consideration of most writers and their advisers. But there are deeper matters that have to be resolved before it makes any sense to talk about money. The issue, the real issue, is death.

Two books have recently focused my thinking about death. The first is *How We Die* by Sherwin B. Nuland.[1] Nuland is a physician whose book explores the various ways in which our bodies can fail us, from congestive heart failure to stroke to cancer. It's a compassionate book, one that ultimately raises important questions of medical ethics and the patient's right to determine his own destiny.

More important, *How We Die* is a confrontation with the certainty *that* we die. Every one of us has an Achilles' heel of some sort. If we're lucky and none of our major organs is prone to failure, if our immune system destroys every incipient cancer cell, we'll still crumble with old age.

We say we know this. We've all heard the platitude that nothing in this life is certain but death and taxes. Some of us wear T-shirts that say CARPE DIEM. Seize the Day, since this is the only day you have. Eventually, we will run out of tomorrows. We know, we know, we know.

But how many of us really live with a full awareness of our mortality? Not many, as Ernest Becker reminds us in *The Denial of Death,* though everyone lives in *some* awareness of death.[2] In fact, Becker writes, death anxiety is the very thing that makes us human and drives many of our complex behaviors.

Human beings are dual beings. We are symbolic, and we are animal. In our symbolic aspect, we are self-aware, and our minds can encompass the vastness of the universe and the astonishing complexity of even its smallest parts. This power to understand, to be conscious, means that we also understand our animal aspect, our "creatureliness" as beings that must die.

As soon as we are conscious enough to understand our ultimate helplessness against death, we work to escape the realization. It is a terrifying truth that we could cease to be at any moment, and certainly no child is ready to cope courageously with this certainty.

So Becker (standing on the shoulders of Otto Rank and others) concludes that Freud was wrong. Sex isn't at the core of our humanity. Death is. Becker writes, "If the child's major task is a flight from helplessness and obliteration, then sexual matters are secondary and derivative. . . ."[3]

As children, we develop strategies for repressing our death fears. To do otherwise is to succumb to terror and paralysis. But as adults, life compels us to stir up that ancient anxiety and confront the reality that we die.

Life compels us to confront death, but some of us will evade the compulsion. Repression is a coping mechanism. If you're happy with the way you're coping with your death anxiety, why stir up trouble by confronting it? Entire cultures are built around maintaining what you might call a "healthy" repression. It's as if the culture had evolved to say, "Don't think about that death stuff. Here's something to occupy your thoughts instead." If you're happy with what your culture has given you, why challenge it?

Sticking with coping mechanisms is hard for most writers, though. To the extent that writers are self-conscious about their own culture, the distractions of that culture are liable to fall flat. We see through the distraction because as artists we tend to examine things closely, to ask questions. This is not, by any means, going to be true for every writer. After all, some fiction is written by people who believe that our various distractions really are the answer to all questions of ultimate meaning. In fact, such writers may be fabulously successful in the culture because they so unquestioningly believe in the current cultural obsessions.

And that's fine. The work of such writers will provide psychological armor for vast numbers of people. As I'll discuss shortly, there are various ways for a writer to serve her culture, and one of those is for the writer to help the readers distract themselves. The writers of formula romances or rich-and-famous glitz novels are reflecting some of the culture's death distractions right back at it. That's one function that writers can serve.

But those writers whose goal is the discovery and expression of their unique individuality—the ones who want to make a gift of themselves to the universe—must first deal with death. Otherwise, they are speaking out of repressive reflexes, not out of their own authentic selves.

To experience the truth of death while still alive is what religious thinkers originally meant by being "born again." Martin Luther urged us to "die, [to] taste death as though it were present."[4] To do this is to embrace the death anxiety, which enables us to let go of thoughts and behaviors that were adopted entirely to protect us from this anxiety. Confrontation with death does mean embracing a looming fear, but it's also a step to defining ourselves on our own terms. As Becker writes, "The flood of anxiety is not the end for [us]. It is, rather, a 'school' that provides [us] with the ultimate education, the final maturity."[5]

Artists often make this confrontation with death quite deliberately. The best example may be the poet John Donne, who near the end of his life posed for a portrait showing him dead and wrapped in a shroud. He contemplated this portrait as a meditation "to remind him of what he was soon to be."[6]

Writers who are trying to ask and answer serious questions in their work are likely to come at least to an abstract contemplation of mortality. Who hasn't heard that the great universal themes of literature are love and death?

But death isn't likely to remain an abstraction to most writers. We are introspective. We tend to imagine vividly, and personally. Killing off imaginary characters now and then, we're likely to take the imaginative leap of visualizing our own deaths.

If your thoughts don't naturally tend toward such considerations, you can choose to turn them that way deliberately. I've seen a T-shirt design that depicts a Zen Buddhist image of a dancing skeleton. Just wearing the image on a shirt isn't much of a meditation on your "creatureliness." But you can at any time try the practice, as a "walking meditation," of being aware of your bones, a part of yourself that will outlast you.

A quieter meditation, also from Zen, is to sit still and visualize the image of your own skull half buried in the earth, amid fallen leaves. Just keep the image in your mind and let whatever thoughts arise flow around that image.

Coming to terms with your mortality can, paradoxically, give you courage. Next to death, other threats pale. Whenever I feel fearful about a course of action that I nonetheless want to take, I practice the Power of Negative Thinking. I ask myself what it is about the action that frightens me. If I take this course of action, what is it that I'm afraid will happen? Whatever my answer, I ask myself, Could I endure that? And I could, of course. So I ask myself again, What is it I'm really afraid would result?

If I can't make enough money, I'm afraid that I'll be dependent on others, or out on the street. I'm afraid I'll look foolish. But these are things I can endure. They might distress me, but I could handle them, could come out victorious on the other side. So I keep digging. I keep asking, What's worse than that? What am I afraid would happen?

And it turns out that all my fears lead eventually to death. Death is the one thing I'm sure I can't see myself through. And if I've already accepted that I must die, then I might as well choose to live on the path that I'm passionate about. That way, I'll die in the process of living a life that has meaning for me. (For more on Negative Thinking, see chapter 22.)

In one of Carlos Castaneda's books, don Juan says something similar when he tells Castaneda that Death is an adviser. Whenever you feel anxious, says don Juan, look to your left. That's where your Death stands at all times. Ask Death for his advice, and Death will say, "I have not touched you yet. That is the only thing that matters."[7]

Again, we've heard all of this before. What empowers us is not hearing it, but living by it. Are you living authentically? If you die tomorrow, will you die on a path that you chose for yourself? Is it a path worth dying on, of "spending" your life on in the sense that one spends an inheritance?

Now we've come pretty far afield from the question of when you should quit your day job. To come full circle, let me tell you about my visit to the hospital ultrasound room a few years ago.

I went for a kidney sonogram. Polycystic kidneys run in my family. My grandfather died of the disorder in his early fifties.

Lying on my side in the darkness of the sonogram room, I asked the technician to turn the screen to where I could see it. She did, and I started to ask questions.

"So what are we looking at?"

"See that bean shape?" she said. She outlined it with her finger. "That's your kidney."

"Okay," I said. I could sort of see the shape, though the edges seemed indistinct. There were other shapes that were much more clear. On the sonogram, they looked like black holes. I said, "And what are those black structures?"

"Those," she said, "are cysts."

At that moment, I had no idea what my prognosis might be, and the technician was in no position to tell me. So what loomed in my consciousness, as clear and sharp-edged as those black holes on the sonogram screen, was death.

My first thought was fear. And my second thought was, "Thank God I've been writing." And my third: "I am still wasting too much time."

What will become of me? The nephrologist who interpreted the sonograms had the perfect perspective on my prognosis. "You may not have problems for twenty years. Before then, we may develop drugs that arrest the growth of the cysts. It's possible that you will die of a heart attack before your kidneys give you trouble."

In other words, I may yet live to be eighty-five. Or I may die in a traffic accident before this book sees print. Such considerations aren't morbid. They are the basis for deciding how I should live the next hour, and the next.

You are going to die. Before you do, what kind of life do you want to live?

Should you quit your day job? We haven't answered the question yet, but perhaps we have properly reframed it.

If you fully understand and accept that you are going to die—could die tomorrow of some stupid accident—then your perspective on the question of a day job is bound to shift.

But this shift in perspective isn't going to affect all writers in the same way. Before you can draw any conclusions, you must do some more thinking about what sort of writer you intend to be. And this brings us to the existential question.

Existentialists, as you may know, are not interested in the *essence* of human beings. Whether we die forever, are reincarnated, or have an incorporeal afterlife are not questions existentialists find worthy of pursuing. Questions of essence will take care of themselves in due time, they say, and we can't answer such questions with certainty in the here and now. What we can explore, though, is what it means to exist.

To put it another way, questions of essence ask *what* we are. Questions of existence ask *how* we manage ourselves.

So the existential question is, "How are we to be in the world?"

Previously, I brought up some ideas from Ernest Becker's book *The Denial of Death*. I'd like to turn now to Becker's reading of the existentialist thinker, Sören Kierkegaard.

In the 1840s Kierkegaard, writing from a theological foundation, was coming to conclusions that Otto Rank would later reach in his reexamination of Freud. The essence of all our troubles, Kierkegaard concluded, was our duality. In Kierkegaard's terms, we are above the beasts but below the angels, and this is why we can experience the dread of death. If, like the angels, we were unanimal, we need not die. If, like the beasts, we were unselfconscious, we would not know that we were fated to die.

So our psychological or spiritual struggles arise from our union of opposites. Each of us is both a consciousness and a body. Consciousness makes us aware of our possibilities, and our bodies make us aware of our limitations.

In addition to producing a fear of death, Kierkegaard wrote, this duality produces a fear of life. So we're stuck in a paradox. We fear possibility because the more we express of it, the more we are going to lose when we die. And we fear death because it is the end of possibility.

In a fix like this, how do we go on? How do we act in the world?

Kierkegaard pointed out several answers as they are expressed by the people living around us. At one end of the spectrum are paralysis and madness. These won't concern us too much here, because to the extent that these are defined as ways of *not* acting in the world, they preclude getting much coherent writing done.

That leaves us with three more active and creative ways in which to respond to our death awareness. In short, we can be Philistines, Culture Heroes, or Cosmic Heroes.

The Philistine is the person who "tranquilizes [himself] with the trivial."[8] As I noted earlier, it appears that we humans have evolved superficial cultures to help keep our minds off death. Activity can absorb our concentration, and thus our fear. If we don't want to be aware of our existential paradox, we need to keep busy.

There's quite a range of things with which the Philistine can keep busy. Turn on the television, and you can get a heavy dose of concentration absorbers: a new car, a sexier mate, an enviable two-week cruise. In America, Philistines have the consumer society to work with, but the distraction game can be formulated in other ways, too. The transformation of political leaders or celebrities into idols—what psychoanalysts call transference—is another distraction. Rather than accepting the full range of our own powers, we project those powers onto our idols and then worship them. Busy, busy, busy.

Notice, please, that any of these—a car, a lover, two weeks in the Tropics, or devotion to a leader or a celebrity—any of these can be positive and even wonderful in its own right. What Kierkegaard finds wanting in the Philistine is the reluctance to live expansively. "Devoid of imagination, as the Philistine always is, he lives in a certain trivial province of experience as to how things go, what is possible, what usually occurs. . . ."[9]

Writers can be Philistines, and as I suggested earlier, this isn't all bad. To be a Philistine is vastly better than being paralyzed or mad. This narrowness of life is a kind of armor against the awful dread of mortality. The Philistine writer's job is to help fashion the armor with which people protect their psyches.

Of course, one can be a "good" Philistine writer or a "bad" Philistine writer according to which distractions one chooses to show readers. Some of our distractions are more destructive than others. Fixating on romantic love is a distraction, and this gives us the most simple romance fiction. Answering death anxiety by pretending to *be* the angel of death is also a distraction, one that gives us the SS on one hand and shoot-'em-ups on the other.

For the Philistine writer, the question of when to quit a day job must boil down to distractions. Which gives you more of the distracting goodies you crave, the day job or full-time writing? For Philistines in the developed world, distraction usually costs money, so writing full time will only make sense when it pays better than the day job and can buy more distractions.

The Philistine who confronts his own mortality can slow down to consider what really matters to him, and at this point he may evolve into what Kierkegaard calls an "introvert" and Becker calls a "Culture Hero."

This is the upstanding citizen. Knowing she will die, she is concerned with the legacy her life will leave, and she defines herself by the enduring cultural, social, and historical values that are life-affirming. The Culture Hero as a writer will be concerned with consoling humanity with humanity's own values, reflecting back to the culture only the best that the culture has to offer. This perspective is certainly a step up from the Philistine's because it is so much more thoughtful. The Philistine writer reflects the culture back at itself by reflex. The Culture Hero writer sifts through the culture and selects before reflecting.

The Culture Hero answers the existential question not by avoiding it, but by asking, "What endures?" The answer she is reasonably certain of is "Culture." So culture becomes the repository of her unique self. If she can't endure physically, she can endure symbolically in the memory of the culture. If she isn't a writer, the Culture Hero might instead try to leave her legacy through raising children to be good citizens, or she might run her business in a way that reflects her highest values.

For the writer who aspires to be a Culture Hero, the question of when to give up the day job will come down to a question of where she can make the greatest and most lasting contribution. She may find that she can express her cultural heroism as a mother, an employee, and a fiction writer all at the same time. Or her job may offer little in the way of lasting contribution to her culture, in which case she'll want to make the leap to full-time writing as soon as she knows it doesn't mean that her children will suffer for it.

The limitation of the Culture Hero is that she answers the question "What endures?" on society's own terms.

The *Cosmic* Hero, on the other hand, answers the question of what endures in a broader sense. She knows that cultures and even species are temporary. The only infinite repository for the unique self is . . . the infinite. What endures is eternity. Since she can't transfer herself into immortality, she is limited to addressing herself to it. If the Culture Hero asks, "What will I leave behind?" the Cosmic Hero asks, "What will I say to God while I have God's attention?"

The Cosmic Hero concentrates on her self, on her authentic identity distinct from all others. Her task, while she breathes, is to express that idiosyncratic identity. If she writes, she writes across the sky. She may write across the sky by writing novels, and she may intend for others to read her novels, but she is not writing for other people as much as she is writing in service to the infinite. She is writing because this is the way she has been called to express what she is while she lives.

Becker, who doesn't consider the possibility that there are Philistine and Culture Hero artists, puts it this way:

> The whole thing boils down to this paradox: if you are going to be a hero then you must give a gift. If you are the average man you give your heroic gift to the society in which you live, and you give the gift that society specifies in advance. If you are an artist, you fashion a peculiarly personal gift, the justification of your own heroic identity, which means that it is always aimed at least partly over the heads of your fellow men. . . . The artist's gift is always to creation itself, to the ultimate meaning of life, to God.[10]

The courage of the Cosmic Hero is to say, "So I am to die. Very well. I can accept that as if it has already happened. Now look: While I lived, this is what I was."

This is a saintly sort of existence. Kierkegaard called such a person a "knight of faith." This is someone who has given over the meaning of her life to her Creator. The knight of faith must be sustained entirely by her faith, her "trust in the invisible dimension." She doesn't need distraction and she doesn't need cultural immortality because she has faith in the absolute "rightness" of the universe. Her faith might take the form of a belief in an afterlife, but it might instead be expressed in a trust that is less specific, a trust that however matters of mortality turn out, they are in God's hands and God is worthy of her trust. Whatever is, is right. She dreads death as much as any of us, but her faith keeps being reborn out of her fear. That's what it means to be in a state of grace.

Should she quit her day job? She doesn't even ask the question. Whatever is the handiest expression of her authentic identity, she's already doing it.

The Cosmic Hero, the knight of faith, is an ideal. I think it's an existential state worth striving for, even if we fall short. Kierkegaard, one of those who envisioned this ideal, did not live it. Indeed, it's an ideal at the core of many religions, and only a few human beings ever seem to embody it.

I certainly don't claim to be anywhere near that myself. So far, it's hard enough for me to alternate between being a "good" Philistine and a Culture Hero. Sometimes, in all honesty, I have been a "bad" Philistine. Only in a few instances have I worked in a way that might be worthy of a Cosmic Hero.

I want to be absolutely clear, too, that our knee-jerk categories of "high" and "low" art often have nothing to do with the writer's answers to the existential question. There are Culture Heroes writing science fiction, just as there are "bad" Philistines holding tenured positions in university creative writing programs. Some people who are living close to the ideal of Cosmic Heroes are subsisting on peanut butter in cold-water flats, and some of them are living in Beverly Hills.

When should you quit your day job? Before you can answer the question in monetary terms, I think you need to examine it in terms of faith and death and courage. You need to know what you can endure, and what sustains you.

Answer those questions, and timing your leap into full-time writing becomes a question that answers itself.

Part Three

Step-by-Step

When, Where, and With What?

As a beginning writer, I suspected that more experienced writers knew about some almost magical combinations of place, time, and tools that could help my writing go more smoothly. After a visiting writer had read in the university auditorium, I'd be the student who stood during the Q&A to ask, "Do you write at the kitchen table? Do you keep regular writing hours? Do you write your first drafts by hand? On what kind of paper? With what color of ink?" And the visiting writer might patiently answer all of these questions, but would more often answer only part of them and then say something about how the particulars of writing practice did not matter as much as finding some way, any way at all, to get words onto the page.

Now, of course, I am a more experienced writer. I no longer rise from the audience to ask questions. No, now I get myself invited to the reception after the reading, because in that setting it's much easier to corner the writer and interrogate her until she gives a more complete and satisfactory account of where she writes, and when, and with what tools. At this stage in my career, I don't just *suspect* that place, time, and tools combine to make the writing go more smoothly. I know it.

Well, all right. I don't really corner honored guests at their receptions. But I'm tempted. I *do* eagerly scan interviews with writers to see if they'll talk about the details of how they get their writing done. I'm delighted when I learn, for example, that South African playwright Athol Fugard likes to grind his own ink. For each new play that he writes, Fugard selects a new pen, which he then retires once the play is finished.

I won't necessarily adopt many of the writing practices I run across, but I do learn something from most of them. Fugard's ink grinding may be a sort of ritual, like pencil sharpening, that helps to put him in the frame of mind that he needs for writing. While I don't know what Fugard gets out of having one pen dedicated to its play, such a practice appeals to me in at least three ways. I could imagine that the play was already known to the pen, and that all I needed was patience to let the pen write it out. A pen so special that it could only be used for one task would remind me of the grand nature of that task. And the urge to retire the pen would give me a concrete event to work toward, since it might be a long time after I finished the play before it was performed and "finished" in the eyes of the world.

Does Fugard keep his retired pens or give them away as gifts? Which practice would appeal to me if I were to retire *my* tools? What tools do I use that I could dedicate to just one project? The notion of retiring some object after a work is finished appeals to me, and I might find it motivating and fun to find an analogous way to mark the completion of stories or chapters or books.

The right combination of place, time, and tools will do three things for a writer. First, it will keep him writing enough (rather than researching or thinking about writing or daydreaming) so that a reasonable quantity of work gets finished. Second, it will help him to feel good about writing, encouraging him to keep at it. Third, since we all know that it's easier to enter and record the fictive dream on some days than others, it will help him have more good days than bad ones. That is, a good writing practice will help the writer to dream the dream that is his fiction and record it.

The details of my writing practice tend to be fluid, changing little from day to day, but varying considerably from year to year. Here are some thoughts on what I do now, and why.

Where

Most days, I do my writing in one of two places: reclining on the couch, or sitting at my desk. If I'm on the couch, there's a very good chance that I have a cat in my lap. She'll complain if I don't stay settled, so she helps to enforce the discipline of staying put and working instead of getting up to see if the mail has come. I don't have any comparable method for staying at my desk, since the chair I use has me kneeling as much as sitting. Hence, no lap for the cat. But the wall beyond my computer monitor is covered with little signs, such as the reminder from Isak Dinesen to write every day "without hope and without despair."

Both settings are comfortable. My back is well supported when I'm lying on the couch, and the half-kneeling chair at my desk encourages a posture that I can maintain comfortably for a long time. My office has big windows, so I have plenty of natural light in the summer. For western Oregon's gray winters, I have brilliant halogen and fluorescent lights for both the couch and the desk. From either place, I can look out at trees in the middle distance and give my eyes a break from focusing on a page or a screen that's only a foot or two away.

All of these comforts are important. They make it possible for me to stay on-task for a long time and get some words down on the page, but comfort does more than increase my endurance. Being comfortable helps me to forget that I am writing at all, and I can lose myself in my story. Conversely, if my back aches or if eyestrain gives me a headache, my discomfort will constantly remind me that I'm not really in another place and time with my imaginary people.

Working on the couch gives me an additional benefit. It makes me feel cozily decadent, like I'm getting away with something. That's fun.

It's partly for the pleasures of decadence that I sometimes leave home to work in other places. *Look at me! I'm sitting under a tree in the park! This is my* job, *writing in this notebook and occasionally watching squirrels!* But working away from home can also be a way to jog myself out of a rut when I feel stuck on a story or chapter. When I'm pacing back and forth on the footbridge over the Willamette River, notebook in hand, muttering, I'm writing. Sometimes my pacing takes me over the river to a shopping mall's food court, a hotel lobby, or a bookstore with comfy chairs. I've written in all these places. (I've also ended up killing an hour or two browsing in the bookstore—some destinations are hazardous.)

I've written in cafés, libraries, bus stations, and museums. There are times when it feels necessary to have other people around, when silence or music or white noise just isn't the right background sound for the kind of work I'm doing. And it's not just writers who sometimes want the murmur of human voices for background. Accountants in a new, superquiet office building at the British Broadcasting Corporation found the silence so stressful that management decided to install a special "mutter" machine that would provide simulated background conversation and occasional light laughter.[1] We are social animals. Sometimes we're starved for the sounds of our kind, even when we're concentrating and don't want any actual social interaction.

When

I get up at 6:00 A.M., and from then until 3:00 is my writing time. That doesn't mean that I'm actually on the couch or at my desk for the entire nine hours. Generally, I lie on the couch under the intense light for ten minutes or longer before my reptile brain stirs. I review my to-do list for the day, and then I write for fifteen minutes. Sometimes those first fifteen minutes are journal writing, dream recording, or just desultory mad scribbling that might include lots of cheerleading or whining. I might write about the day's main writing project, circling it, sniffing it, and maybe growling at it. Sometimes I use the fifteen minutes to write three off-the-cuff five-minute stories. Only rarely do I actually begin to draft something in these first fifteen minutes, but these first scribbled pages serve as a sort of inoculation. I have already written, so whatever I write later won't represent the first writing of the day. I already have some momentum.

After that, the next few hours are devoted pretty much to either writing or doing nothing. I eat breakfast, take a shower, meditate, dress, et cetera. Some mornings I may drive my wife to work—a round trip that takes me half an hour. But except for those occasional bad days where I'm sloppy and undisciplined and don't get anything done, that's about the limit of what I do that isn't writing. I don't check my e-mail, read, or listen to the radio. I'm free to stare at the wall all I want.

In short, I either start writing because I want to write, or else I bore myself into writing. I give myself "half an hour" for lunch (which is more often an hour altogether), when I get a little respite from the ban on reading. That's when I open the mail and read the newspaper. After that, I'm back to writing or doing nothing.

I rise early and write early because I'm at my most creative early in the day. Early, but not too early. Many writers I've met get up very early (Katherine Stone gets up at two o'clock in the morning to start her writing day) or stay up late so they can write in the predawn quiet. Six is as early as I want to rise because I'm seldom fully alert when it's dark out. If I got up at five, I'd just be in a waking haze for an hour longer. Writing early also makes it easier to not do some of the things that are less important than writing. Often, there isn't time left for them at the end of the day. Better that unimportant things get neglected, rather than the writing.

Of course, I'd rather not neglect anything at all. I'd like to find a way to follow every one of my dreams, but I've gradually become more realistic. Long ago, I secretly envied a friend of mine whose chronic pain kept him from sleeping more than a few hours a night. He spent part of every night writing at a twenty-four-hour café, then slept his three or four hours at home before getting up at seven for a full day of teaching and study. I used to think that by force of will, I could live like that, too. Think of all the writing I could do with those extra hours, and I'd still have time for everything else! I tried to wean myself of "excess" sleep.

Writing during the wee hours may have been a good way for my friend to deal creatively with his persistent inability to sleep, but trying to get by on five, six, or even seven hours a night didn't work for me. I don't think or write well on less than eight hours of sleep. The fictive dream I'm trying to dream onto the page requires mental alertness. Going to bed at ten is as important to my writing day as getting up at six.

With What

For writing on the couch, I use either pen and paper or my palmtop computer. Pen and paper are for making notes, outlining, or writing around the edges of a project with finger exercises about character or back story. Most of these notes go into a Mead notebook. Each large project gets its own notebook, so ideas for short-short stories go into the notebook for a short-short collection. My stack of notebooks for novels that I haven't written serves as a reminder that I have to stop generating new ideas and write one of these, and then another, if I ever hope to get anywhere as a novelist.

Right before I draft something, I usually jot down an outline and various working notes on an oversized pad of newsprint. For both fiction and nonfiction, I use "cluster" outlining, drawing connecting lines between related ideas. I need the space of oversized sheets to get all the related elements onto one page.

I'm not unnecessarily picky about what pens I use. In a pinch, anything that makes a line will do. However, if I have a choice, I like to work with a variety of colors only because it's fun. Lately, I've been writing with metallic gel roller pens and a two-color roller that lays down an alternately purple or blue line. And although this isn't a very landfill-conscious attitude, I like the gel pens because they put down more ink with every stroke than a regular ballpoint does. A ballpoint seems to last forever, but I use the gel pens up in a matter of weeks. It's silly, but seeing the dwindling supply of ink makes me feel that I must be making progress.

Gel pens also have a very light touch. Since I once bruised my thumb badly by writing for eight hours straight with a ballpoint, I appreciate a pen that I don't have to grip so tightly or press so hard. After that bruise, I couldn't hold a pen for a week—a reminder that driving myself mercilessly now can mean less productivity later.

The palmtop computer's keyboard is so small that I can't touch-type. I have to hunt and peck with my thumbs. But I can do this on the couch, on my back. As I draft the opening paragraphs of something, I compose so slowly that the limitations of the tiny keyboard don't really slow me down much.

The palmtop is so small that I can and do bring it almost anywhere. I can write while the dentist keeps me waiting.

Once I've got my opening paragraphs, I'm ready to work much faster. That's when I move to the desktop computer. I use a split key-board, which reduces the strain on my wrists. Although the finished work will be printed in manuscript format, I compose single-spaced pages in a Times Roman font. I like to see as much of the text at a time as possible.

Colored pens make the writing process more fun; the palmtop adds to my productivity by letting me draft downloadable text anywhere. In both of these cases I'm pretty conscious of my tools as I use them. For dreaming the fictive dream scene by scene and writing it down, my desktop PC is my most helpful tool because I can use it *un*consciously. I touch-type so automatically at that keyboard that I can give all my attention to the story, hardly aware of how I'm writing it down.

That's what works for me. You now know about my own place, time, and tools for writing, in some detail. My point, however, is not that you should do as I do. My point is that we all develop our distinctive work habits in much the same way that we each develop a distinctive prose style.

We learn style by imitation. At least, that's how it worked for me. As a beginner, I copied my favorite writers. In my earliest, mostly unpub-lished stories, an astute reader could point to the adjectives that I bor-rowed from Ray Bradbury, the puns I took from Nabokov, the long sentences I wrote to parallel Faulkner's. As I read more widely and borrowed moves from a greater range of sources, my copycat repertoire grew broad enough that I could pick and choose my effects deliberately. The way that I combined and modified those effects became my own unique style. When I read, I read partly for pleasure and partly as literary espionage, on the lookout for effects that I can steal.

I assembled and continue to modify my writing practice in the same way. Here, then, as an aid to doing the same, is an assortment of other writers' notions of When, Where, and With What.

When

Most writers are regular. Many rise early, as Hemingway did, and write into the afternoon, but most of my writing friends seem to rise late and write either in the late morning and afternoon, or late into the night when the rest of the world sleeps. Timing is often a matter of finding those hours when the house and neighborhood are quiet. When Anne Tyler's children were at school, she wrote until they returned. Such a practice, born of necessity, may continue after the children are grown. James Baldwin wrote nights because his house was quiet then, but even after his children had grown, he continued the practice because he could count on solitude. The phone doesn't ring at 2:00 A.M.

However, being regular doesn't necessarily mean having the same habit every day, or even in every season. My friend Bill Sullivan writes both fiction and nonfiction, but it's the nonfiction that shapes his writing time. Bill makes his living from writing guidebooks for Oregon hiking trails. In the sunny third of the year, he hikes and takes notes. When the rains return, he spends his days at the keyboard.

When Erskine Caldwell lived in Maine, he wrote on even summer days and worked outside on odd ones. During the winter, he switched to shoveling snow or sleeping during the day and wrote at night, every night.

At times when my schedule was too irregular for me to keep to the same writing hours every week, I would make appointments with myself and write them into the calendar so that I could get an hour of writing in on Monday morning, half an hour during my lunch break on Tuesday, and so on. I hated this, and I didn't always keep my appointments, but it was a way to squeeze some writing time into weeks where I wouldn't have written at all otherwise.

Joseph Heller squeezed writing time out of his workdays as a copy-writer. He composed at least parts of *Catch-22* in the office, scribbling away at pages in his desk drawer. If someone entered his work area, he'd close the drawer so they wouldn't know he wasn't creating ad copy every minute.

When you write is also a question of duration. For how long should you keep at it?

Western writer Matt Braun's attitude about hours is typical of many commercial writers. "There is a belief," he writes, "perpetuated through the generations, that a writer can be creative for only *four hours* a day. All but holy writ, the belief has gained widespread acceptance within the literary community. Of course, what it actually represents is the world's best excuse not to work a full day."[2] And it is true that many writers put in forty or fifty hours a week at the desk.

But writing less than one can physically manage may be less a sign of laziness than self-knowledge. Some writers, compelled by financial necessity to write more than they would prefer to, burn out. Others really do have a physical limit. Edward Albee would always get a headache after three or four hours.

Among the four-hour writers were Henry Miller, Aldous Huxley, Thomas Mann, Anne Bernays, and Tolstoy. Anthony Trollope accomplished his staggering output of seven manuscript pages a day during the two or three hours before he went to work.

How long you can bear to write may be a function of what you're writing. John Irving, when he begins a novel, can put in only two or three hours a day. In the middle of the book, he can write for as long as twelve hours, but he slows down again to two or three hours a day when he approaches the final chapters.

Not every writer measures his workday in hours. John Updike writes three pages a day. I believe Fred Pohl manages four.

Some writers are marathoners. Georges Simenon used to get a checkup from his doctor before he wrote a novel, to make sure he was up to it. Then he would write feverishly, living, as he said, "just like a monk." After five or six days like this, he'd be tired of the novel, but he'd press on to finish the damn thing by the tenth or eleventh day, staggering out of his seclusion with a manuscript. William Faulkner wrote *As I Lay Dying* in six frenetic weeks while he was also working as a day laborer, shoveling coal. Quite a few commercial fiction writers do tie-in novels this way, pumping out four hundred pages against an impossible deadline.

On a smaller but still demanding scale, Katherine Anne Porter wrote each of her short stories in one sitting.

There are even writers who were quite successful writing only when they felt like it. Henry Miller would sit down at the typewriter first thing after breakfast, but if he found the words weren't coming, he'd quit. Edmund White agreed with this practice. "If you're not writing well, why continue it? I just don't think this grinding away is useful."[3] Jerzy Kosinski also wrote only when he felt like it, but he also said, "I feel like it most of the time."[4] The extreme case of someone who felt like writing most of the time was Isaac Asimov, who was probably only partly kidding when he said, "Whenever I have endured or accomplished some difficult task—such as watching television, going out socially, or sleeping—I always look forward to rewarding myself with the small pleasure of getting back to my typewriter and writing something."[5] As he also said, "Thinking is the activity I love best, and writing to me is simply thinking through my fingers."[6]

Where

Sometimes, where you write is a matter of taking what you can get. When Raymond Carver's household was too noisy for concentration, he'd take his notebook out to the parked car to write. Many a kitchen table has a second career as a writing desk. Commuting writers have penned novels on trains, ferries, and buses.

My friends mostly have home offices. Only one of them, Michael Armstrong, has his office in a separate building, a cabin that he built a few feet from his home. He built his office as a separate building, rather than as an addition to his existing cabin, to "create a psychological distance between life and work" and to enforce the notion that his writing was a job. "Walking out the door, into the weather, down a short path and out to another building creates a transition: 'Going to the office' becomes a literal act that fosters a working state."[7]

Annie Dillard also writes in a separate building, a shed in her backyard. But Dillard and Armstrong couldn't be more different in how comfortable they think a writing space should be. Armstrong wanted good natural light and an inspiring view. Dillard's shed gets little sunlight. Her desk faces a blank wall so that she can't see out of either small window. "Appealing workplaces are to be avoided," Dillard wrote in *The Writing Life*. "One wants a room with no view, so imagination can meet memory in the dark."[8]

Indeed, View versus No View is a chief debate in the question of where writers should write. "A writer should never install himself before a panorama," said Blaise Cendrars. "Like Saint Jerome, a writer should work in his cell."[9] A view can, after all, be a distraction. William Maxwell's window overlooked nothing but a tin roof. "It was perfect," he said. "The roof was so boring it instantly drove me back to the typewriter."[10]

Norman Mailer, on the other hand, wants "a long view" overlooking "the sea, or ships, or anything which has a vista to it."[11]

In Toni Morrison's case, it's apparently not the particulars of the writing space that matter, but the separation from her home. She rents a hotel room to write in.

Most writers write in a chair, and not a few think that my habit of writing on the couch is strange. But I'm in good company. Truman Capote wrote lying down, as did Paul Bowles. John Nichols reportedly writes while both horizontal and wet, in the bathtub. Agatha Christie didn't draft her fiction in the tub, but she liked to plot there.

Someone once told Virginia Woolf that, as a writer, she had an easier discipline than her sister, who painted. Her sister, after all, had to stand to make her art. Thereafter, Woolf wrote standing up. Hemingway started his writing day on his feet, too, writing in that position until he developed some momentum. Only then would he move to a chair.

With What

John Barth and Anne Tyler write with fountain pens. Tyler feels that the muscular action of moving the pen helps her to recover her imaginative state, to move swiftly back into dreaming the fictive dream. Barth sees the continuous line of ink as helping him to hold the fiction together. "Good old script, which connects this letter to that, and this line to that—well, that's how good plots work, right? When this loops around and connects to that. . . ."[12]

Steinbeck's pencil worked for him something like Tyler's pen. He had to have round pencils. Hexagonal ones were painful to hold for six hours. With the correct pencil in his hand, though, his whole body must have been primed to write. "I really am a conditioned animal," he said, "with a conditioned hand."[13] Some writers vary their conditioning according to what stage their work is in. John Updike writes early drafts by hand, then types them; finally, his secretary enters the corrected pages onto a word processor.

Robert Frost said he always wrote on a writing board, never at a desk or table.

Isak Dinesen dictated some of her early drafts. Erle Stanley Gardner dictated his Perry Mason novels and other mystery fiction. One obstacle to trying dictation is that writing is usually done privately, but dictation is a sort of public performance of the first draft, even if the audience is only one person. Eugène Ionesco didn't want his early drafts to be subject to even unspoken criticism. When his hands shook too much for him to write and he had to hire a secretary, he found one who wasn't particularly sensitive to literature so that she could take dictation without having an opinion about whether something was good or bad. Now voice-recognition programs make it possible to dictate a first draft to a computer. Science fiction writer Wil McCarthy is beginning to experiment with writing fiction this way.

It's not just the tools themselves that matter, but how you use them. I began writing before the era of personal computers. I know that having to retype a complete draft just to fix some problems in the middle sometimes made me fix problems in the beginning that I'd wanted to overlook. I mean, if you've got to retype the whole thing anyway . . .

Fred Pohl knows about this advantage that the typewriter had over computers, and he duplicates the effect by printing out his first drafts and then erasing the file. He forces himself to type the second draft in from beginning to end.

Ultimately, it is true that what matters most is *that* you write, not the particulars of where, when, or how. But by being open to the methods of others, you can sometimes discover new tricks that make it easier to project those moving pictures in your head, write down the words to describe them, and feel like doing it again later.

13

When the Novel Has to Be Done Yesterday

As I began writing this chapter, there was a big difference between *what* I felt and *how* I felt about it. My wrists hurt. My back ached. My brain and body were fried from overwork.

And I was very, very happy.

I had just turned in a novel that I wrote in two months and revised in two weeks. I beat both deadlines. More important, I was happy with the result. *Ashes of the Sun* (by Hanovi Braddock) won't ever stand as one of the great works of Western civilization. It's a game tie-in novel. But I am not going to slink into the shadows when someone points out that Hanovi Braddock and Bruce Holland Rogers are one and the same. I'm proud of the book.

Ordinarily, I'm a slow writer. Landing a novel contract with a tight delivery deadline meant that I had to change how I did things. I needed to figure out how to rush a novel and stay sane, and that called for managing the psychological challenges that I knew I'd face.

What follows are the steps I took, reconstructed after the fact. This is not intended as a formula, but as an illustration of some of the ideas I cover in other chapters. I should also confess that this chapter is much better organized than my behavior was.

So, in a completely artificial order, here's a list of things I did.

1. Start with the motivational Big Picture.
2. Analyze the practical Big Picture.
3. Plan work and rest.
4. Decide on procedural rules.
5. Set performance goals.
6. Energize during the work and after.
7. Reward myself without deprivation traps.

The first item on my list actually *was* the first thing I did when I got the assignment. I sat down with a notebook to write about the motivational Big Picture for this project. I asked myself what writing this novel was going to contribute to my career. Work written under my Hanovi Braddock pseudonym, I reminded myself, isn't intended to be especially deep or thoughtful. Hanovi writes adventure fiction. If I ever write pure space opera or a fat fantasy trilogy, it will be Hanovi who gets the credit, not Bruce.

Money isn't usually my first concern when I write, but it's half of Hanovi's reason for being. I hope that I'll be able to make enough money by writing Hanovi's books in a hurry that I can afford to write Bruce Holland Rogers books by my usual process of slow accretion.

The other half of Hanovi's reason for being is this: Under my veneer of literary sophistication beats the heart of a pulp reader. I love Edgar Rice Burroughs. Yes, I can see the machinery creaking when Tarzan's purely evil enemies do rotten things just to get me to hate them. Yet I still enjoy hissing when they come on stage. I cheer when Lord Greystoke manages an improbable rescue, and I willingly turn off my brain to get through the racism and sexism on every other page. Tarzan is fun, and Hanovi exists because I get a kick out of trying to write slam-bang action that saves the thinking for another book.

So I had agreed to take this assignment because it would be fun and because it would make money to support my other writing. It might build an audience for later adventure fiction by Hanovi Braddock, which would support later serious writing. So my career concerns were for writing quickly, but well enough that readers might look for other Hanovi Braddock books when I wrote them.

I had another important motivational concern: the project's "contribution." I want everything I write to have some positive impact on my readers—even the fiction that I'm doing mostly for money. For Hanovi's books, this is a secondary goal and can partly be expressed in the negative: I *don't* want his books to be sexist or to glorify violence (though there is likely to be violence in them). More positively, I want to discover, in the process of writing the books, some content that appeals to the reader's better nature.

After I had jotted all of this down, I made two little signs to post on my computer monitor. One was a dollar sign—the most compelling "career" motivator. The other, to represent my "contribution" motivator, said, "I am an angel in disguise writing a holy text in disguise." (At one point my wife looked at the sign, looked at me, and said, "Good disguise.")

Why did I bother with this step? Because I knew that there'd be many days when I'd be thinking, "This is hard. Why am I doing this?" Now I'd have ready reminders.

The second step, Analyze the practical Big Picture, was a logistical step. I got out my calendar and did some more notebook scribbling. What were the steps to writing the novel? What did I have to do before I was ready to write the first chapter? (Character sketches, maps, outlines, and so forth.) How many chapters would there be? How many total pages? Also, what other time commitments did I have? I needed to know what needed doing and how much time was available for doing it.

The third step was to divide the tasks so that I could have an overview of what would have to be done when. This was pretty straightforward—a matter of writing in "character sketches" on the first day, "third-pass outline" on the second, and "write chapter 1" on the third. What makes this step worth mentioning is that for once I took into account my bad tendency to overbook and burn myself out. If I commit to write for six hours each day for three weeks without a break, I'm likely to go on strike by the seventh day—procrastinating all day and feeling guilty the whole time. The result is that even though I don't work on that seventh day, I don't relax, either, and end up feeling burned out when work begins on day eight, leading to another strike on day nine or ten. This time, management agreed to labor's terms from the outset. I blocked off some days for relaxing guilt-free.

I was also realistic about how much writing I could do on the day before or the day after the writer's conferences I had scheduled each month. I gave myself a day off before and after each conference. I also had a play script under contract, and I'd have to do requested revisions for that. I blocked four days for working on the play. I was left with forty-one days available for writing *Ashes*. The outline called for a novel thirty-four chapters long. I set aside two days for prewriting and five for the initial revision. That meant that I'd need to produce a chapter a day.

Step four was to plan procedural rules. What approach would best support my getting a chapter done every day? Since I'm a master procrastinator, I told myself that I would always be at my writing desk by nine in the morning. When I wrote, I would not reread what I had done in earlier chapters. If what I said in chapter 6 called for a revision of chapter 1, I'd make a note of that and fix it later. I would not worry about the contents of a future chapter until I came to it. I would start each day with one hour, no more, of brainstorming the chapter's contents and jotting notes. Then I'd write toward a dramatic conclusion.

All of this helped to compartmentalize the various stages of writing. I can't sit down to write a novel—that's too intimidating. But I can sit down to write the tentative first page of the first draft of a novel, especially if chapter 1 is the only chapter I have to think about. The rules helped to clarify what I was responsible for at each moment. Of course, rules don't help if they're applied too rigidly. If a chapter went so seriously wrong that I couldn't bear to set the next one on so shaky a foundation, I went back to revise, even though the rules forbade such revisions. Rules must support getting the work done, and if they become an obstacle, it's all right to bend them.

Step five was also designed to reduce my performance anxiety. I set performance goals.

Performance goals come in two varieties: certainty goals, and expectation goals. The certainty goals are the ones I have complete control over. These are the goals that do the most to reduce anxiety, since anxiety springs from fear over what can't be controlled.

On the small scale, I set an expectation goal of a chapter a day. This is what I fully expected to be able to do, and it was what my calendar called for. But this goal alone would have made me anxious at the start of every day, so it was supported (and ameliorated) by a certainty goal: Every day, I would write on the current chapter for six hours.

I couldn't always produce a chapter every day. Some days I got hung up on some plot difficulty or another. (Thankfully, there were some days when I wrote a chapter and a half.) But every single day, I could guarantee that I'd be at my desk for those six hours.

As I've been saying in earlier chapters, all goals are easier to reach if you atomize them. My real goal was to write for four ninety-minute stints with nature breaks in between. It was easier, that way, to stay in the saddle when my back began to ache. By the time I felt achy, I'd look at my timer and see that just twenty minutes remained before I could take a break. Similarly, beginning a chapter is hard, but writing the first sentence of a chapter is easy, so that's what I commit to do when I sit down for the first ninety-minute session. If I reach that goal, then my new goal is a second sentence. Then a third. Soon I'm in the groove.

My certainty and expectation goals were also set on a large scale, and could be summed up in the phrase, "It doesn't have to be good, it has to be done." August 1 had to be my first concern. (It helped to remember Randall Jarrell's definition of the novel as "a prose narrative of some length that has something wrong with it." I wasn't going to get it perfect even if I had a decade to keep working.) A finished novel of any quality, that was my certainty goal. My expectation goal, though, was a good story. I couldn't guarantee that outcome, but I aimed for it.

Step six, energize during the work and after, was designed to keep me from burning out. Weekly breaks and travel breaks wouldn't have been enough to keep me going if I were working in an unsupportive environment.

Here, you need to know yourself. Social interaction energizes me, and too much solitude saps my energy. Unfortunately, my wife was away at a think tank for all of the first month that I was writing the book. I compensated with social interaction online and by occasionally taking my work to the library, sketching the day's chapter out in the company of strangers.

I also used movie soundtrack music even more than I usually do. Just to keep putting one word after another, I played some cursorial Vangelis music from *Chariots of Fire* and *Antarctica*. I used some music for particular moods, *Krull* and *Universal Soldier* for battle scenes, *Schindler's List* for pathos, but the main function of playing the music was to get my blood moving—a hard thing for an extrovert to do in day after day of solitude.

Finally, I rewarded myself at the end of each working day. It really didn't matter what rewards I chose. What helped to keep me feeling good (and productive) was the feeling that some small thing I was enjoying at the moment had been *earned* with hard work. But I also did not deny myself "unearned rewards." Negative reinforcement works well in some contexts, but I've found that reward deprivation is counterproductive for my writing. It damps my enthusiasm for work.

Thus, on some days I might have decided that a cool shower would be my reward for finishing the day's work. If I finished my six hours and showered, I felt great for having earned the shower. But if it was a swel-

tering hot day and I needed a cooling shower in order to be able to concentrate, I'd take it anyway. It just wouldn't have the I-earned-this buzz
attached. I'd choose something else as the reward for coming back and
writing my last two hours.

That's the essence of how I got to page 441 of *Ashes of the Sun*.

What works for one writer won't work for the next. Indeed, what
worked for me on this project may not keep me motivated and energized the next time around. But I've found that thinking deliberately
about motivation, energy, and anxiety issues helps me to get the work
done even under pressure-cooker conditions.

14
When the Novel Has to Stew

In the previous chapter, my emphasis was on mental tricks for getting the work cranked out, the tricks that made it possible for me to write a novel in two months. I stand by my advice, but I also think I should make clear that it's far from the only correct answer to the question, How do novels actually get written?

Some writers and teachers of writing emphasize some nose-to-the-grindstone rules for writing, rules that sound something like this: Don't dawdle. Get the draft down on paper. Write fast. Don't count research as writing time. Have a bunch of projects lined up so you can move quickly on to drafting the next one after the current one is done. Be business-minded.

All of this makes perfect sense for some writers. And for any writer, it will make sense some of the time. It's true that sometimes the only way to begin the story is to stop thinking about it and just *go*. Writing fast can get you past all sorts of emotional complications that will otherwise bog you down in your own ego. Research can be an excuse for procrastination if drafts make you anxious and research is fun. If you don't know what your next project is, you can spend a long time drifting after you've finished a novel. And if you aren't business-minded, you may write an unmarketable book or be devoured at contract-signing time.

But the overall pressure-cooker approach is disastrous advice for some writers. Novelist Sean Stewart tells me that if he'd tried to follow such advice at the outset of his career, he'd have had a Terrible Writing Accident. Though Sean is amazingly productive, he isn't configured for that sort of speed.

Part of the difference may have to do with the writer's aims. If what you want to do is spin a good yarn, if the novel you propose is plot-driven or sets out to convey a clever conceit that's already clear in your mind, then writing fast may be the best approach. But if you're writing a character-driven novel, or one that conducts a thought experiment about ideas you only vaguely understand and must develop as you go, then writing the novel as if it were due yesterday may keep you from producing the book you really want to write.

To oversimplify, the more a book is genre action-adventure, the better it lends itself to hurried construction. The more literary the book, the slower it must be cooked up.

I can already hear the howls of protest. I *did* say I was oversimplifying. And either approach, fast or slow, can ultimately yield an action book or a thoughtful book. (I am gratified that many readers found *Ashes of the Sun* to be a thoughtful book, even though my first concern was for good adventure.) What's more, an action book written fast can turn out to be thoughtful, and certainly a good character-driven novel can also have a riveting plot.

But the oversimplification works very practically for me. I have written five novels. Four were action-adventure novels. The fifth is a hard-to-categorize (and thus hard-to-sell) novel that has gone through a zillion drafts and transformations, each of which taught me something new about the nature of the characters. In tone and in structure, it is a literary novel. The action-adventures were all written quickly. The unsold literary novel emerged very slowly, and I wrote many pages *about* it before I was able to type CHAPTER ONE.

The slow-cooking technique is the one I'm using now for my novel-in-progress, *Steam*. I'm still discovering very basic things about who the characters are, what they want, where they've been. I'm struggling to define the narrative shape. I am a long way still from writing the first page.

This slow-cooking approach is a little like the way that Orson Scott Card wrote *Ender's Game*. He thought about the book and made extensive notes for two years, then sat down and drafted the complete novel in two weeks. The difference is that Card was spending those two years creating a detailed outline. What I'm doing is more nebulous. I'm creating something less concrete than an outline. By the time I draft the first chapter, I may still be vague about what happens in the middle of the book, but I'll know who it happens to, and I'll know what I think the ultimate meaning will be (though this will shift on me as I write, like sand under my feet).

So what am I spending my time on?

I'm writing character sketches. I'm writing biographies about my characters, covering mundane details like what they look like, but also psychological details about how they perceive and act in the world.

I'm also writing poems written in the voices of the characters. I'm playing metaphor games with them. (If Adrian's name were a color, what color would it be? If Jenna were an animal, what animal would she be? If Blake were a spy, whom would he spy for? With what mission?) I've found many good questions like these in *Writing With Power* by Peter Elbow, but you can certainly make up your own.[1]

Because it's a great symbol system for complicating my simple first thoughts, I'm also using the tarot to explore my characters. I have a CD-ROM program that has laid out a spread for each character's past, present, and future in the physical, mental, and spiritual realms. The tarot is vague enough that anything it suggests requires a great deal of interpretation, but it's emotionally and symbolically loaded. I particularly like the cards from the Mythical Tarot deck because each suit in the Minor Arcana follows a particular myth in developmental terms: Pentacles is the life of Daedalus, Swords is Orestes, Wands is Jason, and Cups is Psyche. These story images in the cards help me to get a feel for the developmental issues represented by the cards.

The setting for *Steam* is integral to the story, and I'm writing about it. Eventually, I may draw maps of the place.

I'm reading. The novel is about steam locomotives, manic depression, and fathers, among other things. So I'm reading an 1889 edition of M. N. Forney's *Catechism of the Locomotive* until I really know how a steam engine is operated. I'm watching videotapes of engine crews running steam engines of various vintages. I'm reading about manic depression, and I'm reading books about father–son relationships and about daughters whose fathers abandoned them.

And I'm writing about the meaning of these things, little essays to myself about what a steam locomotive tells me about the universe, about human beings. I'm writing about manic depression, about my own feelings about fatherhood, about what it means to be or not be a father.

I'm doing all of this in the context of the novel that's beginning to take shape in my mind, and I'm writing about what narrative shape might contain that novel. There are four novels that have something to do with how I want to write this novel. So I'm writing about how

Faulkner's *As I Lay Dying* is like what I want to do, and how it is different. I'm doing the same for *Going After Cacciato* (Tim O'Brien), *Tourists* (Lisa Goldstein), and *Talking Man* (Terry Bisson). I know instinctively that each of these novels has something to teach me about the shape of *Steam*.

Besides these novels, I'm looking at the beginnings of other novels, reading lots of first pages to ask, "If *Steam* opened in the same way that this novel opens, at what point in my story would I be beginning?" I may write the first page of an opening that develops tension the way *Breathing Lessons* does. How did Tyler do that? What would I gain by using a similar strategy?

Along similar lines, I have dabbled with beginnings that used different opening-scene narrative strategies. If I started the first chapter with dialogue, which two characters would be talking? What would they say? Or if I opened with a description of an important object, what object would it be? How about starting with a bizarre action? What action? If I were to start with an expository lump (generally not a good idea), what would I want in that lump? What thoughts might my main character be thinking at the beginning, some arresting thought that he would never dare to speak aloud?

Such exercises do not produce actual first pages, but they do help me to discover what the book is about and what things *might* appear on the first page to announce, symbolically at least, what the book's concerns are to be.

As I do this kind of work, I sometimes have the sort of "Aha!" revelation that shifts my perspective significantly. Last night, for instance, I saw how dividing a character into two bodies so that half of him could have one adventure with his brother while the other half stayed behind with some other characters solved a major structural problem that had been nagging me. This event has to happen in the first chapter, and it changes what the book is about. It also shows me what the chapter-by-chapter structure of *Going After Cacciato* has to do with my book. (I knew there was a relationship, which is why I diagrammed O'Brien's novel, but I didn't know the nature of that relationship until my character offered to perform this nifty splitting trick.)

Not everything I'm doing at this stage looks even remotely like work. I'm walking and thinking about my novel, listening to music while I daydream about the novel. Of course, I have three-by-five cards in my pocket while I do this, and I take them out and write as ideas emerge.

I'm also planning on running the novel through various heuristic exercises, lists of questions that I can ask myself to clarify what my story is and why it's worth telling. As the novel opens, what is one of the characters on the verge of doing? What does this character want most in the world? What opposes him or her?

There is a risk to writing a novel this way if, like me, you have a history of abandoning projects. It's also a very frustrating way to proceed if you're feeling pressure to get the next manuscript into your agent's hands or to get a first novel written to prove that you really can write one.

It can also be a pleasant and ultimately very productive way to write. Certainly, it's slow. But it's also deep. The trick lies in knowing when to shift gears and produce scenes, when to stop and noodle some more.

Blast-scorching and slow-simmering are not the only ways to cook up a novel. I see these as the extremes, and I've been successful with both of them, if you measure success by *my* satisfaction with the finished novel. But there are so many other correct ways of doing it that Kipling was wrong when he said, "There are four and twenty ways of constructing tribal lays, and every single one of them is right." He missed by several orders of magnitude. There are at least as many ways to write as there are writers.

How do you write a novel? I think you have to answer that question one novel at a time. Do what works for this novel. For the next, you may have to invent the whole process all over again.

Part Four
Dangerous Territory

15

The Hazards of Rejection and Acceptance

The letter is identical to the letter that hundreds of other applicants are receiving at the same time. Even so, it seems personal: "We regret to inform you that your grant application was not among those chosen for funding." Long seasons of hope collide with that sentence like a robin crashing against a windowpane.

Rejection feels awful.

Of course, there was the time I opened an envelope from the Oregon Arts Commission. Inside that envelope I found another form letter, only this one began: "We are pleased to inform you. . . ." My whoop of joy terrified the cat, and my triumphant leaping probably registered on seismographs miles away.

Acceptance feels wonderful.

Those twin realities, that rejection feels so bad and that acceptance feels so good, pretty much sum up the hazards of rejection and acceptance. Powerful feelings come with the "yes" or "no" of an arts endowment, an agent, a publisher, a movie studio. And those feelings can change how we behave, how we think, and how we relate to others.

Negative and positive feelings shape our behavior in an obvious way. We move away from what feels bad. We move toward what feels good.

The feelings that come with rejection or acceptance may shape my behavior in ways that I eventually regret, but which in the short term help me to feel more pleasure and less pain. To avoid rejection, I may stop sending out my work, applying for grants, or attending critique sessions. Or I might try to lessen the emotional impact of rejection by submitting my work to markets with low standards. That way, I think I'm more likely to get an acceptance, and if I get a rejection, it's from a publication that I don't respect. Who cares if they don't want my story? I don't want *them*, either.

On the other side of the equation, I've said yes to projects that really weren't right for me just because it felt so good to be wanted.

If rejection makes you miserable, you may draw gloomy conclusions that don't really fit reality. If you feel bad enough, you may forget any good thing anyone ever had to say about your writing. You'll make decisions based on a glum view of both the world and your abilities. An acceptance, on the other hand, may drive you to enthusiastic overconfidence. Confidence is great, but you don't want to end up promising more than you can deliver.

When it comes to relating to others, I have warmer feelings for editors who have bought my work than for those who have only rejected me. At the extreme, rejection can lead us to imagine that the editor's rejection is more than a professional judgment. One of my friends told me that editors who used to buy her work started to reject it again. She reasoned that they couldn't be rejecting the quality of the work, which they had previously agreed was professional. Her conclusion: "They just hate me."

If the editors hate you, then it's only reasonable to hate them in return, right? And some writers take that stance. True story: When the editor of a newer magazine received death threats from one rejected writer, he called the FBI. The bureau began an investigation, and FBI agents showed up in the offices of other magazines asking to see their editors' correspondence from this writer. These other editors complained about this to the New Editor. "But the guy threatened to kill me!" the New Editor said. And the Old Editors told him, "This happens all the time. If we all called in the FBI over every death threat, we'd be too busy cooperating with investigations to read manuscripts." Before long, the New Editor had received enough threats for him to realize that this was so.

Sending death threats to editors is rotten. Such corruption of the soul is bad for all concerned, but adoring the editor who accepts you may also make for an awkward business relationship. And in all of these scenarios of altered behavior, diminished reasoning, and distorted relationships, the price you pay for not dealing well with rejection or acceptance is the same: You lose your flexibility. The pain or pleasure becomes your whole experience of sending your work out and getting a reply, and you get less information out of the exchange than you might have, deal less resourcefully with whatever comes next.

Since we're going to have powerful feelings in response to rejection and acceptance, it's important that we not be overwhelmed by them. So how can you have a healthy, flexible relationship with rejection and acceptance?

Among the many how-to-write books on my shelf, the advice for handling rejection is almost always: Don't take it personally. That's good advice. But I also think you should sometimes take rejection personally in the right way.

When I receive a rejection, I take a moment to discover how I feel about it and to decide what combination of impersonal and personal responses will help me to feel that I have answered the rejection. And it is very important to do *something* in reply to a rejection. Otherwise, the rejection is getting the last word.

To respond without taking the rejection personally, I often console myself with truth or history, analyze the meaning of this particular rejection, and then put my work back into the mail.

Why are stories rejected? The first reason is that the work is not yet fully realized. The writer is not yet writing stories that other people will pay to read. This truth may not seem like much of a consolation, but it can be. If the piece isn't ready for its audience, then I need to work more and learn more. There is something that I can do about such rejections, even if it takes time and effort.

The second main reason that stories are rejected is that the editor can't use them. The story may be a good one—well written, interesting, and moving. But an editor builds a magazine just as a carpenter builds a house. If my story is a twenty-by-thirty-by-thirty block of polished mahogany, it may be some of the most gorgeous wood the carpenter has ever seen, but he can't frame with it, can't cover the roof with it . . . he can't use it. Stories have to fit the issue that the editor is assembling, and new titles have to fit the book publisher's list. I take consolation in knowing that a rejection for "poor fit" has little or nothing to do with how good the story may be.

The consolation of history is one that you've heard before, but it doesn't hurt to be reminded: Editors have rejected wonderful work. Robert Pirsig's best-seller, *Zen and the Art of Motorcycle Maintenance*, collected 121 rejections.[1] *The Clan of the Cave Bear* by Jean Auel was rejected because it was judged too long a novel to be profitable. "We don't think we could distribute enough copies to satisfy you or ourselves," an editor wrote.[2] Another publisher has distributed millions of copies in several languages.

James M. Cain was told that, although unpublishable, *The Postman Always Rings Twice* showed that he might be able to write a successful novel eventually.[3] Tony Hillerman was instructed to "get rid of all that Indian stuff" if he wanted to revise and have the editor reconsider his first novel.[4] Before Irving Stone's *Lust for Life* sold twenty-five million copies, it was rejected many times, once by an editor who called it "a long dull novel about an artist."[5]

John Le Carré, H. G. Wells, John Knowles, and Rudyard Kipling are among the many writers rejected on the grounds that there was no future for them as writers.[6] Dr. Seuss was turned down early in his career because he was writing and illustrating work that was just too different from what publishers of children's books were selling.[7]

The foregoing consolations are general responses. But what about any particular rejection letter that I've just received? To respond to it, I might reread my submission. Does the story say what I intended? Do I still think it's written well? Is a revision called for? Perhaps I should reconsider my ambitions for the piece. Is it right for a general audience or a specialized one? Is it too sophisticated or too simple for the markets I had in mind?

If the rejection letter is more than a printed form, I can also reconsider my submission in light of what the editor said. Did the editor miss my intention? Why? Was it my writing that missed the mark, or his reading? Sometimes you may decide that the editor read inattentively. It happens. But the editor's "misreading" may actually point to a problem that you can now recognize and correct.

Incidentally, unless an editor invites you to revise and resubmit, you should be wary of taking any advice offered in the rejection letter. Some editors have form rejection letters with language that sounds as if it were written for you and you alone, and you can go crazy looking for the inconsistencies implied by the remark that your work was "generally consistent." The words may mean nothing at all. One editor's rejections told almost every writer that his or her submission was "generally consistent."

Even if the editor writes a rejection specific to your submission, the gesture may be an expression of courtesy more than it is the result of thoughtful analysis. Giving you a detailed reason for the rejection seems more attentive than just saying "not right for us," when the latter may, in fact, be more accurate.

Finally, I can respond to a rejection by rejecting it. I can put the manuscript right back into the mail to a different editor.

In none of the strategies above am I taking the rejection personally. But often rejection does feel personal. I don't like to attempt a stiff upper lip. It doesn't take long for the rest of me to stiffen up as well. So in addition to being reasonable, I make rituals, and I get righteous.

I have shredded rejections. I have burned them. I have taped them to the wall. Ideally, each rejection should elicit its own response, reflecting how you feel. Sometimes it's enough to file the rejection or throw it away. But certain rejections deserve something special.

My favorite rejection story comes from a friend whose eight-year-old son collaborated with another boy to write and submit a story for *Cricket*. The story was returned with a standard rejection notice. The boys then collaborated on an appropriate response to the rejection. They took the offending letter into the backyard. They burned it. They mixed the ashes with dog shit. They buried it.

As a ritual for dealing with rejection, that's perfect. The boys recognized what they felt, they responded creatively with an expressive gesture, and they offended no one. I'm sure they felt better.

If you're angry about a rejection, getting righteous lets you be angry in a constructive way. As Sean Stewart once told me, "I don't wish to advocate blind rage and senseless vindictiveness, but as the comic said, it worked for me. If you have a choice between fury and despair, go fury."

Sometimes I seethe. Rejected, I resolve to keep writing, keep improving, and *show the bastards!* But to do this without damage to my soul, I have to keep some perspective on my fury. I understand that the bastards I'm going to show up aren't real people. Living, breathing editors, publishers, and even their accountants deserve my compassion. The bastards are straw men, the System, Them.

If rejection builds a fire under you, stoke it. We can all use the steam. But burn straw in your imagination, not people.

Staying flexible in the face of acceptance is just as important as a flexible response to rejection. My first instinct is to take acceptance personally. And I do. I celebrate. An editor wants me! Hooray!

Then I *don't* take the acceptance personally. I analyze the deal I've been offered. I consider the reasons why I might want to decline. I talk it over with another writer. And because I have already celebrated the acceptance, turning down the deal doesn't mean turning down the good feelings. I've already enjoyed and expressed those feelings.

Rejection, of course, remains the greater challenge.

What will I do the next time I am rejected? I've got matches. There's plenty of dog shit in the neighbor's backyard, and the neighbor has said, "Sure, help yourself."

I'm ready.

16

The Hazards of Writing Workshops

Writing workshops are great. They give writers a chance to learn from one another, to find solace for some of their shared difficulties, to cheer each other on, and to share market news and survival tips.

And writing workshops are awful. They give writers a chance to vent their hostilities at each other, to shoot the wounded, to sabotage one another's efforts.

Both of these perspectives are true enough that even though I'm a fan of workshops, I understand why Sharyn McCrumb once said, "I wouldn't show a novel to anyone who couldn't write me a check." But the problem for a writer who relies entirely on editors is that editors miss things, especially in the current marketplace where many editors are largely purchasing agents. Even if you get an editor who is more involved and capable, she can make suggestions that are just plain wrong for the work, but knowing when the editor is off base is harder when you're relying entirely on your own judgment. It helps to have vetted your work with your peers.

Workshops are more likely to help, less likely to damage, if you have a sense of the dangers going in. Here is my map of Workshop Hazards, followed by some possible ways around them.

Hazard One: Ego Damage From a Righteous Critique

This is the most basic hazard of a critique session. We come to a workshop with something that has taken us long hours over days or months or years to create. Even if it's a very strong story, there are going to be flaws. So much can go wrong in a narrative, and success is so subjective that getting it right for all readers is impossible.

In the space of an hour, then, we subject ourselves to hearing a dozen or so opinions about where we went wrong. That's hard enough, but in most workshops there are one or two critics who are famous for unloading without much tact. These may be critics whose observations are acute and useful. They are so direct, however, that their comments feel a bit like a sledgehammer between the eyes.

This might not be so bad, except that many of us come to workshops with a secret little fantasy. We think, "This time, with this story, I'm going to blow everyone away." That's the fantasy that I've harbored in twenty years of workshops, anyway. I have always wanted to hear everyone say, "I love it. It's brilliant. Don't you dare change a word." But no one ever says it, except as a joke. (The fact that these sentences always work as a joke is, I think, an indication of how widespread this fantasy is. We're all hoping to hear these words in a workshop, and we are always disappointed.)

So we come hoping against all experience that we'll be praised, even adored. Instead, we get a detailed assessment of imperfections and shortcomings. That's hard to take. Sometimes it's so hard that people will quit a workshop or even quit writing.

Hazard Two: Ego Damage From Hostility, Insensitivity, or Grouchiness

I've met quite a few workshop participants who used critiques as a way to tear down other writers in order to make themselves feel bigger or more "real." Writers who see themselves as avant garde are especially prone to this. Since their own work will appeal to only a small audience, they tell themselves that their audience is the only one worth reaching . . . and they belittle writers who try to reach anyone else. (Actually, such hostility can come from commercial writers, too, who also may belittle any audience but their own.)

In a workshop this hostility is expressed as a rejection not of the work itself, but of the whole desire to produce such work. This is harder on the ego, because now it's not your particular efforts that are found wanting, but your basic objectives, your aesthetic judgment, your *self*.

There's accidental damage, too. Many years ago in a senior-level poetry workshop, a freshman woman read aloud her Tragic Suicide Poem, and when she got to the end, I laughed with one great explosive "HA!" I am sure that she felt I was laughing at her poem. But what had amused me about her ten-line melodrama was that I had written one just like it when I was a freshman, and so had many of my friends. I laughed because I recognized suddenly that there was a developmental progression to writing. Years earlier I had been where she was now, and the realization gave me a jolt of pleasure.

Nowadays if I didn't control such an outburst, I would at least have the decency to explain why I had laughed and try to apologize. But I said nothing to soothe the wound I had insensitively (and unintentionally) inflicted. She suffered accidental ego damage, I'm sorry to say.

Finally, you'll sometimes get leveled when the person who is critiquing your work is simply in a bad mood. Such damage isn't personally hostile, but it isn't exactly accidental, either. And all such injuries hurt, whether they arise from malice, insensitivity, or grumpiness that had nothing to do with you or your story.

Hazard Three: Critiques May Lead You Astray

Here I don't just mean that the readers in your group may be wrong about whether you need a different title. I mean that a workshop or one person in that workshop can become your main audience, and you'll end up tailoring your work to please them.

At a recent workshop, Damon Knight said of my story, "This isn't up to the standard I've come to expect from you. It's not your kind of story. I don't know why you wrote it. I wish you hadn't."

Sheesh.

Fortunately, I'm at a stage in my career where I already know that I write lots of different kinds of stories. So while I respect Damon and think he's a wonderful teacher, he's never going to convince me that I should abandon the subgenre of slight and silly SF. It's one of the things I sometimes do. But if I were younger and newer at this writing business, I might have taken those words to heart and resolved to write only the kind of sophisticated story that Damon expected from me.

Being led astray is an even bigger problem if the workshop is full of writers who do work that's very different from yours. If they don't recognize and honor your objectives (which is hard for them to do if *you* don't recognize and articulate your objectives), they may persuade you to do work that fulfills their dreams more than it fulfills yours.

More generally, a bad critique can make writers feel socially desperate, as if they need to prove their value to the group. This can warp not only the writing, but the writer's interactions with group members as well. I've seen folks get either shrill or obsequious in workshops. In fact, I've been pretty shrill or obsequious myself. If anything, this raises the emotional stakes and will make the next critique of your work that much more devastating.

How to Protect Your Ego From Righteous Criticism

The first step in keeping a good workshop from wounding you is to have a clear sense of why you're attending.

Are you trolling for compliments? That's not a bad thing if it helps motivate you to finish work and bring it to the workshop. But it is important to separate the fantasy from the reality—most of the time, your stories will not make all the other writers go slack-jawed with amazement.

Success, more than anything else, can take the sting out of criticism. The more stories you've sold, the better you'll be able to hear criticisms without thinking that you're no writer at all. But it's not just sales that will do this for you. There are other forms of "publication," after all.

Public readings are a good way to have an audience for your work. Reading aloud, hearing and seeing your audience react, can do a great deal to bolster your confidence. You might also try forming a "reader's workshop" of other writers where you read aloud to one another from works in progress but *do not critique!*

How you receive critiques will also affect how you feel about them. It helps to take copious notes as your critics speak. This keeps you occupied (so you won't be mentally defending your story), gives you a record to consider later when you're not in the hot seat, and encourages your critics. (It's hard to criticize. It's made easier if you think the person you're speaking to is really paying attention.)

If you do find yourself wanting to defend your story, this is usually a sign that your motives are skewed, that you're placing your ego ahead of the story. After all, you won't be able to stand next to every reader and explain things once your story is published. Workshop readers are giving you information about what they didn't understand, or what blocked them from enjoying the story. Just absorb it. Think of it not as a judgment, but as data that you must think about and interpret later.

Remind yourself that social acceptance doesn't depend on opinions about your stories. (If it does, find another group. The one you're in is poison.) One of my friends abandoned a workshop after it shredded one of her stories. Months later, she ran into the workshop leader in a grocery store. He said that he missed her and wondered why she'd stopped coming. When she told him it was because of that story's poor reception, he couldn't recall what story she was talking about. Chances are, *you* are always going to be more memorable than even your best work.

Again, it's success that will do the most to protect your ego. So keep in mind, as your precious words are dragged over the coals of righteous criticism, that it's better to suffer now for the sake of your eventual success, rather than mailing out a story with flaws you just couldn't see.

How to Protect Your Ego From *Un*righteous Criticism

The first thing to know is that some hostile workshops can't be fixed. The whole point of some avant-garde groups is to create a social environment where marginalized artists support one another, and hostility to anyone who isn't part of the in group is one form that the support takes. So choose your workshops carefully.

Also, it's a good idea to get the feel of a workshop before you bring in your most "sensitive" material. As one of my friends puts it, you shouldn't expose yourself fully "until you know what the level of savagery is." So start with what you know are lesser works, or with a few trunk stories dusted off and revised for the occasion.

Then know and follow the workshop's rules. Some hostility or grouchiness is caused by writers bringing it on themselves. One time I brought a dozen short-short stories to a workshop. A dozen. In aggregate, they weren't any longer than the stories we usually critiqued, but the participants felt they couldn't say more than a sentence or two about each piece. It made them mad, and some of them gave very grumpy critiques. I've seen the same thing happen to a writer who regularly brings fifty-page stories to a workshop that reads the stories on site before critiquing them. The norm is fifteen pages, with an unspoken ceiling of about twenty-five. So this writer's stories are usually read last, in haste, by readers in a bad mood.

But even when someone else behaves in a way that puts you in a bad mood, a great way to protect yourself from unrighteous criticism is to refuse to engage in it yourself. Make an effort to be wise, compassionate, and complete when it's your turn to criticize. If someone has submitted something that has made you grouchy (manuscript too long, a difficult font, et cetera), admit it up front, ask them not to do it again, and then deliver thoughtful criticism anyway.

How Not to Be Led Astray

Some things that I've already mentioned are helpful in keeping your workshop from directing you where you don't want to go. Success helps. If you're already succeeding at what you want to do, then a workshop isn't likely to lead you too far away from that. And separating story criticism from social censure (or story praise from social success) also helps. So does a noncriticizing reading circle. Or a public reading of your work. And of course, you should avoid workshops where the whole point of the gathering is to diss the kind of writing you love.

But what about an otherwise good workshop that threatens to lead you astray by always nudging you, perhaps very subtly, to write what the other members write, to become more like everyone else? You can abandon that workshop, but in practical terms *most* workshops will tend to lead you astray, at least some of the time. Even careful critics will lure you toward writing the way they themselves write. There's an unavoidable tension between how you write and how all the other members write. There's no workshop without this tension, and even if you created one, a cultish workshop devoted to writing just what you write, then you'd have a hard time resisting that group's conservative urges when it was time for you to grow in a new direction.

The most practical remedy to being led astray is to see to your roots. In addition to getting feedback from the workshop, read work that's similar to what you're trying to produce. Talk to readers who like what you like. You don't need to get critiques from these readers. What you want instead is to continually reconnect with the work that inspires and excites you.

A Sense of Humor

This, finally, is the remedy for most workshop ills.

Not everyone can get away with this, but Damon Knight makes curmudgeonly pronouncements in his workshops. A famous one: "The universe would have been a better place had this story not been written." That may bruise your ego, but you have to laugh about it eventually.

You can also make light of the unspoken cravings of the ego. In our monthly Eugene workshop, Leslie What designates the "winner" each time. To the author of the story that got trashed the least, showed the most promise, and received the mildest revision suggestions, Leslie will say, "You won."

Of course, it's a silly thing to do. The first time that Leslie turned to me and said, "Bruce, you won," I told her just how silly it was. Writers aren't in competition with one another.

Then I went home and my wife asked me how the workshop had been. I pumped the air like the winning pitcher in game seven of the World Series and exulted, "I won!"

That made it easier, in the following workshop, to lose by a wide margin.

If everyone in your workshop laughs a lot, then you're probably doing more good than harm.

17
The Hazards of Reviews

The one undeniable virtue of book reviews, from the author's perspective, is that a positive review in the right place is likely to increase sales. There are other possible benefits, such as validation. The first time my name was mentioned in a *Publisher's Weekly* review (one positive sentence about my story in an anthology), I made a dozen copies to send to relatives. This was one more step toward feeling *real* as a writer. Sometimes, a writer will even get some insight from a reviewer about a flaw that tends to crop up repeatedly in her work, a flaw that the writer is happy to correct once she knows about it.

That's the sunny side of reviews. For most writers I know, however, that sunny side of reviews is like a crescent moon—just a sliver of light at the edge of massive shadow. There are obvious negatives in that shadow, starting with the disappointment of not getting a rave review that will make the book fly off the shelves. A less-than-stellar review is usually the writer's first solid disillusionment, the first signal that her dreams for this book may not be realized. Then there are reviewers who trash the book with comments that the writer grudgingly agrees with, leaving her with the feeling that she's been "found out." More often, the reviewer misrepresents the book, attacks it for its virtues, or just doesn't get it. How can a writer not feel slighted by that?

Even a positive review can leave the writer feeling miserable if it praises her for virtues she doesn't agree that she has. She feels like a fraud. Or if the review is full of praise, if the work is cited as a Notable Book, then the writer may feel queasy about the inevitable bad review that's bound to follow this one. And as with many positive rewards in publishing, a favorable review may make the writer timid about striking out in a new direction with the next book for fear of losing that reviewer's favorable opinion.

The solution for many writers is to filter their review reading. James Dickey ignores reviews unless he's told that they're fabulous. If the review is negative, he says, "then I don't read it, because I don't want to go around filled with resentment for some stranger. That bleeds off your energies; you take them out in useless hatred."[1]

Others read no reviews at all. Lawrence Durrell found that a positive review would swell his ego so much that he had a hard time getting on with the writing. Sean Stewart says that even reviews of *other* writers make him unhappy. "Good reviews make me envy the recipient and wonder how I ended up on yesterday's dust heap. Bad reviews make me dread when it will happen to me. Most reviews, good and bad, rather tend to miss the point."

But reviews are like gossip. Good or bad, most of us want to know what's being said about us, *exactly* what's being said. Besides, most of us can't afford to hire publicists, and most agents expect us to be partners in our own promotion. Positive reviews can help to sell foreign rights, for example. So we hunt for reviews of our work, read them, and, one way or another, feel miserable about them.

What can we do to feel better about reviews, then, other than avoiding them? Here are seven suggestions.

1. Consider the Reviewer's Motives

The first thing to keep in mind about reviews is that the reviewer owes it to his audience to be entertaining. One of the Cat Crimes anthologies containing a story of mine was given a lukewarm review in *Publisher's Weekly* in which the reviewer mentioned a few stories that he did like (no mention of mine), then said that the anthology also included "a few hairballs."

Was *my* story a hairball? In a fit of insecurity, I e-mailed the anthology editor. "Yeah, I read that," he told me. "Don't worry about it. The reviewer was being clever. Remember, reviewers are writers, too. They want to show off as much as you do."

It is much easier to be clever about a work's faults than about its virtues. I know that as a reviewer, my lamest efforts were for works that I really liked. Trying to articulate why I think a novel is excellent can turn my brain to mush. It's easier to write entertainingly about another writer's flaws, and it's more fun, too. Keep that in mind when you read someone's review of your book.

Consider, too, that every reviewer has his or her own agenda and tastes. There are some reviewers who hate science fiction and fantasy; who feel, as Lionel Trilling did, that any work of art that isn't naturalistic (that is, mundane) is an irresponsible waste of words. On the other hand, there are reviewers of science fiction interested almost exclusively in the originality of ideas, and they're often blind to any other sort of qualities that may make a story special. If you wrote a romance novel and the reviewer for *Aviation Weekly* complained that your story had no airplanes in it, how bad would you feel?

In general, reviewers tend to be aesthetically conservative, and sometimes morally and socially conservative, too. A reviewer who is comfortable in the very artistic, moral, and class structures that you're challenging with your work is unlikely to say cozy things about what you've written. This is why Jean Cocteau advised, "Listen carefully to first criticisms of your work. Note just what it is about your work that the critics don't like—then cultivate it. That's the part of your work that's individual and worth keeping."[2]

2. Remember Your Readers

Whether a review was positive or negative, your emotional reaction to it can distract you from your true audience, as if you were turning your back on the paying customers and speaking your lines for the critic who watches from backstage.

If you're writing for reviewers, or if you're hesitating to write something because of what the reviewers might say, you've lost your soul. (Not irretrievably, I hope.)

I can't tell you who your true audience is, and you may have a different audience for every book. But it's likely that you're writing first to please yourself, then perhaps for a circle of friends, and finally for an audience of people you'll never meet. Some writers write for one particular person. Kurt Vonnegut says he always wrote for his dead sister, a specific and somewhat idealized audience—and one unlikely to be critical of the result. I've known writers whose first audience is a spouse, an old friend, or one particular child.

Readers who send you fan mail, who review your work positively for Amazon.com, who seek you out at signings, they are your audience more than any reviewer. Reviewers have ambitions. Your readers just want a good book.

3. Be Deliberate About Your Choices

If you've chosen to write the work that was closest to your heart, the work that you most wanted to write, work that only you could do, then you'll have the satisfaction of making an artistic contribution. You may not like what the critics say about your work, but your work will at least be *yours*. You can take some real consolation in Christopher Morley's observation that "A critic is a gong at a railroad crossing clanging loudly and vainly as the train goes by."[3]

If you've chosen to prostitute your talent, taking on projects that you knew were unimportant, substituting easier achievements for your true work, then you've boarded not a train, but a handcar, and the critic at the crossing, whether praising or faulting your work, serves to remind you that the work is just a handcar.

One writer's handcar is another writer's train, but *you* know the difference.

4. Stay Busy

It's as true of reviews as it is of editorial rejection: Work-in-progress is a healing balm. A bad review doesn't sting as badly if you can say, "Wait until they see what I'm working on now!"

The downside, of course, is that a positive review may make you nervous, especially if you're being praised in the review for qualities that the work-in-progress won't have. Still, your performance anxiety for a work-in-progress will be much easier to manage than performance anxiety over a work you haven't even begun yet.

5. Lament

"The appropriate response to a bad review," says Sage Walker, "is to wail, gnash teeth, feel depressed, and eat chocolate." She also notes, "Even the good reviews tend to be way off the mark."

Reviewers who don't actually trash us often see the work in ways that strike us as pudding-headed. A reviewer's misreadings and misrepresentations are bound to make you feel awful, and it's wise to allow for some expression of those feelings. Call another writer to complain. Wear black. And chocolate is never a bad idea.

6. Seek the Consolation of Philosophy

"It is advantageous to an author that his book should be attacked as well as praised," wrote Samuel Johnson. "Fame is a shuttlecock. If it be struck at only one end of the room, it will soon fall to the ground. To keep it up, it must be struck at both ends."[4]

7. Don't Do the Dirty Deed Yourself

There are some writers who manage to both write books and review books without too much emotional entanglement. I'm not one of them. I once reviewed an editor's novel, and when he later rejected a book of mine, I could have sworn that his rejection letter contained several echoes from my review.

Probably I'm wrong about that. But I worry enough as it is. Publishing is a small field, and I don't need to add any unnecessary complications to my already commingled social and professional affairs. I will, on rare occasions, still review books, but they have to be works outside of my field by writers I don't know.

I'm not alone in this. In the *New York Review of Science Fiction*, James Patrick Kelly shredded one of my stories. "If Rogers had stayed onstage for three words longer, this short-short would slip over the edge into preciousness. As it was, he got off just as I was reaching for a tomato."[5]

"Ouch," I wrote in an e-mail.

"Frankly," Jim wrote back, "writing negative reviews gives me the creeps. In fact, based on your and several other reactions . . . I've decided to give the [review] column up."

Some fiction writers can also write reviews because they don't care that other writers may hate them forever on the basis of a less-than-glorious review. For a while, I took the approach of writing reviews only for books that I liked, but even a positive review can strain a friendship if the other writer thinks you wrote a *stupid* positive review.

If you can write reviews without giving yourself the creeps, great. If not, there's no dishonor in admitting that you'd rather not play this game.

There are two responses to reviews that I avoid.

The first is talking back, at least in public. I think it's perfectly all right to say, "Oh, yeah? Well so's your mother!" But privately, and not in the critic's hearing. It's pointless to take the whole procedure too seriously and defend yourself against a review, though simulating back-talk can be a good way to lament.

An artist who fights back in public makes a fool of himself. The one certain exception to this rule was German composer Max Reger, who wrote to a music critic, "I am sitting in the smallest room in my house.

I have your review in front of me. Soon it will be behind me." You can't top that. Why try?

The other unproductive response is *ad hominem,* attacking the reviewer. This can be great fun, of course. "Sneeps wrote a nasty review of you? Let me show you this review of Sneeps's own novel. Tore him to shreds! Sneeps flunked out of Yale, you know. I don't think he's very smart, in spite of his impressive vocabulary. Look! His participles dangle! Did you know he was once arrested for stealing library books?"

The problem here, as with envy, is that the *ad hominem* response tends to poison everyone involved. As an example of how bad blood can linger, consider the remarks I heard among some members of a professional writers' organization when they were electing officers. Writers ruled out voting for certain candidates on the basis of reviews that those candidates had written years before. Talk about holding a grudge!

Disraeli, Coleridge, Dryden, and countless others observed that critics must be frustrated artists. That truism may sometimes be accurate, but it fails to give reviewers their due. Good review-writing is its own form of art. Rather than dressing down the reviewer, I think it's better to remember how difficult is his task . . . and how exposed his errors may be. Take a look sometime at the little book *Rotten Reviews,* a collection of negative reviews for works that went on to be fabulously successful and widely admired. As George Moore observed, "The lot of critics is to be remembered for what they failed to understand."[7]

Posterity will judge our works, and will judge our critics, too. If a critic savages you, the best response is to keep writing anyway.

That'll show them.

Part Five

Matters of State

Manic Depression and Matters of State

In this chapter I'm going to tiptoe across a minefield. I'm going to discuss the psychological state that best supports the day-to-day labors of fiction writing, and I'm going to compare that state to hypomania, a mild "up" episode of manic depression. The metaphor is irresistible.

Even so, I have three reasons for thinking that this is a dangerous thing to do.

The first danger is that I'll be seen as romanticizing a mental illness, and that's not my intention at all. Untreated manic depression, whether severe or mild, makes life harder for those who suffer from it, and for the people who love them.

The second danger is that I'll be adding support to the argument that creativity and madness are the same thing. It's tough enough to choose a life of writing fiction, bucking the expectations about how responsible grown-ups are supposed to live. We don't need to add support to the notion that anyone who spends hours alone writing about imaginary people is crazy.

The third danger is best clarified with a warning. It's the same warning that my Abnormal Psychology professor repeated at the beginning of every lecture, and it goes something like this:

> WARNING! We're about to discuss a mental illness in some detail. This is a risky thing to do because like any first-year medical student, you may find yourself exhibiting the very symptoms that you hear about. As a result, you may come to the conclusion that you're suffering from this illness when, in fact, you're perfectly all right.
>
> Remember, all the symptoms of mental illness are extremes of normal behavior and feeling. It's normal to sometimes think you heard someone say something

when, in fact, they didn't. Mild auditory hallucinations
like this don't mean that you're having a psychotic
episode and "hearing voices." Also, it's normal to get
into a funk sometimes. One day of wanting to stay in
bed with the covers over your head does not mean that
you're clinically depressed.

What makes the warning doubly necessary is that I'm going to discuss a form of mental illness, manic depression, that has some statistical connection to writing. A fifteen-year study of writers who taught
at the Iowa Writers' Workshop found that 80 percent had experienced
some episode of affective illness—mania or depression—at some point in
their lives. A sample from the general population should yield a much
lower number, closer to 10 percent.[1]

This statistical connection works both ways. A study of people with
cyclothymia (a mild form of manic depression) found that they scored
very highly on a scale designed to measure lifetime creativity.[2]

With these statistical connections, it could be easy to lose track of
what I'm saying here. Please keep in mind that the point I'm making
with manic depression is *metaphoric*.

Manic depression is a mood disorder. Those who suffer from it
alternate between periods of extreme stimulation and extreme depression. The stimulation is often experienced as a rush of excitement,
though it can also be felt as irritability, instability, or impulsiveness. In
the depressive cycle, sufferers often feel suicidal.

At its worst, mania produces symptoms that look a lot like some
cases of schizophrenia. The sufferer may hear voices, have delusions of
being "chosen" for a great mission, and talk in a rapid stream of
thoughts so hard to follow that it sounds initially like schizophrenic
"word salad."

Again, manic depression is no fun.

There is, however, a state experienced by some manic depressives
that has a certain appeal to it. This is the "hypomania" that I mentioned
in the opening.

In hypomania, you'd feel tremendously confident, swarming with
great ideas. Goal-directed behavior (such as writing) would fill hour
after effortless hour, and your need for sleep would diminish. When

you're hypomanic, three hours of sleep is enough, *has* to be enough, because there's so much wonderful work to do! Every project is touched with genius. Every story or painting or musical composition you create is sure to sell for an enormous price, win an award, and be admired as the apotheosis of your art.

In full mania, with its more out-of-control symptoms, you might feel a rush of enthusiasm, and ideas might stream through you almost faster than you could keep track of them. It's likely that you'd feel marvelously creative, but when you returned to a state of euthymia (not manic, not depressed—normal mood), most or all of what you had produced during your mania would turn out to be worthless.

Hypomania, for some, is different. They get the elation, the confidence, the energy to go and go and go . . . and the work that they produce is *good*.

It's easy to understand, then, why some creative patients stop taking their lithium or other stabilizing drugs. The hypomanic high for them is such a productive high that they're willing to risk the suicidal crash that generally follows it.

If you've written regularly for very long, there's a good chance that you've felt a high like this at least once. (Remember what my psychology prof said about the symptoms of mental illness being exaggerations of normal states?) Maybe what you produced in this state was good, and maybe it wasn't, but that hardly matters since writing can always be revised. The point is that you wrote like crazy. It felt good. You didn't want to stop.

All right. Let's shine the light for just a moment on the other half of manic depression. And this half *needs* light, because it's gloomy indeed.

We've all been depressed at some time. We know how the color goes out of the world, how things look pointless, hopeless, and gray. Clinical depression, whether the kind experienced by manic depressives or the more gradual (and perhaps blacker) "unipolar" depression, seriously interferes with a person's ability to function. It's a struggle even to get out of bed—not because of sluggishness, but because the whole world is dead.

Now here's a really depressing observation, courtesy of the confidence and decision-making branch of psychology: Mildly depressed people are better at making estimations about outcomes in the real world than are euthymic (normal mood) people. That is, a euthymic person will tend to be overconfident. Mildly depressed people make self-predictions that are more accurate. When you're depressed, you're being realistic about the world and what you can accomplish in it.[3]

You can easily examine the flip side of this and see that "being realistic" is depressing. For example, what are your chances of getting a story published in *Playboy*? The magazine buys only thirteen or fourteen stories a year, and most of them come from Joyce Carol Oates, Harlan Ellison, Donald Westlake, and other thoroughly established writers. One or two stories a year might be from a writer who isn't already well known, but it's unlikely that those stories were selected from the slush pile. Those lesser-known writers had some connection somewhere so that their story was read more carefully than most. Let's estimate that one story in a hundred published was found in the slush, submitted by a writer who had no connections. That's one story every eight years coming out of an eight-year slush pile of some fifty or sixty thousand manuscripts, maybe more.

One in sixty thousand. Even if you write a terrific story, what are the chances that it's the only one in that pile of sixty thousand?

But here's the good news from that same branch of decision-making psychology: Realism is a handicap.

Another study demonstrated that people who overestimated how much internal control they had over an outcome tended to hang in there and keep working, whereas more realistic people gave up.[4] Think of it this way. If you believe that all that matters is writing a good story, you'll keep busting your butt to write one. In truth, there are external factors beyond your control that can shoot down even a great story—the editor may be in a lousy mood when your story crosses her desk, for example. But your attitude really is everything. Even if the overall odds are terrible, a story that you wrote in the glow of overconfidence has an infinitely greater chance of publication than the story you *didn't* write while you were feeling more realistic.

You can see this sort of useful inflated confidence in a number of successful writers. T. Coraghessan Boyle said in an interview that the supposedly poor prospects for literary writers and professors didn't discourage him as he pursued both of those vocations. He always thought, "[If] one person is going to do it, it's going to be me." Or as a slightly manic guidance counselor said to me once, "There will always be a job for you if you're the best in the world at what you do."

If you're going to write, if you're going to keep going in the face of this difficult marketplace for fiction, you probably can't do it with willpower and discipline. Willpower and discipline will burn you out. What helps more is to profoundly overestimate your chances for success. This isn't just a matter of positive thinking. You'll perform best if you actually change your state to something that's close to hypomania.

Real hypomania brings painful side effects, including poor impulse control. In hypomania, people do a lot of things they later regret. But in that loss of discipline is a hint about the lure of hypomania, a hint of why I think it's such a great metaphor for an ideal writing state. All those pages and pages of creative work are done in a state of ecstasy, in the confidence that this new story will be the first science fiction novella to win the triple crown of Hugo, Nebula, and Pulitzer. It doesn't take discipline to write furiously. It takes overconfidence.

So how do you develop such a positive state?

It doesn't happen overnight. I don't get there every time I sit down to write, but I do get there much of the time. I use the techniques that you'll find in the next four chapters.

19
Altered States

When I first wrote in a magazine article that the kind of work we do as writers probably can't be done on willpower and discipline alone, I heard from a few readers who thought that I was discounting discipline altogether. I wasn't. Discipline is one of the useful items in a working writer's toolbox, but it's a limited tool, as I've already noted in the chapter on Writer's Block, the mythical beast.

But changing your state is easier than enforcing discipline. I like easy. If I can get similar results by an exercise of will or by establishing a fun routine, I'll take the latter, thank you.

Here, then, are some basic techniques that you can use to change your state. I think they're fun. They work for me. However, no technique is going to be universally useful. Some of these exercises may not appeal to you, but that's why I'm giving you so many of them. Something in this chapter and the ones that follow it is bound to suit you.

To set the stage for our first set of techniques, I want to tell you about a psychological effect called "misattribution" of emotion. I'll cite some studies, but I want to admit up front that I'm warping the science slightly for the sake of making my point. Research psychology, like any good science, tries to limit the claims for its findings. I'm stretching the interpretations by assuming broader applications than the researchers can guarantee.

Here's a frequently cited experiment that illustrates the misattribution effect:

Men aged eighteen to thirty-five who were walking across a bridge were stopped by a young female researcher. She explained that she was conducting a psychology experiment dealing with "the effects of scenic attractions on creative expression." She asked the men to tell her a story about a card from the Thematic Apperception Test. (These cards illustrate a scene that is ambiguous, but with clearly identifiable human figures, unlike the Rorschach Inkblots.) Half of the men surveyed were stopped while crossing a solid, sturdy bridge a few feet above a small river. The other subjects were stopped while crossing a narrow, wobbly wooden bridge spanning a canyon more than two hundred feet deep.

After she completed the interview, the young woman offered each man her phone number in case he had further questions about the experiment.

The men on the wobbly bridge, whose hearts were pounding and whose adrenaline was surging, mostly told stories about the TAT card that were romantic or erotic. In the days that followed the interview, nearly 39 percent of these men phoned the interviewer.

The men on the low, sturdy bridge were far less likely to tell steamy stories about the TAT card, and only 9 percent of them phoned the woman.

The researchers realized, of course, that the sort of man who chooses to cross a dangerous bridge might be more generally thrill-seeking, more easily aroused, and more inclined to phone a woman he has just met. So they adjusted the experiment and interviewed the men ten minutes after they had crossed the bridge, when the hikers' arousal states should be about the same regardless of which bridge they crossed. This time, the men who had crossed the dangerous bridge behaved about the same as the men who had crossed the safe one.[1]

First lesson: When love is what you want, take your date on the fastest, highest, steepest rickety roller coaster you can find.

Second lesson: Arousal is a general state. Fear, ecstasy, sexual excitement, and artistic enthusiasm are not very different physiologically. Given a particular physiological state, the emotional state that follows is largely determined by how you label it. When you're aroused, you look for a cause. The cause you settle on helps you to decide what it is that you're feeling.

So one good way to achieve a productive state for writing might be to achieve the physiological state that you're after, then write before the state subsides. You'll begin to associate arousal with writing. Right?

Actually, things are a little trickier than that, because cognition is the Great Monkey Wrench in the machinery of self-determination. That is, the very fact that you know what you're trying to do can lead you to think sabotaging thoughts. The men on the dangerous bridge really thought they were in love (or in lust) with the researcher. If someone had made them read Dutton and Aron before crossing the bridge, they might very well have met the woman on the bridge and thought, "Sure, my heart is pounding like crazy, but now that I know all about misattribution, I can see that she's not so hot."

(And now that you know about roller coasters, you might feel manipulated and resentful the next time someone suggests a first date at the amusement park.)

In fact, an earlier experiment demonstrated that when we are well informed about the source of our arousal, we're good at avoiding misattribution.[2]

Now you might ask, "What good does it do to get into a great physiological state of arousal and then write if I know that the positive state actually has nothing to do with writing?" And the answer is, "No good at all."

As long as you "know" that your elevated state and your writing behavior are unrelated, you'll continue to attribute your aroused feelings to their first source, whatever that was. But what you "know" is at least partly a matter of choice.

A third study of misattribution showed that people can redirect their attributions of emotional state. Subjects were asked to read a speech into a video camera, a task designed to make them anxious. Some subjects were told that during the task they would hear a subliminal sound that would arouse them. Others were told that they would hear a relaxing subliminal sound, a sound with no effect, or no sound. The presence or absence of a subliminal sound wasn't mentioned at all to a final control group.

The subjects who thought they were hearing an arousal-producing sound attributed their keyed-up state to that sound. They made the fewest mistakes in reading the speech because they labeled their state "arousal caused by subliminal sound." Subjects in the other conditions didn't redirect their arousal, so they labeled it "nervousness at having to read this speech."[3]

When we have more than one possible source of arousal to choose from, we have the power to shift our attribution around. Let's say that yesterday I was working on a climactic scene in my next novel. All the pieces were falling into place just as I needed them, and as I wrote I could feel myself getting worked up emotionally. I was tapping my feet as I typed, my face felt flushed, and my heart rate was up. Every once in a while, I got up and danced around the room saying, "Oh, man, this is so *good!*"

Today, if someone gives me a small shot of epinephrine before I begin to continue writing that scene, I can attribute my elevated heart rate either to the drug or to the excitement generated by my own writing. The drug and the behavior both have the power to make me feel this way. Believing that I have two good explanations for my state, I can direct the attribution where I want to.

Now I'm going to ask for what may be a leap of faith. I'm going to ask you to acknowledge that the natural way for writing to feel is *wonderful*. Writing something you care about will naturally put you into a state of full engagement, of excitement, of flow.

If you don't feel engaged and excited and fluent when you write, it's because you have been disconnected from the original expressive experience of writing. It's not your fault. There are whole phalanxes of forces out there conspiring to make us feel miserable when we write.

But if you can scrape away all the miserable garbage, underneath lies a pure and natural joy. Writing feels as good as love.

If you can scrape away all the garbage. Yuck. Sounds like a long chore of therapy and self-improvement lies ahead, doesn't it? Fortunately, I believe in self-improvement only as a last resort. I'd rather find techniques that work for my unimproved self, things that will work today. I don't have time for much self-improvement.

So here's my advice: Think of just one time when writing felt like flying. If you can think of more than one such occasion, if you can make a long list of great writing experiences, so much the better. But one experience is all you need.

Now go to your writing space and intentionally alter your state. It's not as hard as you may think. Three of the easiest ways are through exercise, breath, or laughter.

For exercise . . . come on, you already know how to do that. Twenty-five jumping jacks will work just fine. Count enthusiastically as you jump.

For breath, what you want is some mild hyperventilation. Try inhaling deeply through your nose, then blowing your breath out through your lips in five short bursts, as if you were blowing out five candles in a row. Empty your lungs completely at the end. Repeat three times.

Laughter is something you can fake until it begins to happen naturally. So pretend to laugh. Make your breath do what it does when you laugh, coming out in short bursts. Add the sound, "Ha! Ha! Ha! Ha! Ha!" or "Hee! Hee! Hee!" if you want to. This technique works very well in a room full of people—you're soon laughing at each other's laughter. But you can work yourself into hysterics alone, too. If you don't believe me, practice in front of a mirror, hands on knees, knees slightly bent. "Ho! Ho! Ho! Ho! Ho!" Seeing yourself pretend to laugh will make you laugh.

In each case, you should feel a buzz that continues as you sit down and begin to write. As you write, notice the buzz. Remind yourself of that past writing-as-flying experience. Didn't writing feel great back then? And now you're writing some more, and you feel great. See? It's happening, just as it did on that earlier occasion. Writing feels good.

There are some shortcomings to the technique I've just outlined. The most significant is this: In each case, the arousal stimulus stops as you begin to write. Sure, you can jump up after a paragraph for twenty-five more jumping jacks, and you can breathe cleansing breaths between sentences or giggle for a minute at the end of each page, but that's still not quite the same as a stimulus that keeps you feeling aroused and energized without interruption.

My favorite "misattribution" technique avoids this shortcoming because, like a drug, it offers continuous arousal. I use music.

There are three things that music does for me. First, it provides initial stimulation. I pick some song with a strong beat, and often with inspiring lyrics, something like Carly Simon's "Let the River Run." I spend some time moving to the music—let's not call it dancing. In fact, I can do something else while I'm shuffling and swaying—the breakfast dishes, for instance.

After five or ten minutes of this, I have altered my state. If I felt tired, lazy, and unmotivated before, I no longer feel that way. Now I switch to getting a second benefit from music. As I sit down at my writing desk, I turn on music that will help me sustain my state without interfering with my thinking. Usually, that means music without lyrics. Often, it also means music that I've heard many times before. That way, I'm not likely to be actively listening to what's new and interesting, which, like lyrics, would be a distraction.

Finally, music provides me with what may be the greatest tool for altered states: habituation. By listening to the same music every day when I write, I come to be cued to my writing state by the sound of the music. Whenever I hear that music, I begin to enter the mental arena of writing.

Of course, you can always just write, waiting for the work itself to excite you. But if you find yourself staring blearily at the screen, low on energy and uninspired, try one of these techniques for changing your state. If the excitement of writing doesn't emerge on its own, encourage it.

20
That's an Affirmative!

On television, a financial planner was talking about the ways that people can shift their thinking about money. "When I started out in this business," she said, "I had zero confidence and wasn't even sure I belonged in the same room with the men and women who were training me. We were of different social classes. I could tell by their clothes, by the way they handled themselves, by the confident way they talked about large sums of money. I wasn't cut out to be like them."

She was ready to drop out of the planning profession before she had started. Then someone taught her about affirmations, positive statements that you repeat out loud or in writing in order to change something in your life. She started every day in front of her bathroom mirror, repeating until she felt the reality of it, "I am a financial planner bringing in ten thousand dollars in commissions every month."

And it worked. Within a few months, she was earning at least ten thousand dollars a month.

To my dismay, she didn't then go on to talk about *how* this exercise in affirmations had worked. I knew from my own experience that affirmations were a great tool for shaping my destiny, but I also knew that they were often presented in terms that irritated me and might have kept me from ever trying them. "She's going to leave a lot of people with the impression that affirmations are magic, not psychology," I said to my wife.

Holly, the psychologist, said, "There's a difference?"

She was reminding me that a lot of what we call "magic" is applied psychology. The stage magician's tricks are based on his knowledge of perception—knowing, for example, that if we see part of an object, we will, under some conditions, imagine the rest of it. Also, some psychological techniques, like affirmations, seem to work "by magic," meaning that we do some inner work and get an outward result. But there's nothing supernatural about such techniques.

As the Buddhist teacher Chogyam Trungpa Rinpoche said, "You can't cheat the phenomenal world." There are some people who will tell you things like, "Affirmations change the vibrational pattern of the universe, bringing your thoughts into physical manifestation." They believe you can exchange mental energy for material goods. I can accept such statements as metaphor, but many people who say such things don't mean them metaphorically at all. They think they are describing the hidden workings of reality, spells of sympathetic magic.

So what's the harm in that? It's twofold.

First, claiming supernatural causes for the effects of affirmations will drive a lot of people away from even trying the technique.

Second, such thinking leads to solipsism. The more you think of your mind as the author of reality (rather than the interpreter of reality), the less you feel obliged to deal with the phenomenal world on its own terms. If you believe in the power of your mind to stop your car on its own, why bother with the brakes? Exaggerating your mental control can lead you to give up the control you really do have.

Most people don't actually stop relying on their brakes, but some do themselves real harm in health matters. While it's true that your thoughts can have some effect on your blood pressure, for instance, the range of effect is limited by biochemistry. For my own high blood pressure, I tried meditating, visualizing, and affirming my good health. I changed my diet. I exercised more. My blood pressure came down, but not enough. Then I discovered that my kidneys were diseased. No matter how I fine-tuned my thinking, my disordered kidneys were going to send exaggerated biochemical signals to my arteries. At that point, relying on a "positive-thinking cure" alone would have been stupid. Affirmations work, but not by cheating the phenomenal world.

Then how do they work?

In his book on general semantics, *Symbol, Status, and Personality*, S. I. Hayakawa wrote that we strive "to make sense of ourselves—to be self-consistent. We like to think that the various aspects of our ideas, beliefs, and goals form some kind of organization—that the various parts of ourselves fit together."[1]

Our self-concept is built out of ideas that could start with the phrase, "I am the sort of person who . . ." Sometimes it can be expressed in a negative. "I am not the sort of person who . . ." We'll do a lot to preserve this image of what sort of person we are. Why did that schoolteacher in Jonesboro, Arkansas, shield a child from gunfire with her own body? Because that's what the sort of person who really cares about children does. Manifesting this self-concept was more important to her than preserving her life.

Affirmations work by changing our self-concept, and in the aftermath of that change, our behavior changes to match what we think of ourselves. Let's consider the financial adviser and her affirmation about earning ten thousand dollars a month. What did repeating her affirmation do for her?

It's clear from her story that she thought of herself as a working-class frog among middle-class princes and princesses, and she didn't think that her frog identity was something she could change. She had been feeling powerless. When she started using the affirmation, she was proving to herself that she wasn't powerless because she was doing something. Maybe repeating the affirmation felt silly, but she was at least taking some kind of action.

So her self-concept was changing already. She had been the sort of person who couldn't change. Now she was beginning to believe that maybe she was the sort of person who could change after all.

With practice, repeating the affirmation and imagining its reality gave her confidence to imagine herself as that planner who earned ten thousand dollars a month. What would that version of herself look like? Like her peers at the company, of course. Guided by her new self-image, the planner invested in new clothes and a new hairstyle that were beyond her present means but matched her new sense of who she really was. Her confidence increased, enabling her to "fake it till you make it" by modeling her behavior on that of the established planners. Well before she was earning ten thousand dollars a month, she was looking, sounding, and acting like a woman who earned ten thousand dollars a month.

Obviously, there are limits to this kind of change. The objective of the affirmation has to be something that you can reach by changing your behavior, and you have to be able to discover what sort of behavior will get you there. You don't have to know this when you start, but you have to be able to find it out.

The planner's environment supported her goal. She started her new career in the midst of an investment boom and in a city with lots of potential clients. If she'd been starting out during a recession in Chugwater, Wyoming, she still might have invented a way to success, but it's certainly not as likely.

Then again, maybe it *is* possible to make ten thousand dollars a month in commissions in Chugwater. An affirmation could help you to believe that if anybody could find such a career in Chugwater, you're the one. Affirmations can give you the confidence to try.

Again, though, You Can't Cheat the Phenomenal World. Though you chant a million times, "I own an imperial red Mercedes 600 SL," the car is not going to just materialize in your driveway. And no matter how many writers chant "I have won the National Book Award," only one writer at a time is actually going to win it.

Any concrete outcome that you concentrate on is, after all, symbolic. It's a motivational emblem, a way of scripting your internal refrain of "I am the sort of person who . . ."

Even so, you should be careful of what you wish for. You may get it.

Everything comes with an opportunity cost. When you finally buy your Mercedes, you give up the opportunity to buy something else with that $130,000. When you sign your contract to write a movie novelization in two months, you effectively give up the option to write a work of entirely original fiction in that time.

You may know yourself well. Aiming for a specific goal and supporting your efforts with affirmations may bring you exactly what will make you happiest. But it pays to consider the opportunity costs of what you're aiming for before you commit yourself fully with affirmations. Arriving exhausted at the wrong goal is bad enough, but it's worse to find that chasing the wrong thing has sent you running *away* from what you really want.

With those cautions in mind, here is the Beginning Course in creating and using affirmations.

Creating Affirmations

1. Write your affirmations in positive terms. If your goal is to put your writing first, don't say, "I will quit procrastinating." That's not an affirmation. It's a negation. Write instead, "When I get up in the morning, I go to my writing desk first thing and begin to write."

2. Use absolutes where appropriate. "I *always* go to my writing desk first thing."

3. State your affirmations in the present tense as if the thing you desired were already so. Not "I *will* have a comfortable office for my writing," but "I *have* a comfortable office."

4. Where possible, make your goal concrete and specific. "I drive an imperial red Mercedes 600 SL" is a better affirmation than "I own a nice car."

5. The more emphatic you are, the better, but emphatic assertions of things that aren't outwardly true may seem silly, creepy, or childish to you. If you find yourself resisting, then try a milder version of the affirmation. "I am the sort of person who owns an imperial red Mercedes" is an unfalsifiable statement. You can be that sort of person whether or not you ever get the car.

Using Affirmations

1. Write your affirmations on three-by-five cards, one to a card. Once or twice a day, go through the whole stack and repeat each affirmation aloud several times.

2. Tape-record yourself reading your affirmations. Read them in the first person, and then read them again in the second person, changing all the "I" forms to "you" forms, and perhaps even addressing yourself by name. "You, Bruce, have a comfortable office." Alternatively, have someone else make this recording. For some people, another person's voice plants ideas more forcefully, perhaps because some of us are vaguely embarrassed by the sound of our own recorded voices. Listen to these tapes while you commute, exercise, or do housework.

3. Write your affirmations, filling a page—or a blackboard, if you have one—with repetitions.

4. Post your affirmations around the edges of your bathroom mirror and recite them.

5 However you review and replay your affirmations, try

to make each statement a sensual and emotional experience. What exactly does your comfortable office look
like? How do you feel as you sit down in your ergonom-
ically perfect chair and rest your fingers on the keyboard?

6. Be faithful. Don't skip a day.

Maybe some of these techniques don't appeal to you. You certainly
don't have to use all of them. I have used them all, but never all of them
at the same time. I'd never have time for writing if I was always listening
to tapes, reviewing a stack of three-by-five cards, and filling notebooks
with the same positive sentences day after day. The two most important
elements are writing good affirmations to begin with and then sticking
with them faithfully.

Graduates of Affirmations 101 are likely to choose affirmations
such as:

"I am a financial planner bringing in ten thousand dollars in commissions every month."

"I drive an imperial red Mercedes 600 SL."

Or:

"I have a Hugo Award on my bookshelf, next to my Edgar."

"My novel is on the *New York Times* best-seller list."

This was how I started. Sometimes I've ended up with exactly the
reality I affirmed or else with a reality I was happy to accept as a substitute. (If you're unhappy with your *yellow* Mercedes 600 SL, you can always
paint the car.) But the selfish focus began to bother me. Now, rather than
stating what I hope to receive, I pay attention to what I'm going to give:
"I write every day." "I get new work into the mail every month." "I'm good
at getting on track and staying on track all day." Extrinsic motivation can
be effective, but I seem to need less and less of it.

As I began to move on to Advanced Affirmations, I became more
interested in changing not my possessions or status in the world, but
my experience of reality. That's the topic for the next chapter.

21

Advanced Affirmations

In *Symbol, Status, and Personality,* S. I. Hayakawa observes that "all languages impose a conventional and more or less arbitrary structure upon the events described," and he provides some examples from North American languages. For a speaker of Nootka, every utterance is a verb. You can't speak of "a house." Instead, you'd have to refer to "it houses," but without any form of "it." A flame is not a thing or an event or a process—these words that I want to use to translate the concept are all nouns, and even "a flaming" is just the convention my language uses to convert a verb into a noun.

In Hopi, a house is a noun, but events of short duration—flames, lightning, meteors, puffs of smoke—are verbs. The Hopi language divides experience according to a time sense that isn't present in English.

A Shawnee speaker caring for her gun does not think of her action as "cleaning the barrel with a ramrod." Instead, she perceives it as "drying action with a moving instrument on the interior of a hole." In both languages, the words are an efficient expression of the activity, perhaps the *most* efficient expression in that language. Different languages draw the gun owner's attention to different aspects of the reality, and no language calls the speaker's attention to everything. Language abstracts. Abstraction is a matter of making choices.[1]

It's easy to forget just how abstract language is, and how much it shapes our experience. I once heard a story about a Puerto Rican man whose new job in Florida required that he determine the race of people he was interviewing. He had a hard time learning the categories of "Black," "White," and "Hispanic." The continuum of skin colors was clear enough to him, but some people who were "White" were darker than others who were "Black."

How would it change our culture if none of us had learned to interpret certain features as "Black," "White," "Hispanic," or "Asian"?

"Human beings live," Hayakawa writes, "in a 'semantic environment,' which is the creation of their symbol systems, so that even the individual who believes himself to be in direct contact with reality, and therefore free of doctrines and assumptions, thinks in terms of the symbols . . . with which communication is negotiated in his culture."[2]

There is a phenomenal reality "out there," but we never experience the whole of it. Our sense receptors respond to only portions of reality—our eyes don't "see" ultraviolet light even though such light reaches our retina. And what our eyes do respond to, our brain interprets. The brain processes the firing of optical nerve cells according to the wiring of our species—you and I recognize patterns better than cats, but cats are better at recognizing motion. Then culture and language sort that already filtered experience into abstract categories. It's popular these days to say that we all create our own realities. That's an exaggeration. But our interpretations do make our *experience* of reality.

Not all interpretations are plausible, of course. Essayist Gillian Kendall used to protect herself from muggers by imagining two panthers walking alongside her all the time. She felt safe and acted confident. She got mugged twice. "I no longer trust such protective devices of the mind," she writes. "They leave me vulnerable, less likely to engage in boring standbys like locking doors and asking friends to walk with me."[3]

Feeling safe and acting confident can protect you from the mugger who wants to choose a weak victim, but they do no good against the two men waiting in the bushes for the next person who comes along. You aren't the only one trying to shape reality.

The *meaning* of the muggings is more flexible. Both times, Kendall was assaulted in a "nice" neighborhood. The second time, two men held a gun on her. She resisted, easily pushing the gun hand away. What do these details mean?

Within the limits imposed by the phenomenal world—diseased kidneys, muggers, the scarcity of National Book Awards—we can examine our assumptions, weigh them, and deliberately select other assumptions. Affirmations, repeated declarations of what we now assume to be true, can help us to internalize those choices.

I sort such affirmations into three general types.

1. Counters to Neurotic Patterns

I used to deny myself the time to refresh my mind, to seek out creative input from whatever interested me at the moment, to play. After all, such activity might or might not result in a story. If it didn't, then I'd used my time frivolously. I had played when I should have been working. Wandering wherever my passions led me often resulted in my most original, most authentic writing, but even so, I didn't let myself wander very much.

I assumed certain things. "Play is not to be valued. Work is what matters. Play that results in better work is valuable, but play that has no result but the play itself will lead to sorrow." Some of these attitudes came from my interpretations of things that my father said about assuming adult responsibilities, though I know now that what he actually said wasn't necessarily what I heard and believed. Some of these attitudes came to me through parables I learned at school: The Ant and the Grasshopper. The Little Red Hen.

Burdened with messages that play wasn't good for me, I wasn't doing enough of the sort of play that I knew *was* good for me.

Sometimes I write long lists of all the things that I *might* write instead of choosing one project, beginning it, and seeing it through to the end. Why? I appear to be thinking, "Whatever I'm working on now, there's something better to do." Or I'm worried about being "typed" by the marketplace and need those lists to remind me that I'm not any one kind of writer. Why do I stall when it comes to tackling my most ambitious ideas? "Ambitious works can be harder to sell. I'll have an easier time selling a more conventional novel first." Why do I abandon my work for a friend who calls in distress? "This is a crisis! It can't wait!"

There may be some truth in these formulations, but they are not *the* truth. In every case where I identify assumptions that have led to unhelpful behavior, I can formulate assumptions that are just as true (or just as uncertain) but which support the behavior and feelings I prefer.

Those assumptions become affirmations. Sometimes they are contradictory, but contradictory assumptions can both be true . . . and helpful.

- Creative play recharges my batteries.
- I deserve the pleasure of playing aimlessly with ideas.
- I can only write one story at a time. Whatever story I choose to work on today becomes the vehicle. It bears the best I have to offer into the world.

- I can't change the past, so I focus on the present task.
- My whole career is made out of days exactly like today. What I do today matters.
- My whole career is made out of variable days. Whatever I do today, I may do something different tomorrow.
- With only the rarest exceptions, anyone else's problem can wait until I have finished writing for the day.
- Rejections are information about the fit of one story with one market at one particular time. I don't exaggerate their meaning.
- Every day, I work first on the project that scares me the most.

2. Statements of Psychological Supports

Rather than countering any particular unproductive thought pattern, formulations like these are intended to remind us of values that support our work. They are statements about what our work as writers does for us, or affirmations of what we're willing to take on for the sake of the work, or reminders about how our work is accomplished.

Such statements are largely true to the extent that we believe them, like the affirmation "Everything that happens in my life is for the good." Not long ago, I saw an interview with a man who'd been blinded in an accident. "I spent five minutes despairing," he said, "and then asked myself, 'What's next? What good will come of this? What *can* I do now that I couldn't do before?'" He founded a company that writes software for the blind. When you're predisposed to find the good in everything that happens, good things happen to you by definition.

- My writing helps me to heal private wounds.
- My writing leads me to forgive myself and others.
- Writing always leads me deeper into myself.
- I am willing to write outstanding work.
- I am willing to create what only I can create.
- Great works are not written so much as they are rewritten. I am patient. I am willing to make mistakes.
- Sentence by sentence, story by story, I am getting better and better.

- No one ever writes a novel. Every novelist has to settle for writing sentences. I can do that.
- In the end, I do all this for one reader sitting alone with my book.

3. Statements of Spiritual Support

These keep me going through the darkest and most difficult times. They focus on the transcendent quality of my work. They remind me of invisible support, a sense of calling, a sense of mission. Some of these statements ask that my work be accepted as my gift back to the divine. I'm surprised and grateful to find that *I am*. I exist! As Buddhists say, I've been given the honor of a human birth. In my astonishment, I write and am thankful for the opportunity. I'm comfortable with, and comforted by, affirmations about the divine, about God. Not everyone is. After I list the affirmations, I'll discuss some possible substitutes for God.

- I am answering a sacred call when I write.
- I am not afraid . . . I was born to do this. (Joan of Arc)
- The work I do is bigger than the person I am.
- The person I am is bigger than anything I do.
- In ways I don't have to understand, God works through my writing.
- God has given me this hunger to write. God has the power to feed that hunger.
- I need only listen, and I will be told what to do or say next.
- My writing heals the world in ways both visible and invisible.
- If I do my share of the work, God will do God's share.
- Writing with faith is how I serve God.
- Writing even in the face of personal crisis and disaster is my gift to God.
- Writing always brings me closer to God.
- I serve. God provides.
- I am willing to be used for God's creative purposes.

Now for God substitutes. First, there's Julia Cameron's alternative. Listing some similar affirmations in *The Artist's Way*, she suggests that those who are uncomfortable with the word *God* think of it as an acronym for "Good, Orderly Direction," for the nurturing and life-supporting essence that inheres in the phenomenal world.

Second, Buddhist gods are understood by many believers to be entities that exist only in the mind. That doesn't make them unreal. It makes them psychological. Imaginary. They stand for something more subtle than the representation. Invent a god—the Great Storyteller, for example. Imagine his or her attributes. Set him or her on an imaginary throne, and try substituting "the Great Storyteller" for "God" in the affirmations.

Third, consider the great tradition you have joined by writing. For God, can you substitute the Literary Tradition? Think of books. Think of all the world's libraries.

So here is how some of the revisions might look. "Writing with faith is how I serve the Literary Tradition." "I serve. The Great Storyteller provides." "Writing always brings me closer to good, orderly direction."

I started the previous chapter by noting my discomfort with the woman whose lesson about affirmations did not include the disclaimer: "Affirmations are not supernatural!" Yet here I am listing my affirmations about God. I could argue that God, as I conceive God, is not supernatural, but I'd just be demonstrating how contradictory my beliefs really are.

We each see the world in contradictory ways. It could hardly be otherwise since, just as the word is not the thing, the map is not the territory. However, all we have is our maps. Affirmations enable us to be our own cartographers. Good maps don't have to be perfectly consistent. They just have to get us where we're trying to go.

22

The Power of Negative Thinking

This chapter is dedicated to my Inner Bitch. No doubt there are some readers who will object to this for one reason or another, but the Inner Bitch archetype cannot be gender neutral and she wears her name with pride. Hers is a repressed voice. She came by her bitchiness honestly. It was the only way to make herself heard.

My Inner Bitch says to those offended readers, "Deal with it."

The persona that I present to most of the world is much more optimistic than my Inner Bitch. I like Bing Crosby's tune "Accentuate the Positive." I use upbeat visualization techniques to shape my attitude and performance in the handball court. I listen to inspirational speakers at writers' conferences and on tape. I believe in the power of positive thinking.

Even so, my Inner Bitch has taught me to believe in the power of negative thinking. She is a powerful force, and if I don't enlist her help, she may subtly undermine all of the good that positive thinking does for me. With every positive thought, she's whispering from the shadows, "You don't really believe that hopeful crap, do you?" She's always ready to provide me with evidence that my best achievements are temporary, that everything and everyone comes to ruin. Her cousin is the Hindu death goddess, Kali. The Inner Bitch is not just cranky. She is in touch with dark truths.

Like any aspect of my personality, my Inner Bitch is ultimately devoted to my success and survival. She reminds me of things that optimism can obscure. Everything *does* come sooner or later to its end. Not everyone has my best interests at heart, and some people may even want to do me harm. Her role is to remind me of my vulnerabilities.

If I repress and deny my negative thoughts, if I never do anything but accentuate the positive, I'm a bit like Icarus flying closer and closer to the sun, humming louder and louder to drown out the voice of the Inner Bitch as she shouts, "Too high! Too high, you fool!"

Positive thinking is good, but without balance, it is reckless.

Thus, a paradox: The more positive thinking I do, the more I need my negative thoughts. So my goal is to guide my negative thinking just as I guide my positive thinking, to make it a tool for my benefit. I'm better off dancing with my Inner Bitch than wrestling with her. (Don't wrestle with your Inner Bitch, folks. She carries a knife in her boot. She'll use it if she has to.)

I have three ways of guiding my negative thoughts: lamentation, exercises, and aikido.

Lamentation

There was once a *Saturday Night Live* sketch that portrayed a couple in bed. The woman was unhappy. "I don't know," she said. "It just seems that I'm thirsty all the time." The man got out of bed, went to the bathroom, and brought back a glass of water. The woman was furious. "Just because I say I'm thirsty doesn't mean that I want you to get me water!"

That sketch was funny because it touched on something that many of us experience but few of us understand about miscommunication between the sexes. In short, most women value lamentation for its own sake, while men generally don't recognize lamentation for what it is.

Lamentation is not about seeking advice, asking for help, or even trying to understand the nature of your difficulties. Lamentation is emotive and social as opposed to rational and practical.

My Inner Bitch loves to hear me lament. I think it reassures her that I have been paying attention after all. Yes, I do know how bad things are in publishing. I have seen how unproductive I've been for the last two months. I noticed that editor's dismissive tone when I telephoned him.

Some men can and do lament, but most of us who care to try it have to learn it as adults. As boys, we were trained to be stoic.

I do most of my lamenting in the company of women because they generally know how to dance this dance better than my male friends. Most men want to offer solutions, make plans . . . bring water.

When I lament, it doesn't mean that I have surrendered to negativity. I'm just temporarily giving voice to the pessimistic side of things. I'm seeking balance.

Two important caveats: First, you mustn't lament with the wrong people. Lamentation is an opportunity for you to express safely all your doubts and worries. *Safely* means that you don't want those doubts to be turned against you. For a writer, this means that you present only your most confident face to agents, your editor, and others who must judge your work. Doubt is infectious. One of my friends made the mistake of lamenting to her editor about possible weak spots in her novel. The editor's rejection letter echoed my friend's lamentation back to her, point by point.

It may be that those really were weak spots in the novel and that the editor would have rejected the work in any case, but the novelist thought otherwise. The novel sold elsewhere . . . to an editor who wasn't primed by lamentation to see problems where there may have been only a lack of confidence.

More generally, it's best not to bemoan the state of the industry with people who are deciding how to handle and present your work. If you have to fake confidence when you talk to your agent or editor, fake it. You can balance this forced positive thinking by lamenting later to a different crowd.

The second warning: Mix the good with the bad. Those you lament with should also be those you celebrate and laugh with, ideally at the same dinner party. If there are friends with whom you do nothing but lament, they may not remain your friends. You'll wear them out.

Exercises

I recently heard a story about Milton Erickson's use of paradox in psychotherapy. According to this account, Erickson visited a pubescent girl who had become severely withdrawn. She hardly ever got out of bed. Erickson talked to her in her bedroom for a while, and then created some pretext for getting her to get out of bed and help him move a piece of furniture. As the girl worked next to him, Erickson stepped on her bare foot, *hard*. Then he said, angrily, "That wouldn't have happened if your feet weren't so big!"

The girl's foot was bruised, but soon her mental state improved. She went to school the next day and resumed her normal life.

Erickson had reasoned that her withdrawal was her reaction to the changes in her maturing body. She felt big, awkward, uncomfortable. She was afraid of being embarrassed by the consequences of these changes. So Erickson staged just the sort of embarrassment she was afraid of, and once she had survived it, she was better.

I think this approach to psychotherapy is hazardous, not to mention ethically questionable. But Erickson's success in this instance is a great illustration of how the thing we fear is often the very cure we need.

When my Inner Bitch whispers her dark truths, my tendency is to distract myself somehow. If I'm avoiding work, it may not be the work itself that I'm leery of, but the shadowy self-talk that may start up as I try to write. I avoid the work to avoid the negativity of my Inner Bitch.

Exercises, then, are a way of stepping on my own big foot. Some things that have worked for me are Hard Times, Writing What They Will Say, and the Worry Wall.

Hard Times is an exercise that I learned from Barbara Sher's book, *Wishcraft*.[1] It's a bit like lamentation, but more structured. With a partner, I complain about how bad things are and talk about the terrible consequences that lie ahead for me. I won't finish this book by deadline. The editor will back out of the deal. I won't be able to sell the book elsewhere. The editor will tell all the other editors that I was a pain in the ass. No one will want to work with me . . . et cetera. I start out with rational consequences and get more emotional and irrational as I go.

My partner's role is twofold. She can cheerlead or she can amplify. Cheerleading rewards me for being imaginatively negative:

Me: "Then the editors will create a listserve about annoying writers, and they'll name it after me."

Partner: "Yes! That's a good one!"

When my partner is amplifying, she doesn't just cheer me on. She adds her own negative thoughts: "And then one of the Year's Best anthologies will print an appendix of the Year's Worst stories. And the appendix will be named after you. And all the stories listed will be by you."

"Including stories I wrote years ago, because their badness is so enduring that they have to be listed *every* year."

Hard Times exercises lead to many absurd outcomes and, usually, to an ignominious death.

A solo version of Hard Times is to Write What They Will Say. Compose a vicious but knowledgeable rejection letter or scathing review of your own work. What is the worst that someone might say about you? Write it down. Exaggerate it. Make it really awful.

Finally, there's the Worry Wall. This wasn't an exercise that I did. It was something that was done for me, but I'd have done it myself if I had thought of it first.

About ten years ago, at a time when I was even more anxious than usual, I did a lot of worrying out loud in Holly's presence. What if I couldn't sell the novel I was working on? What if I didn't sell anything in the next six months? If I ran out of money, could I get my teaching job back? Did we have radon? What were those ants doing in the woodwork?

Holly was listening even better than I knew. One day I came home to find one wall in the house covered with sheets of paper, one worry to a sheet. I laughed. I was teaching a seminar at home, and I invited my students to tour the Worry Wall. They laughed, too.

I don't know if I actually worried less in the weeks that followed, but I did get more work done. That's what it means to dance with my Inner Bitch. After each of these exercises, she's still there, as negative as ever. But I feel better. She and I are at peace.

Aikido

The main principle of aikido, a Japanese self-defense style, is redirection. Instead of blocking a punch or throwing a punch of his own, a student of aikido moves along with the blow, using his attacker's momentum against him.

If you can encounter negativity with a light heart and a sense of the absurd, you can move with it in a way that captures its energy for your own use. This is a particularly useful technique for dealing with negative social exchanges. Take the example of a man whose wife looks much younger than he does. At a party, a stranger turns from the husband to the wife and says, "And this lovely lady must be your daughter." The husband may feel angry or ashamed. It doesn't matter if the comment was a deliberate slight or an innocent error. What matters is moving in the direction of the negative feeling, moving it slightly into a more absurd direction. A perfect aikido move would be for the husband to say about his wife, "My daughter? Actually, this is my granddaughter."

Writers often complain about the questions that strangers ask them. From a writer's perspective, some of these questions seem rude. I think that most often, the questions are innocently intended, but in either case, an adept reply is one that raises the level of absurdity, moving in the same silly direction as the question.

"A writer, huh? Have you published anything?"

"Heavens, no! If you publish, they sometimes make you take money for your work!"

Or:

"What have you published that I might have heard of?"

"Not a thing. I'm careful to publish only in the most obscure magazines because I'm sensitive to criticism."

Of course, sarcasm can be applied with a light heart or a bitter one, and it can seem rude even if delivered with a light, apologetic laugh. This isn't a technique everyone can use well.

There are times when something as innocent as loving encouragement can get tangled up with my resistance to writing. When Holly leaves for work, she customarily wishes me a productive writing day. I usually appreciate the support, but there are times when I'm struggling and her wish just adds her expectations to my own frustrated ones. At such times, I've asked her to turn her farewell upside down. She says, "I hope you aren't going to write today." I assure her that I have plenty of other more important things to do, so she doesn't have to worry about coming home to find me finishing a manuscript.

Silly as that sounds, that exchange helps me to write.

Here's another way of thinking about aikido. The way my karate instructor explained it, an aikido master would defend himself by capturing the attacker in a hold, waiting for him to calm down, and letting him go. If the attacker attacked again, the master would capture him in another painful hold, time after time until the attacker's desire to fight was spent. This kind of patience is a good way of dealing with negative thoughts, with "laziness" and anxiety and all the other symptoms of resistance.

Say it's your writing time. You have something to work on, but you're not taking the next step. You don't even want to think about what the next step would be.

Try being an aikido master. The negative feelings can't defeat you, and you don't have to defeat them. Sit with them. What good reasons do you have for resisting? What are you afraid of? When answers occur to you, don't try to dismiss them with positive thoughts. Notice them.

Acknowledge their power. Wait for them to get tired without your doing anything at all.

Then write.

Here's to the Inner Bitch in all of us. Dealing with her can take time and energy. Sometimes we've got to dance her into the ground before we can get to work. But while we're writing, being vulnerable and taking risks, she's watching our backs. And she doesn't miss a thing.

Part Six

Other People

23

Who's Your Buddy?

At a plenum session of a writing conference where I was teaching, the keynote speaker asked about goals. "How many of you have, written down somewhere, a list of things that you intend to accomplish within a specific time period?"

I raised my hand and expected most hands in the auditorium to go up. After all, this was a gathering of aspiring writers. They all must have concrete ideas about just what it was that they aspired to, right?

Perhaps half a dozen hands went up. And most of the people raising their hands were, like me, instructors for the conference.

I'd like to think that this sample was skewed, that the same question asked at a different conference would show more attendees who planned their work and worked their plans. But if the sample at this conference was indeed typical, then I think the speaker's question had pointed out a key difference between working writers and occasional writers. If you want to get the work done, it helps to have goals.

However, I'm not convinced that sitting down and writing down a list of goals is enough. That might explain why more hands weren't raised. Quite a few of the people in that room might have written down their goals at one time, but then not known how to get from goal to realization. If you write down your six-month objectives and, at the end of six months, don't find yourself any closer to reaching them, then the exercise does seem pointless. Why repeat it?

For all the years that we've been together, my wife and I have used a system of goal-setting, goal-tracking, and mutual support that has helped us identify the life we wanted to live and then live it. It's called the buddy system. We first encountered the idea in Barbara Sher's *Wishcraft*, though we have adapted Sher's model.

Here's what we do. Every six months, Holly and I sit down to talk about how we'd like our lives to be different. We've done some thinking in advance, so we come to the discussion with some goals already in mind. We talk about long-term goals, things we'd like to have happen in ten years or five years or three. Some of the goals are school or career goals, and some are about lifestyle, such as the goal to live with less rushing around and more calm, or the goal to spend more quality time together. Obviously, some are individual goals and some are joint goals. We include in this discussion outcomes that we can't control, outcomes—such as getting a book contract or winning a contest—that depend on someone else's decisions.

We write down these ideas in a planning notebook. At this point, we don't really have any goals, but we do have a sense of direction.

The next stage is to translate these wishes into concrete accomplishments with the question: What things can I do within the next six months that will move us in the direction of these wishes? Here, the outcomes we can't control are viewed from the perspective of what we *can* control. I can't require the contest judges to hand me a prize, but I can write a story that will be eligible for the contest and send it in by the entry deadline. And fuzzy guidelines are made more concrete. What do we mean by "more quality time"? For the next six months, we can commit to the goal of spending every Friday evening together.

This stage of turning general longings into specific goals often requires some strategic planning and practical suggestions, and that's one of the benefits of setting goals with a partner: You can solicit ideas about how to get from A to B.

The next step in the system is to translate the six-month plan into action. Six months is still too long-term to translate easily into daily action, so we atomize those six-month goals into things we intend to accomplish in the coming week.

From goal-setting, we move to goal-tracking, which Holly and I do in a weekly buddy meeting that goes something like this:

First, we review our long-term wishes and six-month goals.

Second, we review the weekly goals that we set for ourselves the previous week, noting which ones were accomplished (or exceeded) and which ones were only partly accomplished or weren't done at all. Writing down what happened, whether it's good news or bad, is an important step in bringing the previous week to a close. Sometimes we decorate the page with celebratory stickers. Gold stars, even.

Third, we whine, lament, gnash our teeth, and resolve to do better.

This is an important step. Lamentation lets you emotionally finish the business of the previous week, which probably included falling short of one or two of your goals, especially if you were being ambitious. Even if *you* were perfect, there's a chance that the universe threw a wrench in your plans. Lamentation is good for telling your buddy how unfair it all is. Like confession, lamentation shrives you, frees you from the baggage of your imperfections. But it shrives the unfair universe, too. You thus wipe the slate clean of everything that was wrong with the previous week before you go on to the final step.

(This isn't for everyone. Any number of people have told me that the whole idea of lamentation seems self-defeating, stupid, or like a waste of time. As with so much in this book, one size does not fit all.)

That last step is to set new goals for the coming week. If last week's goals were too ambitious, you might scale back the next week's goals, or you might instead discuss a different approach to organizing your week so that the goals will be better accomplished this time around.

Holly and I spend perhaps an hour to an hour and a half at our six-month planning sessions, and our weekly meetings rarely take more than half an hour, lamentation and strategic planning included.

I think the buddy system works because it incorporates the whole range of goals, from general aims for the distant future to discrete tasks that you'll do by next Monday. It provides a feedback system for seeing whether or not you're on track and for correcting your course if you're not. And that's the right metaphor, the right way to think of the weekly buddy meetings; they're course corrections, not tests you pass or fail. Because your buddy knows what your goals are, there's the mutual expectation that you're going to accomplish them, and such expectations can motivate you much more than your own secret goals would.

That's the What and How of the buddy system. Another important question is the Who. Who should you seek out to be your buddy?

Clearly, your buddy does not have to be another writer. In fact, if you're inclined to feel competitive, anyone *but* a writer could be a good buddy. However, if you aren't the envious sort then another writer, even a writer who writes the same sort of fiction that you do, could be an excellent choice for two reasons.

First, someone who's on the same journey as you can help you to map the territory. When you have practical problems, a buddy who also

writes might have ready solutions, or might at least know of resources
you could use. Your buddy could share market research with you or
might trade story critiques.

Second, a buddy who shares your goals may be especially well
equipped to appreciate your lamentations. This is why Holly has often
had a second buddy for working on academic goals, from finishing her
dissertation to getting tenure. Holly's dissertation buddy, Mele, was also
working on a psychology dissertation involving statistical analyses. She
was much more appreciative of the difficulties Holly faced and could
groan much more sympathetically than I could when Holly said, "I have
to rerun all my anovas because I coded the missing data wrong, and two
of the items on one of my subscales are *negatively* correlated. Can you
believe it?"

The same goes for a writer complaining that a story, one resub-
mitted after a rewrite request, came back with a *form* rejection. It's a
better lamentation if you don't have to explain why that's irritating.

Another Who question is whether it's a good idea to turn your
spouse or lover into a buddy. For me and Holly, being buddies has
worked out well, and there are some clear advantages to the arrangement. We mix relationship goals with professional ones, so we're getting
periodic relationship checkups. We like that, but not everyone wants to
be so deliberate, so systematic about marriage.

Because we're very aware of each other's current work goals, Holly
and I are able to be more supportive of choices that might otherwise
seem selfish. I feel better understood when I have to say, "I know I didn't
get the laundry done last week and you're out of socks, but, look! Thirty
pages! I met my goal!" And knowing exactly what Holly needs to accomplish in a week when she's feeling overwhelmed puts me in a better position to anticipate her needs and support her.

The buddy system also helps us keep track of our common history.
We have this six-month planning notebook that traces the journey
we've been on together.

For us, the disadvantages have been few, but sometimes bother-
some. There are times when it would be nice for your buddy not to
know that you goofed off all week and had to stay up all night to meet
your goals. Sometimes Holly has caught me in the midst of behavior
that's running counter to my stated goals. Often she's right and I'm

grateful for the midcourse correction. But sometimes her midweek reminders have felt like nagging even when, or especially when, she was right. Your buddy's job is to help you be your best self, but sometimes you may *want* to do a little bit of unseen backsliding. We eventually concluded that we were happiest when "buddy mode" was limited to official buddy meetings, either the regular weekly ones or the ones convened when one of us is *asking* for extra help.

I can sum up the question of spousal buddies by pointing out that the advantage of having your significant other as a buddy is that your s.o. knows you so well. The disadvantage is that your s.o. knows you so well.

If you do choose someone outside your household to be your buddy, I have a couple of additional suggestions. First, keep two sets of notebooks, but write both your goals and your buddy's goals in each notebook. You want your own copy to remind you of your current goals. And if your buddy calls during the week to say that she's having some trouble with one of her goals and wants to talk about it, it's helpful to have a complete record of her current, recent, and long-term goals to refer to. More important, if you aren't living with your buddy then there's a decent chance that one of you will move away or simply lose interest. If there's only one notebook between you and she takes it, you will be losing a valuable record of what targets you have aimed at and which ones you've hit. My own goals have changed many times since Holly and I have been buddies, and seeing where I've been, what goals I have defined and then reached (or thought better of), gives me encouragement and insight. I can see a progression in the last thirteen years that's harder to perceive without this record.

In any case, it's best to buddy with someone you can meet face to face. While most of the business of a buddy meeting could be conducted over e-mail, it's impossible for your buddy to detect that you're blue and maybe need encouragement. The phone isn't much better. When you take the extra time and trouble to meet your buddy in the real world, you're affirming that you and your buddy take your goals seriously.

If you have to, throw my caveats out the window. A buddy who knows nothing about writing and can be reached only once a month by mail is better than going it alone. With the exception of a buddy relationship with a truly poisonous personality (there are those who want to see others fail), *any* buddy system is better than none. The same is true for goals. Modest goals are better than no goals. And as much as I believe in the buddy system, goals known only to you are more effective than goals you never write down because you haven't found a buddy.

The most important things about goals are the habit of setting them and the practice of reporting your progress.

24

Your Literary Neighborhood and Toxic Golf

According to one romantic vision, writers are among the last truly independent operators. Each one of us labors in isolation to bring forth the fruits of his or her unique genius. We are lone wolves.

There are some truths that match this lone-wolf vision. Like any freelancers, writers enjoy a great deal of liberty; the marketplace or current tastes may influence our work, but we choose what to work on and how. Thinking for ourselves is part of our business; if we didn't stand out from the crowd, why would anyone care to read us? We tend to be such individualists, tend to be so unlikely to run with the pack, that *writers' organization* is practically an oxymoron. And we labor in solitude; when I go to get a drink of water, there are no coworkers at the water cooler.

Also, when I make a sale, I like to stand on the edge of a moonlit precipice, put my ears back, and howl. Arooooooooooooo!

The solitary vision, however, leaves out something important in the life of most writers. It leaves out a community of people who share our commitments, a community that most writers seek out as a necessary antidote against environmental toxins.

By environmental toxins I don't mean such pollutants as PCBs, lead, and arsenic. The poisons I have in mind are far more pervasive than any of those. With untreated exposure, they build up in our psyches and result in a debilitating cluster of symptoms. These symptoms vary greatly from writer to writer but may include loss of enthusiasm, depletion of energy, crankiness, depression, periods of little or no writing, or even the end of all literary aspirations. Like any serious disorder, this buildup of toxicity has a name, and its name is taken from one particular patient's case history. I call it Toxic Golf Syndrome.

A Case History of Toxic Golf

Greg wasn't a writer. All sorts of people can come down with Toxic Golf. Greg was a counseling psychologist at a small liberal arts college. The job paid modestly, but Greg was managing to raise a family on his income, and he found the work rewarding. On some weekends, he golfed on an inexpensive public course. His life was going pretty much as he wanted it to go.

In the winter when he couldn't golf himself, Greg watched pro golfers on television. He enjoyed seeing the experts play, but he noticed that after he had watched a few hours of golf he would feel gloomy. The bad feelings often lingered into his workweek. These blue moods didn't seem to have anything to do with whether or not his favorite players won. He didn't really have favorite players. So why was golf on television so depressing?

Greg began to watch golf more critically, and he finally figured out that it wasn't the golf that depressed him. It was the ads. Golf players, and thus golf viewers, were assumed to be an affluent crowd. Advertising works by creating dissatisfaction, and golf ads were aimed at making the viewers who were already doing pretty well financially feel that they hadn't quite arrived yet, that they needed a more luxurious car, that others would look up to them only if they had a more stylish wristwatch. The message that Greg got was that with his compact car and his Timex, he wasn't even on the radar of Respectable People.

Although he knew that on his own terms he already had the good things in life, Greg couldn't escape the powerful images of this advertising. The ads were undermining his values so effectively that his self-defined success seemed empty. If he stayed at the college and kept doing the work that he loved, he would never be a member of the country club or drive a Lexus.

It was scary, he thought, that ads could have such a profound effect. But he understood why they would do so, even when he consciously resisted. Humans are social animals. We need each other to survive, so we are easily influenced by appeals to fit in with those around us, to value what they value.

In his own living room, Greg was spending hours with the wrong crowd, a crowd that dismissed the importance of things that mattered to him. Running with that crowd was making Greg miserable. He stopped watching golf.

Good Neighborhoods and Bad

Your literary neighborhood can nurture and support you, or it can be like toxic golf, contradicting your own values. Our broader cultural neighborhood is at least partly hostile to our writing ambitions. To nonwriters, we're pretty weird. We spend hours in the company of imaginary people. We're fussy about aspects of craft that most readers won't even notice. Each of us makes less money than we would if we'd brought the same passion to, say, real estate. How we feel about a day's work may have nothing to do with whether it's any good or not, so we can't even say with confidence whether we've had a good day even if everything seemed to go well.

All around us is a culture that sends messages about the incorrectness of our choices. "Don't you think you should have something to fall back on?" "You're a writer? You mean, unemployed?" "Since you're home anyway, I didn't think you'd mind watching my kids for a couple hours." Or else people who have known us before we were writers resist the new identity we're announcing for ourselves. When Australian writer Pearl McNeal told people around her that she was a writer, one of them was likely to say, "No you're not. I know you. You're Pearlie McNeal." So she changed neighborhoods. She left the continent, in fact, to start over in a country where no one knew that she was "just Pearlie."

Of course, even if we emigrate, even if we go to a place where the natives believe that we are indeed writers, they still aren't going to understand and support our values. There's not much we can do about the influence of this broader neighborhood, unless it's to do without neighbors altogether. There are hermits who write. They don't need the support of literary neighbors because, without neighbors of any kind at all, they don't feel social pressure that needs a counterforce. However, for those of us who aren't cut out for extreme solitude, it helps to move into a literary subdivision where the gal next door never asks us if we wouldn't be happier with a real job. This means finding others with whom we can celebrate our successes, trade advice, and exchange inspiration. It means finding people who understand both our discouragement over the hundredth rejection and our commitment to keep sending the work out anyway.

Note, however, that it's not just any gathering of writers that makes for a good community. Some literary neighborhoods are bad ones. I've seen an online group, one hosted by a successful novelist, begin an uninvited discussion of why their host's just-published novel was an artistic failure. This novelist felt attacked in her own online living room by people who probably meant no harm but who sure as hell did do harm.

She didn't want to call attention to her discomfort, but she left the group soon after that, effectively closing it down.

I have heard rumors of another online group whose accomplished host regularly sorts participants into the "real" writers and the pretenders. The marketplace is already obsessed with picking winners and losers. This is not how good neighbors foster a sense of community and work for the common good.

Finding Neighbors

I'm a lucky man. Good fortune picked me up from my exile in the Midwest and dropped me in Eugene, Oregon. Eugene has not just a thriving community of writers, but thriving *communities* of them. I have participated in the weekly Wordos workshop, a monthly workshop with Kate Wilhelm and Damon Knight, and monthly meetings of something called Bovine Smoke West. I have lunch every Friday with four or five writers. I play golf with another writer. (I'm careful not to watch golf on TV, though.) Everywhere I turn, I meet another novelist in Eugene who moves in a circle of writers that may hardly overlap with my own. Not every writer belongs to any sort of writing group, but most are eager to talk about craft or business over lunch.

So if you're looking to land in a supportive literary community, you could come to Eugene. Writers *have* moved here for that very reason, science fiction writers in particular. We'll be glad to have you. If you can't move to Eugene, you can probably expand your literary community wherever you are. Here are some of the ways I've done so in the various places I've lived, or things I've seen others do:

- Classes. Teach a class or take a class. I'm still in touch with Illinois writers whom I met by running newspaper ads and putting notices in Laundromats for a workshop that I taught in my living room. I've met other longtime writing friends in classes that we took together.
- Form a creative group. Here in Eugene, one of the most dynamic groups I belong to is Bovine Smoke West, a group that meets in the home of artist and writer Alan M. Clark and includes writers, musicians, and artists of

various sorts. We aren't a critique group. We're a performance and collaboration group. When we meet, we share our recent work with one another. Some of what we share is finished, and some of it is in progress. Instead of criticism, we offer one another an instant audience and opportunities for collaboration. We're also a support group. The professional frustrations of a fine-arts painter have much in common with the frustrations of a mystery writer.

- Read the contributors notes in magazines. When you discover a good story by a writer who lives nearby, look her up in the phone book or ask the magazine to forward a letter for you. I met Alison Clement, a writer who lives forty miles from me, after reading a wonderful story she had published in *The Sun*.[1] We had coffee to talk about writing and publishing, and I was able to put her in touch with a writers' group close to where she lived, a group that she credits with helping to get her novel published.
- Join a writers' organization. Most come with a directory, and you can search that for other members who live near you.
- Attend nearby writers' conferences or genre conventions. Hang out. Ask the writers you meet where they're from. Except for the very largest events, most of the attendees will be local. Trade business cards not just with editors and agents, but with your fellow writers.
- If there isn't a conference in your area, perhaps you can create one, even without the usual facilities. Celeste Mergens lives on Whidbey Island in Washington. The island has no conference-sized hotels, and the only auditorium space is at the public high school. Friday sessions of the Whidbey Island Writers' Conference are held in the private homes of islanders—nonwriters, most of them. Saturday and Sunday sessions are at the high school. Speakers and attendees stay in small hotels and B&Bs all over the island, shuttled efficiently

by volunteers who get some extra face time with professionals. It took a lot of planning, but now Celeste's writing community of top agents, editors, and writers comes to *her* once a year.

- As a last resort, you can surf the Net. I consider this a last resort because for me, anyway, face-to-face relationships are the most nourishing. I see the Internet chiefly as a way to maintain a long-distance community rather than to start one. The social support of someone whose face you know is somehow more edifying than even the most inspired words from someone you know only on the screen. Still, an all-text community is better than no literary neighborhood at all. I like what I've seen of the Forward Motion site (hollylisle.com), the Rumor Mill (speculations.com), and the Speakeasy (pw.org).

Our work as writers is done alone, but at the end of the day, most of us crave companionship. We aren't lone wolves, and it's just as well. In nature, a lone wolf isn't such a romantic figure after all. Wolves, like people, are social. The lone wolf joins a pack, or he starves.

The fate of the lone writer is worse. If he doesn't find a pack of his own kind, he ends up watching golf on TV, stops writing, and eventually buys a Lexus.

I get a cold chill just thinking about it.

Arooooooo!

25

Athena's Wheel

I arrived in the physical world naked and defenseless. Some creatures are self-reliant as soon as they hatch, but not me. On my own, my prospects were dismal. However, with the love and protection of my parents, I not only survived, I thrived.

Years later, I entered the literary world naked and defenseless. Once again, my prospects were dismal. I was so naive that I had no idea just how dismal my prospects were. My parents seemed to know better than I did that my adventure was taking me into risky territory, but they had little specialized wisdom to offer and absolutely no protection to extend. The world of professional freelance writing was even more foreign to them than it was to me. In classical terms, I was in *exactly* the same situation as the young Telemachus, the son of Odysseus.

Well, all right. Not exactly the same. Some of the details were different.

As you may recall, while Odysseus was off fighting the Trojan War, his son was growing up without a father's guidance. Like any young man, Telemachus saw himself developing a man's body and figured that this made him a man. So he set out on a manly quest: to find his father.

The gods knew that Telemachus wasn't ready to undertake such an adventure on his own. Fortunately, one goddess took pity on him. Athena took the form of a mortal man, befriended Telemachus, and joined him on his journey.

If you're undertaking a dangerous adventure, you could hardly have a better traveling companion than Athena. She didn't arrive in the cosmos small, naked, and defenseless like the rest of us. Instead, when she sprang from the forehead of her father, Zeus, she was already fully formed and clothed in armor. She had the wit to avoid a fight and the smarts to win one. Athena, goddess of wisdom and defense, kept Telemachus from succumbing to dangers that he would not have recognized without her until it was too late. She protected him.

Wouldn't it be great if we could all have the good fortune of

Telemachus? Wouldn't it be handy to have the goddess of wisdom there at our right hand whenever we entered a new realm as dangerous as, say, dealing with editors, agents, and our own terror of the blank page?

In fact, we do.

The name that Athena took in her mortal disguise was Mentor. We remember her role by that name, but to describe Telemachus's side of the relationship, we use a French word: Telemachus was Mentor's *protégé,* "one who is protected."

I have made whatever progress I have made in the literary world thanks to my mentors. And whether you realize it or not, the same is true for you.

If you haven't recognized your mentors, it may be due to some confusion over what mentor and protégé relationships look like. In the business world, we imagine the mentor as a senior executive who spots an energetic youngster, someone who reminds him of himself many years ago. "Do as I tell you," he says to his protégé, "and one day this corner office on the top floor will be yours."

Certainly in some fields there are a few relationships that work like that, but most people become mentors or protégés much less formally. A new writer goes looking for an adviser one problem at a time. One discussion at a time, a more experienced writer points out solutions. We may each have more than one mentor, in sequence or at the same time. And while we are one person's protégé, we may be simultaneously another person's mentor.

This is what human culture is all about. It's as if each person were a point on a circle. Wisdom is transmitted from points ahead of him on the circle, and he sends his own wisdom behind him. If there is progress in the world, it is because this whole circle is slowly turning. I call the circle of mentors and protégés Athena's Wheel.

A mentor-protégé relationship may not be recognized as such for a long time, if ever. Or the mentor may not recognize his importance, though the protégé does. The SF, fantasy, and horror writer Edward Bryant was a vastly more influential mentor to me than he knows, even though I've tried to tell him about it. He accepts my thanks with a touch of embarrassment, as if I must be exaggerating. I'm not. I was driven as a young writer, but I might have driven myself right over the edge of the world without Ed. He gave me stars to steer by and helped me to be patient with myself. I learned a lot by just watching him *be* a more experienced writer.

I might still have been a writer without Ed or Wayne Ude or Kevin McIlvoy, to name just three of my mentors. But each of these men taught me something about being serious, devoted, and regular in my writing habits. Each of them schooled me in the mysteries of publishing and of my own creative psychology. *In loco parentis,* they gave me a brand of approval that my parents did not have the credentials to give. I might have been a writer without them, but not without *someone* standing where they stood.

Stood? Actually, Wayne mostly sat. I stood in the doorway of his English department office asking long-winded questions and delaying the hour when he could go home to supper. Bless him. And bless Kevin for telling me, when I hung around his office starry-eyed with admiration, that I wrote better dialogue than he did. That alone kept me fired up for years.

Often what the mentor offers is a small thing to him, something that he will soon forget even though he himself forever remembers similar gifts from his own mentors. That may be part of why mentors sometimes don't fully appreciate what they've done for their protégés.

Athena's Wheel turns whether we're conscious of it or not. But if we *are* more aware of our work on the wheel, then we can do a better job of it. A mentor who is aware of the role may not only do a better job of transmitting wisdom, but he may more fully appreciate and enjoy his position as an elder artist.

One way to be a conscious mentor is to formally accept the role. At last count, sixty-four of *Fortune* magazine's "One Hundred Best Companies to Work for in America" had official mentoring programs. What works for corporations can work for freelancers, provided that you and your intended protégé share your perceptions of seniority. In a company, the vice president of finance will clearly be a potential mentor for a midlevel manager, and not the other way around. For freelancers, though, you'd better make sure that a potential protégé sees you as being farther along in your career before you say, "I'd be happy to serve as your mentor, if you like." Otherwise, your presumption may be insulting.

The status difference obviously was not an issue when I served as mentor to a high school student. We met regularly, and each time I read a few pages of the endless novel that she wrote longhand in spiral note-books. I didn't critique her writing. A protégé is not an apprentice, and she hadn't developed to a point where criticism would have helped her, anyway. She was still writing chiefly for herself. We chatted about what mattered to us, in life and in literature. I answered what few questions she had about publishing. My chief contribution, I think, lay in regularly confirming for her that she was a writer and that what she was doing at the time could be an early point along the line that would lead to what I was doing at twice her age. Many schools would be delighted to hear that you have some time to be a mentor in this way.

If you do take on the role formally, here are some traits of a good mentor:

Dispassion. Value your protégé's independence, his or her own distinctive life. Many academics make terrible mentors, because they're controlling. They try to shape the protégé's tastes and ambitions to mirror their own. Disapproval from your mentor is a sign that he isn't really much of a mentor. A mentor does not manipulate. Also, a mentor can't be vested in the protégé's success. You can't mentor your spouse, for example.

Judgment. Discriminate. Although a good mentor is dispassionate, he nonetheless shares his thoughts about the good or bad consequences of the protégé's decisions.

Attachment. Care. This is another seeming contradiction with dispassion. No, you don't want to be vested in the protégé's success, but you do want to care about the protégé as a person. Talk about something other than writing some of the time. You might even play golf together.

Wisdom. Spill the beans. How does the writing world work? If there are unspoken rules about how a writer should fire an agent, seek a review, or get a complacent publicity department more excited, say what those rules are. If your protégé is unaware of a social error that could have professional consequences, tell him.

Persistence and Resilience. Show how it's done. When you write in the face of disappointments, it encourages your protégé to do the same. And be willing to talk about how it's *not* done. We all make mistakes, and a mentor who admits to making a few himself can offer trustworthy guidance on repairing the damage.

Generosity. Give even when it hurts, sometimes. Being a mentor does have a price. It costs you precious time. But this is a priority relationship, not something you can do only when it's convenient.

Being a conscious mentor can help you to be a better protégé, too. On the flip side of the mentor's generosity is the protégé's moderation. A protégé has needs. A good protégé, however, manages not to be *needy*. When you're the one seeking another writer's experience, don't be an energy vampire. A protégé takes more than he gives—though ideally, he gives this back, and then some, when he becomes a mentor himself—but be mindful that you *are* taking.

Being a good protégé also requires that when you outgrow your mentor (and you most certainly will in some way), you do so gracefully. Protégés, too, need a certain degree of dispassion. If you find one day that you embody your mentor's cherished principles better than he does, that you are more persistent and savvy, keep that observation to yourself. Some protégés and mentors have gone to war (Paul Theroux and his mentor V. S. Naipaul, for instance) when the protégé no longer needs approval from the Great Man (or needs it but isn't getting it any longer).[1] Recognizing your own expertise is a good thing, but be tactful about recognizing it aloud. A mentor who says that you have surpassed him is boasting in a generous way. If you say the same thing, you're an ass, even if he said it first. And a mentor who withdraws his support may injure you, but as the junior member, you'll look childish if you strike back. Theroux has been widely attacked for publishing a memoir, *Sir Vidia's Shadow,* about his estrangement from Naipaul.

Acrimonious splits do happen, but I think they're the exception. Many mentors, as I've said, don't even know that they are mentors. However aware or unaware he or she is of his or her role, your mentor probably won't be your mentor forever. At some point, you'll either drift apart or the relationship will evolve into a friendship between peers. But if the prospect of a bitter split puts you off, there's another sort of mentor: the one who was dead before you were born.

Raymond Chandler is one of my mentors. He has advised me by example—good and bad—ever since I read Frank MacShane's *The Life of Raymond Chandler.* The same is true of dozens of other dead writers whose lives I've read. Biographies and biographical movies about writers and other artists can teach us a lot about this path we're trying to walk, its hazards and its rewards. And a dead writer offers a perspective on the whole of your career, the shape of your whole life, that a living mentor can't supply.

I came into this world naked and defenseless. My mentors, living and dead, are helping me to have quite an adventure while I'm here. I'm picking up bits of wisdom. Before I make my exit, I hope to pass some of them on to the naked and defenseless human beings who are just today arriving.

26

Writers and Lovers

The inclination to write is common. Sometimes every other stranger who hears that I write confesses a desire, even a plan, to do the same. It doesn't surprise me that so few of them ever follow through. Consider how much is required. Time on the grand scale: years of patient practice to develop craft. Time on the ordinary scale: a few daily minutes or hours, getting a draft down, rethinking it, polishing. Concentration: the right environment, and freedom from distracting worry. And above all, conviction: the belief that the words on the page matter and the confidence to hang on to that belief in the face of a skeptical world.

A writer's romantic partnership can make it easier to cope with these challenges, or it can make writing much harder than it already is. In this and the next two chapters, I want to consider some of the common challenges that writers and their lovers face.

This whole exercise will be more descriptive than prescriptive. In matters of the heart, each path is as individual as one person's idiosyncracies . . . squared. But reading about the challenges other writers have faced can remind you of places where your own relationship may need work, can reassure you that some of your struggles are typical, and can remind you of how fortunate you are to have solved some common problems. (In which case I *will* make a prescription: Say thank you. Even if you're already good at expressing gratitude to your partner, express it again. With chocolate.)

As I see it, there are six main areas where a partnership can hurt or help a writer: Identity, Sex Roles, Work Habits, Play Habits, Audience, and Blame.

Identity

Especially early in our careers, the world denies that we really are writers. Before we are published, what are our credentials? Some manuscripts? Well, says the disbelieving world, those pages prove that you've been typing, not that you've been writing. As for the hours we say we've put in, who saw us? And even if we have a witness, we could have been loafing, daydreaming, or pretending. For proof, the world wants publications. And once we're published, the world wants to know if we were paid, if the publisher is prestigious, if we've won any prizes, if we're famous.

It helps to say to ourselves, "Well, I am a writer. Really, I am." But as I keep saying, human beings are social animals, and we like to have our realities confirmed by others. Otherwise, declarations of our identity start to feel akin to the repeated declaration, "I can fly. I know I can fly."

If the person you're most intimate with joins the wider world in doubting your identity as a writer, then even just being around your partner while you're trying to write is going to keep you busy second-guessing yourself. It seems silly, but the burden of domestic doubt is so distracting that it can force the writer to go to some neutral site like the library to get any writing done.

On the other hand, a partner who identifies you to others as a writer and who mirrors your writer identity back to you every day can help you to build a separate reality, one in which you've already achieved recognition. In that reality, you can get to work.

Beyond a mutual understanding that you're a writer, it's important that your partner understand what sort of writer you are. If your goal is self-expression, a partner who is always talking about how wonderful it will be "when you write your best-seller" can damage your enthusiasm as much as a lover who doesn't think you'll ever complete anything worth reading at all. One of my friends was so paralyzed by her husband's commercial expectations that she stopped writing. When she was finally able to talk to him about it, he changed what he said to her and to others about his hopes for her work. She started writing again.

Sex Roles

A shared sense of the writer's identity can be a first step toward addressing some practical concerns that arise in a literary household, concerns about sex roles.

In the "traditional" division of middle-class sex roles, there's a husband who (mostly) provides and a wife who (mostly) nurtures. It hardly ever works that way anymore. Most couples find it hard to get by on one income, especially if they have children. In a lot of marriages, the husband works one full-time job and the wife works two, bringing in an income and taking primary responsibility for running the household.

Make one of those partners a committed writer, and now there's someone who (mostly) writes. Or wants to, anyway.

Ideally, an artist should be able to do all three things: make art, help support a household financially, and nurture the partner and children. An artist *can* do all three, but being committed to three roles doesn't bring with it a threefold increase in available time. Making art provides some income to some of us, but in most cases, not an income you'd want to live on.

One of my friends once suggested that the solution was to add an extra husband or extra wife to take over the writer's traditional role. If you can make that work, you have my best wishes.

The more likely solution is to recognize the extra demands that a writer brings to a relationship and to do some realistic planning. After he or she has finished the day's writing, how much time does the writer have left to contribute to family life? Or, to look at it the other way, perhaps more realistically, how much time can the writer squeeze out of family life and outside work in order to write? How willing is the non-writing partner to sacrifice time or alter his or her own expectations, given the available resources?

Even the frankest discussions and most creative divisions of roles can still make partners uncomfortable. Many of us who like to think we're free of rigid role-typing still feel guilty when we don't behave as we're "supposed" to. Men who aren't providing tend to feel guilty. It's the same for women who aren't running the household the way their mothers, or an idealized mother, did. Because of that guilt, it takes some work to build a heterosexual partnership that violates cultural defaults. If you're in a gay relationship, of course, it's less clear what the default settings are. This may make it easier to develop, and feel comfortable with, innovative role systems. (Whether you're straight or gay, others may have trouble accepting your arrangement, but that's a different issue—to be covered in a later chapter.)

Two of my male friends married women with very conventional and rigid expectations. When his first child was born, one of those men stopped writing. The other friend wrote full time while his wife was full-time mom and domestic manager; there was no steady provider, and even though his work did sell, it didn't bring in enough to save them from bankruptcy and divorce. My female friends who lived up to a husband's conventional expectations typically abandoned writing and didn't return to it until their children were grown. Often, if there isn't some role flexibility, if expectations aren't adjusted, then writers either stop writing or else the partnership fails.

Work Habits

Writers are fussy. Some of us insist that our work space must consist of piles and piles of papers in which ideas are fermenting. Others have to have a tidy work area. Some of us are habituated to using a certain tool—a special pen, a particular notebook—or to working in a particular space. A partner who doesn't respect such needs, who tidies the piles or clutters the tidiness, who borrows the pen, who parks his butt in the writing chair, is more than aggravating. He's creating unnecessary barriers to the writer's productivity.

Besides respecting whatever arrangements a writer is fussy about, a partner can be understanding about how continuously some of us write. At an odd, inconvenient moment, we may have to pull the car to the side of the road to write down an idea. Worse, there are times when dinner won't be ready as expected or when a social engagement will have to be missed because for an hour the work was going splendidly and just couldn't be interrupted.

Writing takes concentration, and concentration for most of us requires freedom from even the friendliest interruptions. When Holly and I were first adjusting to life under the same roof, our biggest fights came when one of us was working and the other was feeling lonely or playful or just wanted to feel connected. If I closed my office door, Holly felt shut out and I felt more isolated than either of us wanted. If she growled at me for wanting a kiss while she was wrestling with a paragraph, I felt rejected. Gradually, we talked (and bickered) our way to better understandings. I learned that I could bring her a cup of hot tea or wordlessly rub her shoulders as a connecting gesture, and I came to accept those same gestures from her. We learned to read each other, but we are still making adjustments, still apologizing for interruptions. At least we both acknowledge that the other has a right to his or her concentration.

Another area that can require continuous adjustments is each partner's general appetite for activity. One thing that strained my first marriage was that my first wife got cabin fever easily. She couldn't stand to spend much time in the apartment. She wanted to take a walk, go hear some music, go dancing, see a movie, anything but hang out at home. I was content to sit on the couch and read or write (though in fact, I didn't write very much during that marriage). When we went out, I was resentful, and when we stayed home, she was. If we'd actually worked to plan a compromise (society three nights a week, domesticity for four), we might have been happier together. In truth, though, three nights out a week might not have been enough for her, and was too many for me. This is one of those cases where the real problem may have been that we should have married more wisely. (Later, we both did.)

Play Habits

Some writers keep playing at narrative even when they aren't writing. Fourteen stuffed animals live in our bedroom. Holly and I talk to them. They talk to us. They have long histories and dynamic personalities. One of them, a penguin named Around Here Somewhere, likes to explore; when she's not on the bed she could turn up anywhere, including in Holly's briefcase when Holly opens it in class to take out her lecture notes.

Other writers play word games, relentlessly punning or seeking round after intense round of Scrabble. (Holly loves Scrabble. I don't. But losing yet another game to her by a hundred points is not a huge sacrifice to make for my partner's happiness.)

Such play isn't unique to writers, but it is probably more common in us than in most adults. I'd have a hard time living with a partner who didn't also play, who wasn't willing to enter spontaneous fantasies. I wouldn't stop fantasizing. I'd just be lonely.

Then there are less obvious categories of play, like research and sex. Sometimes I don't know a research opportunity until I see the billboard for the World's Largest Prairie Dog, and my sexual appetite depends a lot on how the writing is going and what I've been writing about. A partner who was irritated by these traits would be irritated a lot. The ideal, I think, is to have a partner who is eager to spend part of the vacation researching steam locomotives because there might be a story in it, who isn't offended and is maybe even delighted when an afternoon of writing love scenes "inspires" the writer.

Audience

How convenient, even inspiring, to have a partner eagerly waiting to read the next chapter! Editorial responses can take a year or more, and then books may take another year to reach bookstores and readers. Even critique groups only read once a month or once a week. Some of us want an audience right now, as the printer spits out the last manuscript page.

But not every partner can take on this role. I know of a few thriving relationships where the partner faithfully supports the writer's identity and ambitions but can't read or appreciate the writer's work. Obviously, then, it's not essential for a partner to be the writer's first reader.

Usually, friction over the partner's role as audience is the writer's fault for expecting some sort of response that the partner can't provide or for expecting a particular kind of response without saying what it is. Not every partner is a good manuscript critic. And a writer who just wants an enthusiastic gush over the good parts ought to say so up front.

Blame

Which brings us to our last source of friction, another one that is the writer's fault: blaming the partner for writing difficulties.

I mentioned earlier that my first wife and I might have married more wisely to begin with. Some partnerships, usually for a combination of reasons, fail, and both partners are glad (after a period of grieving) to move on.

But blaming the partner can be a bit like the poseur sort of writer's block. You sit in a café drinking coffee with your literary friends, bitching about how you just can't write. You get to feel literary without facing the hard work of writing. The same can be true of sitting at your writing desk and brooding about how your partner doesn't support you enough. I've heard one writer admit that he almost ruined a good marriage by indulging in this sort of thinking, blaming his wife for his own creative frustration or using her supposed lack of support to avoid his writing. Fortunately, he recognized what he was doing in time.

Partnerships need to be flexible to work. That includes the flexibility to see where the other person can't move, where you have to do the adjusting. Not all problems in a relationship can be solved, but most of them can be worked around. Every difficulty really is an opportunity for you to deepen your own soul, and soul work is good for writers. Or as the great acting coach Sanford Meisner said, "That which hinders your task *is* your task."

27
Writers Loving Writers

Novelist Leonard Bishop didn't think writers should set up house-keeping with other writers. He wrote, "What promises to become a stimulating, exciting life, with mutual interests in each other's work, usually becomes a ritual of daily torment." Bishop acknowledged that some two-writer marriages had worked out fine, but he insisted that these were "phenomenal exceptions."[1]

If that's true, then I see phenomenal exceptions all around me. I'm happily married to a writer. Right here in Eugene, Oregon, there are at least three other successful writer–writer pairings just among the science fiction writers. There must be more here among the university's creative writing faculty and the many other Eugene writers I haven't met. If we look not just for writer–writer unions, but all sorts of writer–artist or artist–artist couples (that is, other unions that are likely to have the same characteristics that made Bishop uneasy), I can name dozens of romantically and professionally successful partnerships.

Bishop was wrong to make such a sweeping pronouncement. The "stimulating, exciting life" of mutual interests and shared commit-ments is a reality for many of us, and we find a lot of advantages in living with another writer.

The first of these advantages is sympathy. Even when you've been collecting rejection letters for twenty or thirty years, even when you know that "it's just business," there are some rejections that sting. Wrestling with a problem story is always frustrating. Losing the enthusiasm that carried you for the first hundred pages of a novel is depressing. Or, on the positive side, there's the elation that comes with selling that rejected piece. When the problem story or novel presents you with its own solu-tion, you may express your delight by making excited-ape sounds at your keyboard. In each case, it's great to be able to share what you're going through with someone who goes through it, too.

Related to sympathy is an understanding for your odd habits. Not all writers have the same odd habits, but all of us surely have some. Just as we're drifting off to sleep, we sit up suddenly and grope for a pad of paper. In the car, we mumble exchanges of dialogue between imaginary people. We ask not to be interrupted the next time we're staring out the window like that because, damn it, we were *working!*

Your partner may have writing habits exactly the opposite of your own. You may keep to an obsessively regular schedule while your partner writes irregularly, drifting back to the desk for short stints all day long until, hitting a hot streak, he or she stays at the keyboard past dawn and then sleeps into the next afternoon. It's not the similarity of habits that matters to writing couples, but the understanding of how necessary one's habits are.

If your partner *does* have writing habits similar to yours, then you get the benefit of *entrainment,* and just being together can act as a cue to write. My wife has an office at the university, but she does most of her reading and writing at home. When she's writing, I find it very easy to do the same. In fact, I feel vaguely guilty if she's working and I'm not working, too, even if I have officially knocked off for the day. Often we're in different rooms, but the whole atmosphere of the house is directed toward concentration. She writes, I write.

The only drawback I can see to this is that our mutually reinforcing work habits can lead us to work too much, to never go dancing, to never take a weekend off, to go a whole year without seeing a movie. But besides sharing work habits, we share the worry that we'll shut ourselves up like hermits. We've arranged our life so there are some regular social events and enforced vacations.

Two writers or two artists are likely to share the same, or at least greatly overlapping social circles. Moving in the same circle of friends probably does more for the union than for the writing—couples with friends in common seem to have stronger partnerships. Actually, moving in the same social circles *can* do some real good for the writers' careers, too, if those social circles include editors. Couples who sell to the same markets can share professional contacts, getting twice the mingling time out of one publisher's party.

Another professional benefit is almost automatic: shared publicity. Writers can mention each other's books in their own bio-blurbs and public appearances.

Then there's the matter of collaboration. Many artistic couples collaborate at least in the sense of reading one another's work. Even if you only trade suggestions, it's easy to come to see each person's work as a project you hold in common, a contribution you make to the world as a couple.

Holly is my first reader, and nothing—well, almost nothing—goes into the mail without her approval. Sometimes she suggests ideas or sentences that I incorporate in the finished work. Except for some teaching materials on creativity, we've never collaborated in the usual sense of conceiving and shaping a work together from beginning to end, but our two chapbooks of poetry were shared projects. In one, she wrote the book's first section, I wrote the second, and Holly did all the illustrations. In the second, all the poems are mine, but Holly did the cover art.

Some couples collaborate in the more usual, interwoven sense of writing alternating chapters of the same book, or dividing the writing task between them. One of my friends married a man whose prose sparkled and whose individual scenes were great. He was at a loss when it came to plotting a whole novel, however. So she wrote outlines and he filled them in.

Then there are collaborative artistic lives that, like the marriage between poets Donald Hall and Jane Kenyon, are themselves works of art. Hall had cancer twice. He and Kenyon both wrote powerfully moving poetry about the likelihood that he would die first, perhaps soon. Then Kenyon was diagnosed with advanced leukemia. She died. I recently heard Hall read his poems about her last days, and what struck me was the sense that at the end, both writers were intensely involved in being awake to what was happening, awake to each other, and awake to the poetry that they were weaving out of her dying.[2]

I don't think that Hall and Kenyon did any overt collaboration, sharing a byline, but they borrowed from one another. Hall notes that his line about Kenyon's last breath is lifted from one of her poems. Their greater collaboration was the artists' life that they made, supported, and *lived* together.

So the promise of a stimulating, exciting life can be fulfilled fairly often. Even so, some unions between writers really do become rituals of daily torment.

Bishop's main concern was that two literary egos under the same roof couldn't help but clash. "Every writer," he wrote, "possessing the character of an authentic writer, knows that he or she is one of the finest writers in the literary community."

In fact, a big ego is useful to artists. Enrico Caruso used to warm up for performances not with scales or a rehearsal of what he was about to sing, but by belting out, "I AM THE GREATEST SINGER IN THE WORLD!"[3] Ego inflation, even overconfidence, can help us to shut off fear of criticism and dive into our work with gusto.

I can see Bishop's point about clashing egos in cases where husband and wife are at their respective keyboards:

"I am the greatest writer in the world!" he says.

And she says, "No, *I* am!"

That's bad enough, but if her career starts to take off and his doesn't, he could wind up seething with resentment. And this has happened. Some of those writers who agree with Bishop that writers shouldn't marry other writers were once married to the resentful writer who was "left behind."

Many couples find ways to protect themselves against such outcomes. One way is to share the belief that their work is a mission held in common. "*We* are the greatest writers in the world!" The life's work for both of them is to create their own art and to support the partner's efforts. If one writer is doing better in the marketplace than the other, the couple can focus on the opportunities that the success presents: shared publicity, perhaps, or more income to support the work of both.

No matter what the couple does, though, they can't control the perceptions and actions of people outside the relationship. Let's say you both write novels. You are still laboring in relative obscurity while your partner has just had an artistic or commercial smash hit. You're careful not to make comparisons. You're in this together. But outsiders will make comparisons for you. What can you do about the person who calls up on the phone and asks to speak to the writer, then says, "No, not you. I mean the *author*. The *novelist*." What *can* you do, but grimace and hand over the phone?

As hard as you may try to keep competition from poisoning your partnership, other people may be poisoning it for you. It's hard not to feel resentful when your public identity has more to do with whom you married than what you've contributed in your own right. And if you're *not* married to your partner, if you "just" live together, you may be made to feel even more invisible.

In heterosexual partnerships, the woman may find that her work is valued less than her partner's just because it was produced by a woman.

Some couples are helped by writing very different kinds of work, so that a glowing review for the mystery writer doesn't leave the partner who writes literary short stories wondering why she doesn't get such good notices from that reviewer. That reviewer *never* reviews work like hers. But it's hard not to at least muse wistfully about how nice it would be to get similar treatment in your own area, whatever that would be. The inevitability of comparisons is what keeps some agents from representing a client's spouse. Who can blame them for not wanting to be caught in the middle when they land better deals for one spouse than the other?

Issues of ego can bring down marriages. Harry Turtledove and his first wife both wanted to write. He pursued publication single-mind-edly. She didn't. The marriage broke up a week after he sold his first novel. "There were a lot of other things going wrong, too, but that one didn't help," he says. Writers can resolve these problems, as Turtledove has in his second marriage to writer Laura Frankos. It takes work, though. It takes sensitivity and toughness on both sides.

There are other disadvantages to two-writer unions. Even though it's great to live with someone who shares your passions, you're effec-tively doubling the negative side effects of those passions. When your obsessive writing sessions overlap, the dishes pile up, you both run out of clean underwear, and you have cereal for dinner three nights in a row. There aren't any grown-ups in the house, just writers.

And then there's the issue of money. If you can't live on your joint freelance income, then how do you divide the responsibility for taking a day job? Does the partner who can earn the most outside the home have to take on the full load? Do you work two part-time jobs? Or does one of you work a day gig until the other's novel is finished, at which time you'll trade off? What's hardest about these decisions is balancing practicality with passion. If one of you brings in more freelance money than the other, does that mean she gets more freelance hours while the other works more day gigs? Is that fair?

Sometimes, one partner doesn't fully honor the other's identity as an artist. I've seen that break up marriages, too. Husband and wife are both writers, and one of them takes an office job. The one who gets to stay home writing takes on more and more of the writer identity, giving the spouse's art less and less respect.

Mutual commitment to your work can also backfire. A writer who changes, who wants to drop the sort of work she's known for and branch out into something new, may find that her partner has a lot of emotional investment in the former work. He doesn't want her to change. He may not think her new work is legitimate, and he may undercut her enthusiasm for it.

Partners who collaborate closely may grow to feel confined by the arrangement. Or, worse, one partner may feel confined while the other doesn't. In such cases, it can be hard to separate the desire to change the working relationship from a desire to dissolve the union.

Leonard Bishop said that the romantic assumptions of two-writer relationships "collapse under the weight of reality." In fact, the creative rewards of such relationships can be tremendous. They do require deliberate care. The challenge for two-artist couples, it seems to me, is to keep asking the question, "What is our common calling, and how do we best serve it together?" As long as the answer always provides creative outlet, encouragement, and validation for both partners, these unions can be happy, productive, and strong.

28

Writers Loving Nonwriters

As you might guess, domestic unions between a writer and a nonwriter are loaded with advantages that are pretty much the flip side of a writer–writer partnership's *dis*advantages. Nonwriters (by which I really mean nonartists) aren't given to a writer's obsessions. They're more likely to notice the pile of dishes in the sink and do something about it, even if it's only to say, "Honey, did you notice how bad the kitchen's getting?" At least there's some adult supervision in the house. Nonwriters are also more likely to earn a reliable income, possibly putting them in a position to subsidize the writer's efforts. And whatever ego issues there are in the relationship at least aren't issues of artistic rivalry.

There are other advantages. A nonwriter is probably in solid contact with the extra-literary world, so even if the writer spends long hermetic stretches inside her own imagination, she's not as isolated as she'd be with another writer. For her part, the writer gives the household some status diversity. Whatever cool things the partner does in the world, there are plenty of people who think that doing those cool things *and* living with a published writer is cooler still. Some nonwriting partners even get a creative buzz from subsidizing a lover's writing—they had a hand in bringing that work into the world, and they're proud.

But there are disadvantages, too. In a partnership between a writer and a nonwriter, worlds collide. The negative products of that collision, from most to least serious, are the Poisonous Problem, Ordinary Problems, and the Itchy Problem.

The Poisonous Problem is deadly, a serious impediment to a healthy relationship.

Here's a true story, in disguise. A group of us were having lunch, talking about a party planned for the weekend. Hugo confided to us that his girlfriend didn't want to come to the party. Most of the people there would be writers. She didn't like writers.

All of us, Hugo's friends, his *writer* friends, had heard this before. Someone said, "She doesn't like *us?* That's a bad sign, Hugo!" We laughed. If that had been the whole story, we would have left it at that. A joke.

But there was more. "She keeps bugging me about how much I write," Hugo said. "She keeps asking why I'm banging my head against the wall, since I've only sold a couple of stories. We've been going out for a year, but she acts like writing is a bad habit she can talk me out of. She says, 'You're not succeeding, so why do you torture yourself this way?'"

"Dump her."

Although I'd been thinking the same thing, I was surprised that anyone had actually spoken the words. But after a moment's hesitation, the rest of us chimed in. We qualified the initial harshness of those two words, acknowledged that the relationship might be good in other ways. Then all of us, men and women, straight and gay, partnered and single, advised Hugo to cut his losses and leave this woman. She didn't get what he was about, we told him. Probably she never would.

Did our harsh reaction serve Hugo's best interests? I think it did. Had they stuck it out, I imagine Hugo and his girlfriend would have had the same fight day after day for as long as they were together. They might be arguing about the unwashed dishes, what kind of car to buy, where to go on vacation, or whether Hugo should seek a promotion at work. But in every case, the real argument churning beneath the surface would be over whether or not Hugo was okay, whether he had the right to be who he was, a man committed to writing.

Having to fight again and again with your closest companion over your basic values makes for a poisonous relationship. Eventually, with that much poison around, something dies. Sometimes it's the relationship. Sometimes it's the writer's devotion to writing.

In theory, the nonwriter could change, could develop a true appreciation for the writer's identity and work. Personally, I suspect this third outcome happens about as often as abusive spouses are changed by their partner's love. I wouldn't want to risk my life or my creative fire on it.

More often, the collision of worlds is less extreme and leads to more Ordinary Problems. Each partner has to bend a little to accommodate the other's assumptions about what matters and how things should be done—which is, of course, what any couple does, but everything is worked out in the context of one partner's writing. How are you going to divvy up the traditional sex-role assignments to allow some time for the writer to write? To what extent do you both agree that writing is "real work"? Under what circumstances would it be reasonable to expect the writer to write less and earn a more reliable income or do more around the house? What matters more, dinner or a finished poem? In short, how are you going to collaborate on a relationship that gives you both what you need and enables the writer to be productive?

I'm not going to say much here about Ordinary Problems, but not because they aren't important. Indeed, even though Ordinary Problems don't threaten the foundations of the relationship or the roots of the writer's identity the way that the Poisonous Problem does, they can gradually corrode a union in which they aren't addressed.

But I've already said most of what needed saying about these problems in the "Writers and Lovers" chapter. Every issue that I discussed there is liable to need working out in a writer–nonwriter partnership, though some extra communication may be required. Unlike a writer–writer pairing, there aren't a lot of things that a nonwriting partner will easily and automatically understand about what a writer needs.

One Ordinary Problem that's a bit different when only one partner writes is the matter of a bruised ego. While it's true that a writer and nonwriter don't compete directly, one partner's success can still leave the other feeling diminished. The writer who is struggling in obscurity can feel left behind by a partner whose hard work is more apparent and legitimate in the Wider World. And the nonwriter can feel left behind, too, if the writer publishes successfully and the couple increasingly enters a social milieu of publishers' parties and awards banquets at which the non-writer, who's used to having the most outward status, has none. It helps if you're both successful in your respective spheres. Realistically, success isn't likely to find you both at the same moments or in equal portion.

Finally, there's the Itchy Problem, which isn't likely to destroy a relationship even if you ignore it. And for some couples, ignoring it is the easiest thing to do. But there is one wrinkle to watch out for.

I call it the Itchy Problem in honor of my ex-mother-in-law, who gave me a sweater every birthday and most Christmases. A wool sweater. I'm allergic to wool. Wearing it makes my skin itch. Inhaling the fibers makes me wheeze. So for five years, I collected sweaters I couldn't wear.

Did my ex and I tell her mom that I couldn't wear wool? I'm sure we did, though it's possible that we did it so timidly and apologetically that she can hardly be blamed for not noticing. We went along to get along. The sweaters themselves weren't really important. The two cotton sweaters I already had suited me fine, so I lost nothing by accepting these useless gifts and eventually giving them away. It was a little irksome not to have this aspect of who I am recognized, but I could deal with that lack of recognition from in-laws. It's not like I lived with them. It's not like having allergies is a treasured part of my self-concept.

The Itchy Problem is the lack of recognition from people outside your primary relationship. If you're a writer, single, unattached, it's a problem you're going to have to deal with on your own. The main thing you do is just get used to it and hang out with other writers and artists. The source of potential tension in a relationship is how the *partner* deals with the wool sweaters that other people hand you.

As I noted two chapters back, you can make all sorts of creative arrangements for the division of labor and other responsibilities, for nourishing each partner's needs in the relationship. You and your partner control the shape of your relationship. What you can't control is how your relationship is perceived.

Sometimes it seems like it's the partnership against the world. If your in-laws don't understand your arrangements, how much less likely are your workaday colleagues and neighbors to understand?

"She works so hard," some gossip says, "and he just stays at home, sitting around, I guess. He says he's writing a book. Do you know I went by there in the afternoon once, and he answered the door in his bathrobe?"

Or alternatively, "He's an engineer. As for her, well, she doesn't work. Have you ever been in there? With all the time she has on her hands you'd think she could do something about that house!"

To put this in practical terms, let's say you write best after midnight, when the rest of the household is sleeping. As a result, you sleep until noon every day. You and your partner have resolved this Ordinary

Problem. Your resolution works for your partner, and it works for you. But your parents don't get it.

Your mother calls at eleven in the morning and is aghast to hear your partner report that you're still in bed at such an hour. Mom wants to talk and suggests that your partner wake you up. Your partner can (A) wake you up and let you deal with your mother, (B) refuse to wake you but, for the sake of good in-law relations, agree that sleeping until noon does seem pretty slovenly, (C) fight the good fight by explaining to your mother that you were up late working because that's what you do, you write, and the best hours for it are from midnight to four.

What I want, and what Holly would do for me in such a case, is C. And bully for the partner who defends you vigorously. But mine is a two-writer relationship, and the refusal to recognize one of us is effectively a refusal to recognize either of us. Vigorously defending our identity comes naturally. We're both oddballs. When only one partner is the oddball, the outside social forces tend to line up on one side, trying to enlist the partner in pressuring the oddball to be more ordinary.

It's important for a writer–nonwriter couple to understand that this pressure is going to come. And then it's important for the writer to not worry, since worry about itchy sweaters is just about the only way that they can become a real problem.

Will the litany of disapproval eventually convince the writer's partner that the writer is indeed a bizarre loon whose habits ought not to be tolerated? Does the partner's unwillingness to tilt at every windmill of disapproval indicate an imperfect commitment to the relationship?

No.

Explaining why you live the way you do is your job and no one else's. If you aren't persuasive, don't blame your partner if she or he isn't persuasive either. As long as your partner believes in you, count yourself lucky.

You and your partner are swimming against the mainstream. You do this because you must. Your partner does it because he or she wants to be with you, strange as you are.

I don't think you should ask for more than that.

29

Writing with Children in the House

This chapter is a transcript from a panel discussion that never happened. I lack the credentials to talk about writing with children in the house, so I have assembled—from e-mail—the words of some writing parents. These actual quotes and a few outright fabrications are presented here as a panel that might have happened had all these people gathered in one place. The result is an amalgam of experience and some inevitable disagreements: Nothing is more personal than parenting, although writing might come close.

The panelists are all writers: Sean Stewart, Maureen McHugh, Billie Sue Mosiman, Wil McCarthy, Leslie What, Linda Nagata, Beverly Suarez Beard, Susan Kroupa, Valerie Freireich, and K. D. Wentworth. All but Ms. Wentworth, who has spent twenty-five years in the grade school salt mines, are parents.

The discussion covers how writers change when they have kids. Parents develop new powers of concentration. In order to write, they change their own schedules or their kids' schedules. They modify what they write according to what the demands of parenting are at the time. The discussion also touches on how the writer can change the family, or at least the family's perceptions about the writer's hours alone with the keyboard.

Moderator: So let's talk about what I gather is the main problem of writing with children, which is concentration. Children are great interrupters. At various ages, they break your concentration by keeping you awake all night, by trying to pull heavy objects onto their heads, by asking endless questions, by playing loudly, by playing *their stereo* loudly, by making sure that you notice that they are silently sulking, and by keeping you awake waiting for the call from the police. In every instance, these interruptions are important. Your kids need your attention, or the attention of another responsible adult. So how do you balance their needs with the concentration that writing demands?

Mosiman: You change. You learn to concentrate. When my daughters were small, I kept them in the room where I was writing and gave them toys or pans or spoons. I learned to write even while the kids were banging pots, playing their two-girl band tunes. You split your attention. When they were older, the girls could have the run of the house and I still supervised as I worked.

Moderator: How?

Mosiman: I trained myself to concentrate, blocking out sounds except for those that told me an emergency was brewing. I grew used to the sounds of children fighting, knowing from the sounds that it wasn't serious, just squabbling. I noticed when water was running and when, or if, it was shut off, and attended to other sounds that might indicate that the children needed to be seen after.

Kroupa: That's tricky, though. You can concentrate *too* hard. More than once, I remember not hearing one of my children, who had come up and was talking to me, until he shouted at me and shook my arm. Of course, that only happened when I was writing music reviews for the newspaper, on deadline. It's always been harder to work on fiction with the children underfoot. When my children were small, I usually tried to get away for a few hours to write at the local library or coffee shop while my husband baby-sat.

Moderator: One writer tells the story of receiving a phone call while she was concentrating on her work. "Sorry," she told the caller. "There's no one here by that name." Some time after she hung up, she realized that there *was* someone by that name living in her house. Her son.

McCarthy: I can't concentrate like that in the midst of household chaos.

Beard: You have to give up the expectation that you need the right environment for writing. You have to learn to write in a situation of extreme disorder. You sit with a laptop at the dining room table and edit stories while feeding yogurt to your toddler. You write while a small person runs in and out of the room, and smile and comment on what he tells you while not losing your train of thought.

Mosiman: Yes, not losing your momentum is important. I learned how to hold on to the end of a sentence I was about to write, stop, leave the computer or typewriter, change a diaper or get water for a kid, or make lunch or get a snack, then return to the work with the partial sentence still there so I could write it.

Nagata: I wouldn't even try that. My rule is "Do not write while there is a conscious child in the house." They don't deserve your temper tantrums; they deserve you. They are a lot more important than whatever you're writing.

Moderator: But not every writer will feel frustrated by such a divided attention. Trying to do two things at once doesn't make everyone throw a temper tantrum.

Stewart: I'm with Linda. It's ridiculous to try to write while the kid is awake and mobile. Kids are to grown-up work as cats are to newspapers, and you only end up enraged with one another.

Moderator: And that's why a lot of writers change their schedules to get in sync with the children's daily rhythms. Blessedly, children sleep. Quite a few novels have been written during nap time.

Beard: And written efficiently. I take more time to think before I furiously set those words down on the page. I think about what I'm writing a lot, during times when I can't do it.

Moderator: You can also nap when the kids do, and then get up early or stay up late.

McHugh: Raising children is already an exercise in sleep deprivation, so this only works in the short run. But, yes, if you have to, you can write from four o'clock to six o'clock in the morning. Hey, it's what Sylvia Plath did, and look what it did for her.

Moderator: Assuming that there's someone else who can look after the children for a while, you might adjust your schedule by spending some time away from home.

McCarthy: Sometimes I go to the library to concentrate on a first draft. If I stay home, I'm liable to play with the kids even if my wife has agreed to look after them.

Kroupa: Dave Wolverton maintains an office away from home and commutes to his writing desk like any working stiff.

Moderator: Working at home sounds cozy, and I know I've heard some of you say that it's important to have a good sturdy door to your office. But having Mom or Dad just tantalizingly out of reach can make everyone miserable.

Nagata: I can't fathom banishing the children from my presence while we're all at home.

Mosiman: They're not banished. You're at work. In an emergency, there you are.

Nagata: I'm not saying it's wrong, just that I couldn't do it that way.

Mosiman: Writing is my *profession*. I am a *professional*. Working with children at home does not mean you must deny your work in order to raise them. Like I said, you work *and* raise them. It's hard to accomplish, yes, but if you want your profession badly enough, you learn what you need to know to do two things at once, sometimes three and four things at once. The children aren't taking second place. No, they may not have your complete attention *all the time,* but my children didn't suffer. They had me at home and with them every second, and when they needed me, I was there. They're grown and successful and happy adults now. Ask them yourself if they loved their childhood and they will say "Yes!" Ask them if they were neglected or if they suffered and they will tell you "No!"

Moderator: This can be a heated topic.

Mosiman: It's so personal. Parents can get bristly about how they chose to do things. What matters is your results. My grown daughters wouldn't have swapped me for any other mother and have turned into very fine mothers themselves. I must have done something right. I did not neglect them.

Moderator: With writing and parenting, it seems to me you've got a conflict between two all-absorbing tasks. Parenting demands 100 percent, and so does writing.

Mosiman: You devote yourself and work around obstacles of child-raising and time constraints and interruptions or you fail, that's all there is to it. Your commitment to writing has to be soul-killing serious.

Moderator: I should remind everybody that this is an imaginary conversation and that none of the participants actually said these things to each other. To get back to my agenda: You can adjust your concentration or your schedule. What about changing the children's schedule instead of adjusting your own?

McHugh: Yes. Child care. Child care, child care, child care. If you went into the office every day, they wouldn't let you bring your child. If you really can't afford forty hours a week of child care, maybe you can manage three mornings a week?

Nagata: When the kids are in preschool, that's a huge step forward, except that you may then start to ask yourself if you shouldn't get a *real* job. Another lovely guilt trip. There are many of those. It is far easier to justify paying big money for child care when you're producing an income than when you're producing rejection slips.

Moderator: I've met women who applied for writing grants specifically to get money for child care.

Stewart: Trading sleep for writing or paying for child care. You can break your body or your bank. Your choice.

Freireich: Those aren't the only options.

McCarthy: Encourage the grandparents to spend more time babysi—, uh, enjoying the company of their descendants.

Freireich: I used to enforce the strictest, earliest bedtime of anyone I knew and have even now managed to convince everyone involved that it was all for the best and my son's health, welfare, et cetera. But he went to bed at six-thirty or seven until about the fourth grade. I'm a monster. By eighth grade he was up until nine or nine-thirty and I was working much too late at night, and my productivity dropped.

Nagata: I paid for my writing with sleep. But you need to get enough sleep so that you're civil to your children the next day. I guess my advice is to have your children when you're young. I can't imagine going through all that in my late thirties.

Kroupa: People do, though. Writers do.

Stewart: When my older friends had kids, they were much more likely to have the money to arrange day care, nannies, or other domestic help. So a corollary to "Have 'em young" might be "Have 'em when you have money." We can't overstate how much easier money makes this. In short, have money, marry well, and live close to grandparents you like.

Mosiman: We've been talking about the time we take for our writing. But when we don't write is important, too. I've treated writing like the sort of job other people had. I worked all week and did no writing on weekends. That way the family doesn't feel cheated of a mother and wife. On the weekends, they have her full attention.

What: My attitude has mostly been, "You can always write the novel tomorrow, but the children need you today." This has limited my career, by choice.

Moderator: I think you'd all say that you put your children first, but you all seem to have different ideas about how to do that. Some writers change what they work on according to the age of their kids or their care arrangements. Laurel Winter observed one summer that she was writing poetry instead of prose because her kids were out of school. She returned to fiction in September. And that's another strategy I hear about a lot, adjusting your goals, the kinds of projects you take on, according to the kind of attention your children need at a particular stage of their development. Maybe you don't have the concentration for novels, so you write stories. Parents seem to make this kind of adjustment often.

McCarthy: That's because children aren't a first priority. They are more important than that. They trump everything. There are still other things that we want, too, but only in the context that the children must have what they need.

Moderator: What about when kids resist the writing? They want *all* of your attention.

What: And sometimes they should get it. It depends on their age.

Kroupa: I agree. There are times when children need the complete attention of the parent. I never got any writing done for a year after a baby was born—the demands were just too great.

Moderator: So you may adjust what you write . . . to the point of not writing at all for a while. Though none of you waited for an empty nest. If you delayed your writing, it wasn't until the kids had grown up and moved away.

Nagata: Most of what I've said refers to small children. Once they reach the age of computer gaming, they're no problem at all so long as you have more than one computer.

Moderator: Now what about having children help with the writing? I've heard of writers who enlist their kids to help with clerical work or to brainstorm. The point isn't that their contribution is necessary, but that they might enjoy being part of the work and might respect the work more.

Wentworth: Kids respond to being rewarded. They'll see their own behavior of keeping quiet for a while as worthwhile if they get praised for it. Mom keeps an eye on exactly how long she gets to write uninterrupted, then praises the child. "Wow! You let me work for fifteen minutes straight! That was really helpful!" With reinforcement, fifteen minutes could become thirty.

Moderator: A painter told me that her family wasn't being supportive of her work. Then she started to pay family members a cash commission for each of her sales. Soon her kids and her husband would say things like, "Mom, shouldn't you be in the studio? Let me do the dishes. You go get busy."

Freireich: Heaven.

Wentworth: Sure, but it doesn't have to be money. If you make a sale, have a family celebration party or dinner out, some experience that the kids will want to repeat.

Moderator: Last words?

Stewart: This has been a lively, funny, spirited discussion. The chance to sit around and have lively, funny, spirited discussions about anything didn't seem to come my way very often for the first years that I was the writer and stay-at-home father. Writing and child-raising in the atomic age may share those traits of endless work that is never enough, weary introspection, bursts of great joy, and all the work done pretty much alone.

Nagata: The good news is, it does get easier. A big fenced yard complete with sandbox and other children is a valuable asset. Living in a rural area where the kids can only go so far—with no highways or open bodies of water in their ranging territory—also helps a lot. Count the days until school starts, but don't forget to have fun.

What: I have wanted to be a writer and a mother for as long as I can remember. Years ago, if someone had told me I could only choose one of the above, I would not have believed it. If someone said that to me today, I would understand the truthfulness of the remark, but would argue that with sacrifice and a flexible long-term plan, anyone can achieve some degree of success for both career paths.

Stewart: Kids are, all in all, a good investment for a writer. They open up such a large terrain of human experience, and vulnerability, and speech, and interaction, that if your art isn't significantly expanded by the experience, you just aren't paying attention.

Moderator: So what you're saying is, if I want to improve as a writer, I should probably borrow your kids?

[Various offers ensued as the panel adjourned.]

Part Seven
Success

30

Nothing Succeeds Like Success

Are you a successful writer?

If you can answer *Yes* without reservation, if you are as successful and productive as you want to be, if you approach every writing task with full confidence, then you don't need this chapter.

As for me, I feel successful only part of the time. When I'm reading one of my stories to an audience and I can feel every person in the room hanging on my next word, I'm a successful writer. When I'm a nominee attending an awards banquet, even if my name isn't called (it really *is* an honor just to be nominated), I'm a successful writer. When I have just finished the last lines of a work-for-hire novel and I feel that, yeah, this time I *nailed* it, I'm a successful writer.

On the other hand, I'm not successful when I balance my checkbook. When I consider the fate of my first, still-unpublished novel, I'm far from successful. On those days when I notice how s-l-o-w-l-y I'm writing my second novel, which is also a quirky hard-to-classify work that will probably get bounced as persistently as the first one has, I'm about as far from successful as I can be.

On the days when I don't feel successful, I also don't much feel like getting down to work. Why bother if after all these years of effort, I still haven't succeeded? And on those days, I tend to discount any past successes I've had. After all, those successes didn't change me, didn't make me ultimately successful, so they must not really count.

However, when I come home from a good reading, I'm ready to stay up all night outlining a new novel. And I'm more productive and enthused than Anthony Trollope on speed after I return from a convention where people knew who I was, where editors invited me to parties, where strangers paid me knowledgeable compliments on my work. And you should see how much I get done in the weeks after an unexpectedly large royalty check arrives!

This change in emotional state has something to do with a truism

we've all heard: "Nothing succeeds like success." When you feel successful, you're willing to tackle work that has an uncertain outcome in
the belief that you're going to succeed again.

Offered as advice to someone who doesn't feel successful at the
moment, "Nothing succeeds like success" sounds like a tautology along
the lines of telling the poor, "In order to get rich, you need to accumulate
some wealth." Even if there's some underlying wisdom to the apparently
simplistic advice (it really does take money to make money), the problem
for someone who lacks the resource is finding where to begin. Where do
you get, on demand, the emotional experience of feeling successful?

There are a couple of good answers to this. One is to work on
changing your belief system so that you always feel successful and at
peace with the universe. That, however, is an approach that takes time
and self-improvement, and as I've noted before, I favor solutions that I
can use on my current flawed self.

The technique I want to detail here is a way of coaching yourself
into a state in which you feel successful no matter what lousy news
came in yesterday's mail. And it's a technique that doesn't take much
time. After all, you don't want to spend half of a precious writing hour
just getting in the mood.

The technique owes a lot to neurolinguistic programming, and I'm
borrowing some NLP terminology to describe it.

Here's what you do:

First, choose a spot on your body that's going to become your
"anchor." This is someplace that you can touch unobtrusively as part of
your routine for psyching up. The spot I've chosen is the web between
my left thumb and hand, and I "set" the anchor by squeezing this spot
with the thumb and forefinger of my other hand. I could just as easily
have anchored to tugging my right earlobe, brushing the side of my
nose, or squeezing my knee. But choose an action that isn't something
you do under other circumstances. You want the action and the sensation to be unique to this exercise.

Most of the time, you'll be setting your anchor as you prepare to
write and are, presumably, alone and unobserved. Still, there may be
some very public occasions when it would be useful to set your anchor,
so it's best to choose something subtle that you won't feel funny doing
around other people.

Next, identify four or five categories in which you've had moments of really delicious success. Some categories you might consider are Romantic (which we can assume includes Seductive and Erotic), Athletic (or just Kinetic), Career, Artistic, Religious/Spiritual, Academic. Make up other categories if you need to. Write each of the selected categories down on a three-by-five card.

Then try to recall three moments of peak success in each of your four categories. Jot down some notes about the moment and how it felt. It doesn't matter whether anyone else would be impressed with the achievement, or even if other people would approve of your noting this moment as an example of success. You're not going to share this information with anyone, and you can even make your notes to yourself cryptic if you like. What's important is identifying moments in which you felt gloriously successful.

One of my success moments came in high school when I was playing a pickup game of football in the park. My neighbor, Bruce Ferris, always played quarterback, and he was a lot more athletic than I was. If I were pass rushing, Bruce could usually just sidestep me. Even if I grabbed him, I couldn't ever topple him. But in one game, though the tackle seemed to take forever, I sacked Bruce. For ten seconds, I was a hero among my friends, in part because no one, least of all Bruce Ferris, expected *me* to sack him. I felt glorious. Without a doubt, I'm the only person who remembers that moment, but I remember it vividly.

That's the sort of memory you're looking for.

When you have identified several moments for each of the categories, give the three-by-five cards to a friend who will help you to set your anchor. Now imagine that on the floor in front of you, there's a circle about three feet in diameter that's made by a shaft of brilliant golden light streaming down. Try to see this circle vividly. You might even kneel down and trace the outside edge with your fingers.

Imagine the source of this light in any way that's meaningful to you.

You can think of the space inside the light as the Circle of Excellence. Or, if that seems silly to you, you can give it another name.

As you stand outside the Circle, your friend reads you the name of one of your four categories (Romantic, Career, Academic, and so on). You then recall one of the remembered events in that category. You remember what the light was like, what sounds there were; you remember if there were any particular smells, and so on. In as much detail as you can, you mentally re-create the event. As soon as you're there in memory, as soon as you feel the feelings of that moment, step into the Circle, be aware of the golden light that surrounds you, and touch, tug, or rub your anchor spot.

If you like, you can also add a word to your anchor, perhaps one that describes how you're feeling. "On," say, or "Excellent." Or something nonsensical, like "Peach pit." The meaning of the word or phrase doesn't matter—it's just another sensation, like touching your anchor spot, that you're connecting to the emotional state. You can say the word aloud or subvocalize.

Then take a step back out of the Circle.

Your friend goes on to the next category, and you do the same thing again. Go through the list three times so that you have anchored a dozen remembered experiences to that spot on your body. If it's the third time through and you can't remember what your third Romantic success was, experience the first one again.

When you have stepped into the Circle a dozen times, your anchor is set. Later, when you want to evoke a resourceful, successful state of mind, touch your anchor spot the same way you did in the exercise and say or think your word. If you don't feel successful and resourceful right away, then close your eyes and visualize one of those success memories while you keep touching the anchor and repeating the word.

Once you have established a connection between feeling successful and touching the anchor point, you can strengthen the connection by anchoring any time you feel successful. I do this on the racquetball court every time I hit a shot that goes exactly where I wanted it to go. Touching the anchor gets to be a little celebration ritual, a way of calling attention to a moment in which everything feels perfect. Naturally, I also anchor those writing-related moments that have me on top of the world. When I gave a reading a few nights ago, I anchored the applause.

I also touch my anchor point during racquetball matches when I have a string of bad shots and just can't get into my game. Instead of getting caught up in the negative emotion, touching the anchor spot helps me to feel resourceful, as confident as I might if I had just had a string of *good* shots.

The technique isn't perfect. It doesn't make you an emotional robot, able to swing from one affective extreme to the other at a push of a button. (Would you want that?) But it can give you a measure of control over the emotions that shape your productivity. The more I practice anchoring, the easier it is for me to feel successful and confident when I begin my writing day.

All of this feels a little magical to me, especially when I stop to consider a paradox: If I touch my anchor to evoke a resourceful state because I'm feeling out of sorts, then why is it that the out-of-sorts feeling doesn't get anchored, too? Why does this technique always work in the direction I want it to? Is there really a classical conditioning response going on here, as NLP practitioners would claim?

I don't know. I suspect that this technique may work because of something similar to a placebo effect. It may be that the ability to control your emotional state is the product of (1) paying attention to your emotional state and (2) believing that your emotional state is under your control.

Whatever it is that makes the technique work, though, it does work well enough that sometimes, in the wake of bad news that has me feeling discouraged, I won't use the anchor to cheer up because I know it will work and I'll be enthusiastic again before I really want to be. Some disappointments are big enough that they need to be experienced, and some squashed hopes deserve to be mourned.

But when I'm ready and willing to use it, I now have a tool that helps me climb back into the writing saddle. Most days, that's enough to make me a successful writer.

31

Common, Ordinary Success

The previous chapter discussed some techniques for feeling successful pretty much at will. I noted that in addition to the quick fix there were ways to change your belief system so that you'd *always* feel successful. That, of course, is a deeper fix for the problems that come with feeling unsuccessful. And as I mentioned, changing your beliefs is a task that can occur only over time. It involves (impatient sigh) self-improvement.

As much as I favor advice that shows results the same afternoon, I have to admit that some projects will yield better results if you take your time with them. There's a difference between feeling successful at will and *always* feeling successful. If lack of confidence were a broken leg, success-at-will would be a crutch that was there when you remembered to use it. But always feeling successful would be like mending the broken bone.

Feeling a base of underlying security is an ongoing project for me. But I've been working on that project long enough to discover three principles that help. They are:

1. Want What You Have.
2. Know the Heart-Sufficient Goals.
3. Trust What You'll Get.

The four words of the first principle, Want What You Have, are easy to read right over without much thought because you know that you've heard that, or something like it, many times before. If I add that this principle is partly about *renunciation,* you may imagine that I'm about to ask you to shave your head, move into a cave, fast, and take vows of celibacy. Well, no.

When I say *renunciation* in this context, I am not talking about separating yourself from your desires. You'd have to drop out of this culture to stop wanting more money, more praise, more status, more love, or more days of life on this earth. Indeed, you'd probably have to drop out of the human race. We want. Desire is our universal state. It's difficult to change the instinct to seek more. So the only thing you give up in renunciation is the feeling that you are entitled to more.

All of this is rather abstract, but it leads to some very concrete practices that go by the names of Attention, Compassion, and Gratitude.

I'm going to touch on these practices here, but if what I say intrigues you, then you might check out my source: *How to Want What You Have*, by Timothy Miller.[1] This book has been enormously helpful to me. (I have it on audiotape and replay it often.)

Miller is a cognitive psychotherapist. His practice focuses on training people to change their thoughts and beliefs in order to change their emotions and behaviors.

Thus, the practice of Attention focuses on giving up unnecessary value judgments akin to, "Why did it have to rain today, of all days?" or, "There's no good reason why I should feel so miserable about this rejection slip." Attention means that you let yourself sense what you sense at the moment, give yourself permission to fully feel whatever emotions you feel. It means that you don't dismiss any sensation as ordinary or trivial. Whatever *is* is preciously real. The Buddhist writer and teacher Thich Nhat Hanh calls this practicing "mindfulness." In its broadest application, it's a way of experiencing everything you do as a meditation. When you're walking, you're doing a walking meditation, aware of your strides, of your breath, of what you see and hear around you. When you wash dishes, you are doing a dishes meditation.

Compassion is the practice of replacing your distancing thoughts about other people. You unlearn your habits of thinking that anyone else is better or worse than you are. You stop considering others to be more important or less important than yourself. I know that a lot of my own jealous reactions to another writer's awards or bookstore dump display have been less than compassionate. Any thought that contains the words *doesn't deserve* can probably be replaced with something more compassionate.

Thinking compassionately does not mean that you become any less assertive. My mantra for compassion is, "Everybody has a hungry heart." It's a thought that can dissolve hate without sapping any of my power to act where anger is appropriate.

Finally, my favorite practice is Gratitude. This means counting your blessings, earnestly. You can't force gratitude, because even though it's based in thoughts, it has a strong emotional component. But you can practice thinking thoughts that open the door to gratitude.

One such exercise is to look at objects around you and ask yourself if you might feel any gratitude related to them. For instance, there's a little statue of Shiva/Lord Nataraja on my windowsill. I'm grateful to the bronze caster in India who made this elegant little object. I feel grateful that I was able to earn the eight dollars that paid for the statue. Actually, I paid on credit. Well, I'm grateful for my credit cards, and for the bills that remind me of past opportunities to buy things I wanted.

As I keep looking at Nataraja, I find that I'm grateful for the teachings of Joseph Campbell, whose books taught me how to "read" the image of the statue. That reminds me that my brother-in-law gave me the Campbell book, and I'm grateful to him for giving me a gift that was so appropriate for me. I'm reminded that at a convention I bought a similar statue and gave it to my friend Sean Stewart, and I'm grateful for my good friendship with Sean and for the wonderful experiences of reading his novels, sometimes in manuscript. I think of Wil McCarthy, who introduced us, and I'm grateful for *that* friendship.

Once I get started, I find an endless chain of things to be grateful for. It's no effort to feel what I feel, but it takes a little effort to remind myself to *look* for gratitude cues.

Of these three practices, the one that gives me the most immediate feelings of success is Gratitude. This shouldn't be surprising, since anxiety about the absence of success usually arises from thoughts about what we don't have, but wish we did.

My friend Jack Balas, a fine-arts painter, likes to stand the longing for more on its head. He does it by plaintively saying things like, "I wish Wes and I lived together in Colorado with a view of the mountains. I wish we owned a house. I wish our paintings were selling. I wish I had a West Coast agent for my art." You see, Jack and Wes own a house in Colorado together. They have a great view of the Front Range, their paintings are selling well enough to support them, and Jack is happy with his L.A. agent. (You can see by this, perhaps, how Gratitude and Attention are related.)

My second success principle is: Know Your Heart-Sufficient Goals.

Probably you didn't start writing because you were attracted to the money. (There are such people, but usually they Learn.) Probably you began because of some feelings you had about words. Or about stories. Perhaps you were in love with the literary life, the life of the mind. Or maybe you really liked the kinds of people who hung out in literary coffee shops and you wanted them to be your kind of people forever. Any of these is an avenue into passion.

Heart-Sufficient Goals are the ones driven by love, and they depend on outcomes that you and you alone control.

For example, there may be one reader whom you love and for whom you want to create a story. The narrative you write is a gift to that one person, and you have arrived at your Heart-Sufficient Goal when that one reader hears your story. A lot of children's books have been written for one particular child, and publication was a happy afterthought.

At one remove, your Heart-Sufficient Goal may be to write the story to someone who isn't here to read it anymore. As I've noted before, Kurt Vonnegut's sister died before he had done much writing at all, but he has said that he wrote each book for her.

Or you may be in love with your characters. Once they begin to come to life on your pages, your Heart-Sufficient Goal is to be true to them, to bring them fully onto the page of your manuscript and share them with someone. Anyone. Your Heart-Sufficient Goal has been met when you're satisfied that the story conveys those characters to the first person to read your manuscript.

More broadly, some of my Heart-Sufficient Goals have to do with living my life so that it has meaning to me even if, on the whole, it looks like I'm failing by conventional standards. My Hanovi Braddock novel *Ashes of the Sun* is about the eventual triumph of love over fear. That's my personal struggle in my writing career, too, and I am meeting this Heart-Sufficient Goal whenever I am true to my vision, whenever I answer financial anxieties with another day at the writing desk. On some days I may blow it, but the overall shape of my efforts, of my life, is that I'm not giving up on my vision.

Role models can help define this Heart-Sufficient Goal. My favorite Art Hero stories tell of artistic or intellectual effort in extremity. Van Gogh, ashamed of his financial dependence, of his inability to sell a painting to anyone but his brother, and of his unaccountable moods (he was probably manic depressive), nonetheless kept clinging to his passion to paint. Boethius wrote *On the Consolation of Philosophy* while awaiting his execution. Raymond Chandler turned his life around, quit alcohol, saved his marriage, and began a new career as a writer . . . in the trough of the Great Depression.

In so many artists' biographies, the one great successful work of the artist was the life that he or she lived. The story of outward failure has often been a triumph of love. Such triumph isn't mere consolation, but a story of success. It's possible to see this form of success even while you're living it. Emily Dickinson did so. In her lifetime, she was virtually unpublished and gently lectured at by male editors who Knew Better how poems should be written. Why, she couldn't even rhyme! But Dickinson was confident that her poems were a hard-won gift to a later generation of people who would have the eyes to read her work. Or, at the least, she knew that her poems were a lasting and precious trace of her life. That's clear from poems such as #675, the one that starts "Essential Oils—are wrung—." (Look it up!)

What I'm really saying about Dickinson was that she trusted that her efforts weren't wasted on the world. That brings us to the third principle: Trust What You'll Get. This follows from the notion that no effort is wasted, that everything we do, whether we act out of fear or act out of love, influences the decisions of others around us.

The influence isn't always visible. It can take a long time for it to be felt, and it often doesn't happen in the arena where we're looking for it.

Here, as an example, is a little fantasy that sustains me:

I may spend my whole life largely spinning my wheels, having small successes that keep me afloat, but never the big ones that will get my most important books into the hands of readers. My first unpublished novel may, because it fits no market categories, remain unpublished forever. The novels that I write afterward may have the same problems. My short stories may continue to see print, but perhaps they will never be enough to raise my literary reputation very high. It's novels that really count, after all.

Meanwhile, these struggles will feed the musings that turn into the very book that you're reading. Perhaps this book will sell only a thousand copies. The publisher, editor, and I all hope for better, but I'm being pessimistic on purpose.

Let's say that in the midst of this muddling, I die.

From my perspective, my life, while I was living it, was a success. I hit some obstacles along the way. Some I negotiated well. Others, especially the ones that I never clearly identified, continued to trip me up, but I managed to do my work.

Some objective evaluator on the outside might look at my body of work and say, "Minor writer."

Now join me in imagining that the fourteen-year-old younger sister of a young man who buys this book at a garage sale loves books and has a hopeless notion of being a writer. Hopeless because she has undiagnosed attention deficit disorder and thinks she is stupid and shiftless.

But she loves to read.

Something in the Hunters and Farmers chapter, or in some other chapter, gives her a technique that helps her to cope, to write in spite of her difficulty with sitting in one place for ten minutes to concentrate on any one thing. Because of my book, she gets help she would otherwise have failed to get for a few more decades. If I hadn't struggled as I have, I wouldn't have learned the tools that she then learns from me.

Suppose she invents a literary form at eighteen and becomes its unrivaled master at thirty. Suppose she is the Shakespeare of the twenty-first century.

You never know. You *can't* know. But unless you're trapped in a hopelessly mechanistic worldview, it's hard to resist the notion that love, diligently applied, finds its targets. We just may have been wrong about what the targets were.

Trust that if you follow your heart, your heart will be rewarded, even if invisibly.

The more I frame my thinking in these ways, the more I feel indestructibly successful.

32
Peacemaking at the Barricades

You can't stroll very far in the City of Literature without coming to an intersection where writers stand at opposing barricades. From behind toppled desks and stacks of books, the two sides hurl erasers and slogans at one another:

"You people aren't professionals! Who the hell reads you, outside of graduate seminars where the students are forced to do it! Real writers are *popular!*"

"Real writers, huh? You people wouldn't know elegant prose if it bit you on the ass! Real writers create *art!*"

"Art, schmart. Real writers write to be read. We've got Stephen King and Edgar Rice Burroughs over here, two of the best-selling writers in the English language!"

"And you're proud of that? We've got Gertrude Stein and James Joyce, two of the most idiosyncratic stylists who ever picked up a pen!"

"And you're proud of that? Snobs!"

"Plebeians!"

"Amateurs!"

"Hacks!"

"Pretenders!"

"Prostitutes!"

If you come back the next day, the barricades may be at a different intersection. The tones of the argument will sound similar, but some of the artsy writers of yesterday's battle will have crossed over to the popular side, some of the popular writers will have defected, too, and the fight will go like this:

"Writing is an adventure!"

"Is not! It's a *job!*"

"You'll never be authentic with that attitude!"

"Hope you enjoy starving with *your* attitude!"

"Hey, at least we'll live lives worth living!"

"At least *we'll* make a living wage!"

"You're losing your souls!"

"You're just lazy!"

"Careerists!"

"Dreamers!"

All of this may look amusing from the outside, but let me assure you that at every pair of barricades, both sides throw their erasers with lethal intent. These arguments generate a lot of serious ill will. It isn't fun to be on either side of the street.

When we choose up sides like this, we do real damage to ourselves and to each other. As soon as we divide up, we cut ourselves off from the camaraderie, experience, and wisdom of the other group. We exaggerate our differences in order to justify the separation. We demonize. Everybody loses.

How do these barricades get erected in the first place? Why are these debates so hot? And what can we do about the problem?

It might seem that the stakes in these disputes are just a matter of taste. One side likes highbrow stuff, say, and the other side prefers lowbrow. However, people are generally pretty sensible about not arguing over taste. If I'm crazy about chocolate and your sweet obsession is licorice, neither of us is going to hotly defend our preference. We might tease one another: *How can you eat that stuff?* But your teasing isn't likely to get to me if I know that I really do prefer chocolate and I'm happy with my choice.

But the sorts of choices we make as writers are seldom so simple. In writing, we often have to choose, at least temporarily, between two things that we desire.

One of my favorite quotes is attributed to Rabbi Zusya of Hanipoli, who said, "In the coming world they will not ask me: 'Why were you not Moses?' They will ask me: 'Why were you not Zusya?'"[1] If I write work that any number of other writers could have done just as well, I know that at some point I'll be asking myself: Why were you not Bruce Holland Rogers? Authenticity is an aspect of the psychological or spiritual success I crave.

At the same time, I was raised to value self-sufficiency and security. Even though my wife now makes enough for us to live on, I want to pay my own bills. I want to know that I could make my own way in the world if I had to. Moreover, my social status and self-worth are tied up in this question of income. Income is another aspect of what I mean by "success."

Some projects offer big rewards in terms of authenticity and only the faintest hope of money. Some promise good money but offer only the faintest hope for self-expression. Very few promise good money and complete artistic freedom, and those projects generally aren't open to anyone but writers who already have artistic and professional reputations.

Not too long ago, I found myself behind the barricade of Authenticity, throwing erasers at one of my rich friends behind the Money barricade. Let's call him Vincent. I was pointing out all the problems of working for one of his markets, a game company that produces fiction. In the past, I had tried writing for that company. They had jacked me around a lot. Working for them was, I concluded, bad for the soul.

Vincent fired back an eraser that hit me right between the eyes, raising a cloud of chalk dust and giving me a nauseous headache. "You let them jack you around?" he said. "If you don't have any business sense, then you shouldn't be a freelance writer!"

I was about to throw back the biggest eraser you have ever seen when a mutual friend pulled me aside. "You know," this friend said, "your career and Vincent's were very similar for a time. I remember when Vincent was wondering if novelizations and tie-in work would rob him of his artistic soul. He turned down such work for a while, but he had to pay his rent somehow. Then he was making good money, he got out of debt, and he decided he liked being in the black. I know he'd like to do more original work, but he'd have to take a serious pay cut. Meanwhile, since you stopped doing tie-in books to focus on original work, your income has been, um, smaller. See where I'm going with this?"

I did.

I don't think any of us thinks of success as just one thing. Today (though the definition will be different tomorrow), I think success is writing what I want to write, writing well according to my own standards, getting critical acclaim, keeping to a daily schedule, piling up pages, getting paid, appearing in prestigious publications, winning prizes, and making a living from my work. By the criteria on that list, I am entirely successful in some areas, largely successful in others, and a miserable failure at that last one.

That's where my wound is.

Vincent has a different definition of success that probably includes many of the same things. He's making a ton of money, winning prizes for his original work, et cetera. But he has a wound, too. I don't know exactly what the wound is. I'd guess it has something to do with all the novels he might have written if he weren't writing someone else's books for money. Or maybe he craves the respect of his peers, and feels that some of them discount his original work because he does so much tie-in fiction.

Whatever his wound, I hit it square on with my eraser. Then he devastated me with the eraser he fired back. If he had said that I didn't know how to write a good sentence, I'd have known he was full of it. I am confident in my success as a stylist. But attacking my business sense, that hurt. I'm already tender there.

When someone is hitting our wounds, making them bleed, no wonder we get defensive. No wonder we get behind the barricades and counterattack. And no wonder these battles are so serious!

Some writers can't be drawn into particular fights because they have no pertinent wounds. A given writer may not take sides in the fight between the Partisans of Entertainment and Forces of Education because he has never had to choose in this arena. He sees both sides as equally important or equally irrelevant. But that same writer might snarl like a wounded boar if you said that the real measure of quality was whether a work outlived its author. He's very successful writing mass-market originals. He knows they're ephemeral, but damn it, they are *good!* As for *your* stupid notions of quality and success . . .

Get ready to duck.

Equipped with a little insight about why we stand at the barricades, what can you do about these disputes with your fellow writers? Three things.

First, you can be gentle with other writers by not making sweeping, self-justifying pronouncements about what success is. We're all bound to emphasize the sorts of success we already enjoy or feel we're on the way to enjoying. We're all bound to deemphasize the success that, though we may crave it, seems more remote to us. Acknowledge that there are as many kinds of success as there are successful writers.

Second, when you're wounded in a debate that others have touched off, acknowledge your wound for what it is. You wouldn't care so much, wouldn't be picking up an eraser to hurl, if you weren't touchy about something the other side gets in more abundance than you do. To put it another way, you wouldn't rise to the bait if the bait didn't appeal to you. So understand that appeal. Try to define and acknowledge your desire.

Third, and this may be the most useful step, ask yourself what the other side might have to teach you. What do those other writers have that you want? Maybe you could learn from each other.

For example, the fight between "Writing is a job!" and "Writing is an adventure!" seems to draw a lot of writers. What they're really arguing about is writing as Product or as Process.

Product writers aim at a goal, such as making money or appearing in a particular publication. They write headfirst, figuring out what kind of work they need to write to achieve their goal and then writing just that kind of work. They market top-down, studying an individual market to understand its needs and tailoring the work for that market. In a sense, Product writers market first, then write.

Process writers have no aim but the writing itself. They write heart-first, figuring out what they are writing only by seeing what they have written so far. They market bottom-up, studying the broad market to find an editor who might be interested in the finished work. Process writers don't think about markets until the writing is done.

Writers who stand at these two barricades proclaim the other side's lack of seriousness. If you're always writing to meet someone else's needs, how can you possibly produce anything fresh, idiosyncratic, or original? And if you're writing only to please yourself, how can you possibly survive in the marketplace? Both sides make dire, puritanical predictions about the fate of those writers across the street. Product writers are sure to lose their souls to Mammon. Process writers are sure to starve.

In fact, both approaches, Product and Process, are useful, and it may be helpful to know how to shift between them. Artist Alan M. Clark won a World Fantasy Award on the strength of his original and idio-syncratic *Pain Doctors* paintings, work that was done on spec, just to see where it would go.[2] Process art. But Alan first established himself as a Product artist "by doing just exactly the sort of commercial work I saw publishers accepting. . . . [I] only began to insert my vision strongly after I began to get work."

From the beginning, Alan wanted to work on projects in that rare middle ground where both self-expression and a good income are possible, but since such work isn't generally available to beginners, he chose to start at the commercial end of illustration and work his way to the middle.

Alan has met artists who were reluctant to take his advice to do likewise because of the myths that are told behind the Art-as-Process barricade. According to Alan, these artists fear that "once they do something commercial, they'll either have compromised their artistic vision to the point that they won't be able to see their way to return to what they love, or they will become blind to the commercial corruption in their work and fail at being artists, living out their lives as broken, wasted imaginations."

It's possible, and often helpful, to switch approaches even as a brief respite from what you ordinarily do. A Product writer who is burning out can often renew her passion by writing without any goals for a week. A Process writer who is discouraged by the market's rough reception can gain a toehold, and get her confidence back, by focusing on one commercial market long enough to sell to it.

The same is true for the barricades of Highbrow versus Lowbrow writing, Fixed Text versus Hypertext, Writing to Inspire versus Writing to Entertain. If you're feeling stuck, what you need may be behind the opposing barricade.

The longer we stand at the barricades, flinging erasers and recounting the myths of how doomed and deluded the other side is, the harder it becomes to cross the street and find out what those other successful writers know that we don't.

Part Eight

Letting Go

33
Celebrate!

Greetings, gentle reader. I have arranged for fireworks to go off in a few minutes. Here's your party hat. May I pour you some champagne? Sparkling apple juice? Here comes the caterer with the smoked oysters. Please help yourself.

My "Staying Alive" columns are being published as a book, so I hope you'll help me celebrate. And while we sip and munch, I'd like to talk about celebrating, about why and how we do it and about some of the psychological complications that sometimes arise.

I have three reasons for celebrating. First is that when I achieve something as a writer, rejoicing with others is a way of giving some support to my writing identity. I've been saying all along that I was a writer, and look, I finished a story! I got my first rejection! I made my first sale! I won an award! I landed a book contract! Here the book is, finally in my hands!

Second, writing is like climbing a mountain range. You see the summit of the first foothill, and you think that's the top. Once you get there, though, you can see there is a higher mountain behind the hills. Climb that mountain, and you'll see an even greater peak. If your focus is always on the things you haven't done yet, you may miss out on some of the satisfaction and confidence that come with recognizing the things you've already achieved. The habit of celebrating helps me to acknowledge and enjoy the distance that I have already come along the writing path. By celebrating early and often I appreciate more of the here-and-now.

A benefit of such celebration, too, means that if you celebrate good news that later sours, you get to keep the experience of celebrating the good news. When one of my friends sold a short story to *Playboy*, she celebrated by calling just about everyone she knew. Friends and family rejoiced with her. Her mother told the dentist, "My daughter sold a story to *Playboy*." Very likely, the dentist was suitably impressed.

The story was twice laid out in preparation for it to run. Both times, it was bumped to make way for something else at the last minute. Months have passed, and still more months, and years. The editor who bought and loved the story recently left the magazine, so even though my friend gets to keep her fee, she may never actually see her story printed in *Playboy*. If she had waited to celebrate until her fiction was in a current issue, she might have missed the chance to thoroughly enjoy the experience. Publishers don't always deliver on their promises, but if you celebrated getting the contract, then the celebration is one thing a reneging publisher can't take back.

Which brings us to my final and most important reason for celebrating a success. It's fun. It feels good.

Celebrations entail a festive break from the routine. If you're able to be festive by yourself, then it's possible to have a solo celebration. You can break the routine by spending money on yourself that you wouldn't ordinarily spend. I've met writers who set aside a proportion of any writing earnings as mad money, to be spent in celebration. If you can't afford that approach, though, there are always inexpensive ways to treat yourself. Devon Monk celebrated her first short-story sale by buying a five-dollar silver ring. At the same time, she bought a second ring "to earn," a ring that she wore as a reminder that if she could sell one story, she could sell another.

For most of us, though, celebrations have to be social to really count. That doesn't mean a party, necessarily. As with my friend who sold to *Playboy,* another friend, Dianna Rodgers, celebrated by calling friends and family . . . except for her mother. "It was an erotic story, after all," Dianna says, "and even though I had been married for seven years and worked with sex offenders for fifteen, my mother doesn't want to think that I know anything about sex."

Celebratory phone calls are great, but I love a party. If I'm nominated for an award that features a banquet, the whole weekend of the event is a party. Whether I win or lose when the envelopes are opened, the evening is in my honor, in the honor of all the nominees. And the celebration may begin long before the official event when friends celebrate with me closer to home. I didn't win the Edgar Allan Poe Award I was nominated for, but at a party the week before the banquet, one of my friends gave me a cardboard crown decorated with fake jewels, my name, and the title of my story. I've kept that crown. A private emblem of recognition like that can be, in its own way, as wonderful as the Official Award. I know quite a few nominees whose friends gave them, before or after the awards event, some homemade prize that was meant to say, "Whatever the result, you're *our* winner."

Writers have I-Sold-My-Novel parties. Sara Backer's first novel sold to Penguin, so penguins were the featured decoration at her celebration. The cake was a penguin cake. Men were encouraged to come dressed like penguins—in tuxedos, that is.

Other writers wait until the book is published. At a publication party, you can show off copies of the book and maybe even sell and sign a few. A publication party isn't just another book signing, though. You may sign your book at many events to come. This is more special. The book has its debut only once.

At Sarah Cowie's publication party, the cake was decorated to look like her book cover. In her case, friends threw the party for her. If my friends don't organize the fete, though, I've learned not to be shy about doing it myself. Sometimes they buy the champagne, and sometimes I buy it myself. What's memorable is the celebration, not who paid for or organized it.

Celebrations may also take place on a very small social scale, just you and one other person. When one of her friends finishes a book, Nina Kiriki Hoffman presents him or her with a big cookie. Christina F. York, whose husband J. Steven York also writes, says that the rule in their house is, "Sell a book, you get a lobster." Or, more precisely, you are entitled to go out to dinner and order anything on the menu. In both cases, the celebration is for a party of two.

Some writers celebrate every milestone, even those that they have passed before, such as selling a novel when they have sold several previously. Kris Rusch and Dean Smith, on the other hand, celebrate only those achievements that are firsts. They have sold dozens of novels between them under a variety of bylines. Another novel sale wouldn't be worthy of a celebration unless it was in a new genre.

Not every writer celebrates. Ray Vukcevich says that when he sold his first novel, *The Man of Maybe Half a Dozen Faces,* "it somehow felt like a death in the family. Not exactly. It felt like a huge life change that I really didn't want to talk about because I didn't want to hear how sorry everyone was, no matter that people wouldn't be sorry; they'd be just the opposite—happy happy happy. There would be balloons! And noise-makers. Cookies and ice cream. But then what about afterward?"

Not celebrating is an impermeable defense against the certain let-down that comes right after the party or the possible letdown that happens if your career doesn't develop as you had hoped. Other barriers to celebration are self-doubt, the envy of others, and other troubling responses that others might have to your celebration.

If self-doubt leaves you unconvinced that you deserve the sale, the award, or the grant, then you won't feel much like celebrating. If you have your celebration with friends, half of whom mutter under their breath the whole time that you must have slept with the judges, it's reasonable not to want to repeat the experience. The same goes for having a family member co-opt your celebration. The mother of one writer (I'll call the writer Sophie) was in the habit of stealing her daughter's limelight. If Sophie accomplished something, it was a reflection of how like her mother Sophie was, and the mother would want everyone to know that the achievement was hers as much as Sophie's. In a sense, Sophie wasn't allowed to have accomplishments on her own, so why celebrate them?

I have some responses to each of these reasons for not celebrating, but of course it isn't *necessary* to celebrate. It's not as if the desire to avoid celebration needs a cure. But if missing the party or being unable to enjoy the party bothers you, here are some things to consider.

The letdown that comes after a big exciting celebration is one of those things that some of us are more prone to than others. As a child, I thought Christmas afternoon was agony. All that buildup, opening the windows day by day on the advent calendar, shaking the boxes under the tree . . . all the glee of tearing paper Christmas morning. And then the mess that Mom wanted cleaned up *now*. The toys had been played with and were just toys. Desire turned out to be bigger than ful-fillment. Outside, it got dark early. Dark and cold.

If you know what I'm talking about and are similarly afflicted as an adult, then maybe the celebrations that will give you the most joy and the least letdown are the small ones. Instead of a party with a dozen friends, take a different friend to lunch for each of three days, for example.

I've found that the best medicine for envying other writers is to dis-cover what you admire about them or their work. Well and good, but the envy others feel toward you is beyond your control. However, you can celebrate with those friends who are least likely to express envy. Here's an observation from social psychology. We want to think well of our friends, but we all have hungry egos. We have a bias toward thinking that we are better than our friends, and this bias conflicts with the norm of equality in friendship. We're not *supposed* to think of ourselves as better. The solution that people tend to work out is this: We grant our friends superiority in whatever is most important to them. We reserve superiority for ourselves in whatever matters most to us. My friend Alan Clark is both a painter and a writer. I am perfectly comfortable with acknowledging that he's a better visual artist than I'll ever be, but I consider myself the better writer. If evidence arises that Alan is actually a better writer than I am, I'm going to get cranky. I may say something envious and catty.

Lucky is the writer whose writer friends can tolerate or even enjoy his successes. Some groups of writers see the success of one as enhancing the prestige of the group. But if your writer friends envy your successes, then maybe you could cultivate friendships with artists who work in different media. That way, when the painter wins a grant, the rest of the group—the sculptor, the dancer, and the writer—can all party with her without a trace of envy.

A similar solution holds if your family co-opted or otherwise poisoned your celebrations in the past. Don't tell them. Don't celebrate with them. Yes, it's painful that they withheld something from you at another time in your life. But you can nourish yourself now.

Celebrating, like so much in the writing life, like so much in any life, is full of risk. I was once pretty timid about celebration. I didn't want my trophy to get scratched because I might never get another one. I didn't want to spend the money on champagne. But great risks attend great rewards. A trophy doesn't belong wrapped up in a towel in my suitcase, safe. It ought to be with me at the party where, yes, it might get scratched or broken. I've found that the more I treat celebrations as a potlatch—that is, the more I risk or give away—the more confidence and joy return to me.

Does your champagne glass need refilling?

That silly hat really does look great on you.

Hand me the matches. It's time for some fireworks.

34
Getting Away from It All

One key difference between writing and most "normal" jobs is that most writers don't ever take a full vacation from their writing. Oh, they may pack up and head to Mexico, but while they're taking in the Caribbean sun they're also collecting information, mulling ideas, considering titles and opening lines, and maybe even scribbling down the odd paragraph on the beach. My wife already knew what she was getting into when she married me, but I managed to drive the point home by taking a medical parasitology text along on our honeymoon. I was researching a short story that I would have to write on our return. So there we were, lying in hammocks at a Cozumel resort, drinking piña coladas, when I looked up from my book to tell her adoringly: "Malaria is so *elegant!*"

No, writers don't really get vacations, but I'm not complaining. I can lie in a hammock at a tropical resort, and by golly, that's my job! Or part of my job, anyway. It's not a bad racket. Indeed, early in my career the whole notion of a vacation *from* writing would have seemed very strange to me. If "vacation" and "writing" occurred in the same thought, it was because I was scheming to get a vacation *for* writing. A weekend without other responsibilities or distractions might be time enough for a short story. I fantasized about sabbaticals at the family cabin for novel writing. I applied for (and never received) residencies at writers' colonies where I could work for two weeks or a month without having to even cook for myself. Now the thing I most wanted to do all those years is the very thing that I am actually doing for work, full time. Every weekday, the writing is my first priority. I am doing what I love.

Even so, I value writing vacations, and I recommend them. I recommend getting away from it all even to those writers who currently struggle to find writing time, who squeeze in an hour during the commute, who set aside one weekend a month for the novel, who look ahead longingly to the wide-open writing days of retirement.

Taking a break may not be necessary for writers, but it sure feels good. Doing the same thing in the same place in the same way all the time gets monotonous even if you love what you're doing. And monotony is draining. Additionally, a respite from your usual writing place and habits may bring you to a very different place in your work, resulting in novels or stories that are different from what you'd get by hewing to the old routine.

What I mean by "taking a break," though, may be a bit different from what nonwriters mean. Remember, I'm a man who spent part of his honeymoon studying up on tapeworms. My notions of taking a break fall into ten categories:

1. Monastic retreat
2. Busman's holiday
3. Staff retreat
4. Hermitage
5. Break in expectations
6. Road trip
7. Artist date
8. Sabbatical
9. Coffee break
10. Nap

Monastic Retreat: Writing with Writers

Just as monks gather in a community of spirit, this sort of writing retreat brings writers together in a community of writing. Writing colonies are monastic retreats, usually mixing private time for work with some community time for breaking bread, sharing the day's pages, and talking.

Here in Oregon, there's an organization called the Oregon Writers Colony. The colony owns a large house in Rockaway Beach on the coast, a four-hour drive from Eugene. Once or twice a year Jerry Oltion arranges for Eugene writers to rent the place for a weekend. Our time together includes some socializing, especially on the first night. Very soon, however, all the participants get down to work. Most of us write in the big common room, though there are a couple of choice spots upstairs overlooking the beach.

We work. And we work. There are some breaks away from our computers. We cook communal meals (stone soup is a tradition) and socialize some more around the food. Between meals and in breaks in the weather—remember, this is Oregon—two or three of us at a time may drift off for walks on the beach, sometimes to talk and sometimes to just stretch our legs and watch the waves. But even when some of us are on the beach, others are back at the house writing. In fact, since we all keep very different hours, there is almost always someone writing at any given time. When I get up to start my morning stint at the keyboard, Nina Kiriki Hoffman is wrapping up the night's work and getting ready to turn in.

There are other groups that use the Colony House for weekend retreats, but the Eugene writers seem to be the most productive. In the main room, there's a bookshelf for magazines and books containing work written at the house, and most of them are by Eugene writers. Probably a large part of what makes these weekends so productive for us is the assumption that we're going on retreat to *work*. That assumption is powerful. The example of all those other writers at work is also powerful, as is the example of the finished books on the shelf. And there is overt social pressure, too. People who talk more than they write are encouraged to take the conversation outside—often an unpleasant prospect, since these weekends are usually so rainy. (Oregon, remember?) Delinquents usually get back to their keyboards.

On the last night of these weekends, participants read their completed work. If seeing others at work is a good social motivator, it's even more powerful to know that everyone else will have a story or chapter or article to read at the end of the weekend. You want to have one, too.

At the end of a Colony House retreat, I paradoxically feel that I have worked very hard and have had a weekend off. I return to my writing desk the next Monday with enthusiasm.

It's not necessary to drive four hours or rent an enormous house for this kind of retreat, though it is a good idea to get out of town and to go someplace without television or other distractions. A rustic, inexpensive cabin with three other writers would probably do the trick. But don't confuse a monastic retreat with a family vacation. With a group of any size, but especially if the group is small, anyone who comes along but doesn't write is going to be a bad example at best.

Busman's Holiday: Getting Paid (Twice) to Write

The term *busman's holiday* comes from the legendary bus driver whose vacation from driving a city bus was to drive a tour bus. If you can do the work you'd do anyway, but get paid for doing it in an attractive setting, that's a superb writing vacation.

For me, a busman's holiday usually means teaching a writing class and writing when the students write. Two summers ago, for example, I taught two weekend seminars. At each seminar, I lectured on Friday and early Saturday, then gave my students a writing assignment to be completed on Saturday afternoon and evening. Sunday morning, we read our work aloud to the group.

For each of these seminars, I didn't just loaf while my students were fulfilling the writing assignment. I wrote alongside them. I always feel a little extra motivating pressure to turn out a good story when I'm teaching a class. I may not always write the best story of the weekend, but I don't want to be shown up completely! Two of my best stories have been written, or at least started, as assignments for one of my writing classes. One thing that contributes to the success of these stories is that by the time I begin writing on Saturday, I know my students enough that I'm writing with them in mind as my audience. I may include or exclude details to please or excite that small group of readers.

Part of the fun of writing in these seminars is the opportunity to double-dip. Of those two summer stories, one sold the day after the seminar and the other is still circulating. If both stories sell, I will have nearly doubled my fees from teaching these classes.

As with the monastic retreat, I go home after such a weekend feeling fired up and eager to get back to work on Monday.

Teaching may be the easiest way for a writer to have a busman's holiday, but there are other ways to combine an interesting experience with an opportunity to write. I'm looking into the possibilities of leading tour groups out of the country for writing/research excursions. I might not actually teach, but just provide an itinerary and leadership to a group that would write as they toured. And I would write along with them.

What other sorts of busman's holidays are possible? Well, what's your day job? How could you combine it with writing original fiction, or with both travel and fiction? If you can't see how to combine a work-related escape with drafting fiction, perhaps you can at least combine doing your work with research for your writing.

Staff Retreat: Remembering What You're About

At a conventional staff retreat, people who work together spend a few days away from the job to get to know each other better, to engage in "team building" exercises, and to look at the big picture of what they do so that they can make long-range plans for their shared mission.

Writers usually think of their efforts as solitary struggles and solitary achievements. To some extent, that's true. It's also true, however, that we write with other people around us and that our struggles and achievements touch more lives than ours alone. Anyone who has a stake in your success, collaborates with you, or simply is a like-minded fellow traveler can join you on a staff retreat for some mutual support.

If you think that you're a team of one, consider the loved ones who have a stake in your writing. A staff retreat might mean time away with your spouse. When Holly and I lived in Colorado, we used to spend one week every year at a resort in Pagosa Springs. We played racquetball, hiked, and read . . . the usual quiet vacation activities. But we also saw this week as our annual staff retreat. Away from the little details of our lives back in Boulder, we could step back and ask ourselves illuminating questions. What, if anything, is missing from our lives, from our relationship to each other? What do we think "the big picture" consists of? What would an ideal day be like for each of us? What would we contribute to the world if we had unlimited resources? What accomplishments would we like to look back on in five years? Ten years? At the end of our lives?

Questions like these helped us to shape goals for our long-range planning. We came up with ways that we could assist each other in pursuing our goals, and we articulated the big dreams that might serve more as stars to steer by than as actual goals.

Collaborators whom you work with now or would like to work with in the future might well benefit from a team-building retreat. I'd love to have a days-long conversation sometime with the writers, artists, game designers, publishers, and other creative people who live here in Eugene. What does each of us want from our work? Even if we aren't working actively with one another now, what can we do to support one another's efforts? Are there unexpected ways in which we might collaborate?

Of course, your team doesn't have to consist of people who might collaborate. When I think of some of the other freelancers and small-business operators I know in various fields, I think that there's a lot we might teach each other in a retreat. You don't have to have goals in common to benefit from talking about the big picture and doing some long-term planning. My neighbor David, who is in the spice business, might be able to give me a fresh perspective on my own big picture simply because his business and mine are so different.

It's possible to have these discussions in a series of weekly or monthly meetings at home, but meetings in the midst of ordinary life rarely yield the kind of focus and free thinking that a few days away from home can foster.

Hermitage: Hiding Out

Getting away from it all can sometimes mean Making It All Go Away. For that, you can become a hermit.

As I've mentioned in other chapters, you can practice hermitage at home. Stock the refrigerator for the weekend. Unplug the TV, the radio, the phone, the computer modem, and everything else that connects you with the outside world. Vanish into your office. If someone knocks, don't answer. Several of my friends do this as a book deadline approaches, and they can pile up a tall stack of finished pages in two or three days.

To be a hermit, it helps if you live alone. But if the people under your roof are part of the life you need seclusion from (however much you love them), then you can always try being a hermit elsewhere. When Wil McCarthy had a novel deadline and found too many distractions at home, he packed up his pipe, his smoking jacket, and his laptop. At a bed-and-breakfast close to home, he found the solitude that he needed—and a bit of pampering, too.

Break in Expectations: Escaping into the New

Everything that you publish establishes reader expectations for what you will do next. If you've written conventionally plotted hard science fiction stories for ten years, then when readers see your byline they expect a science fiction story with a conventional plot and real science. And editors develop those same expectations.

There are lots of reasons to continue to do what you've always done for the audience you've always addressed. You know how to do it. If readers enjoy reading what you've always written, some of them might stop reading you if they found you were now doing something different.

As I said in the beginning, vacations may not be necessary. But they feel good. It's refreshing, if a little scary, to try things you've never tried before. That includes vacations into new and risky realms of your creative imagination.

I recently heard Marvin Bell, the poet laureate of Iowa, speaking before an audience of writers. "Be reckless," Bell told them. "Shock and disappoint your friends." This is good advice, because the expectations of others eventually become a sort of prison. If you're going to remain free to do whatever you want to do as a writer, it's helpful to knock that wall down every so often.

Also, trying to write things that you don't know how to write is instructive even if you never do get the hang of writing for children or plotting a mystery. You get to reexperience the beginner's mind, the freshness of being naive. Sometimes you can carry some of that freshness back to the work that is expected of you.

Road Trip: Triggering Your Imagination

I've heard it said that anyone who survives adolescence has enough to write about for a lifetime. That may be true. I think it's possible to write a rich variety of stories out of a limited experience of the world. However, writing out of varied experience is more fun.

In Richard Hugo's book about writing poetry, *The Triggering Town*, he suggested that although we know our own hometown best, we can write about it evocatively only through the screen of a town that is merely like ours. He reasoned that we know too much about the history of our home place and have too many emotional reactions to sort out, but if we go and look at a town that is similar to ours, our impressions are more superficial and stable, and therefore limited enough that we can make art out of them without wallowing in the complicating details of fact. We have to get away from our hometown in order to see a simplified version of it.[1]

Going away from your usual turf, even if you go just a short distance down the road to the first place where you're a stranger, is a way of seeing with fresh eyes.

When I lived in Wisconsin I sometimes drove twenty miles from home to write in a small-town library or a coffee shop. Just being a writer in a different location, sitting in an unfamiliar place, and looking at the faces of strangers was fun. But even better was making the trip into an assignment: I would find a story idea in this town, or I would find a solution to a problem I was having with a story. The solution might come from an overheard conversation or from the inscription on the town Civil War monument.

Hugo's book includes a list of assumptions that he might apply to a triggering town, statements such as: "The mayor is so beloved and kind elections are no longer held" or "It is not on any map." That is, he would make up things about the town while he was looking at it and eventually craft a poem by combining his inventions with his observations.

A road trip is an opportunity to see the world, remember some of the truth about it, make up lies, and have fun knocking these things around to either generate a new story or to add something to a story you already have in progress.

Artist Date: Feeding Your Heart

Here at last is an example of getting away and not writing or talking writing. An artist date is a vacation, short or long, from your ordinary life.[2] The object here is to feed your heart.

What is it that makes your heart sing? What stirs you? What brings you alive the way you want your writing to bring others alive? Seek it out.

The conventional artist date is just what it sounds like: a date. You dress up and go to the art museum, the museum of natural history, a poetry reading, a movie. You go for a walk in the arboretum. You get out your telescope and hunt comets.

An artist date can also be much longer, an artist vacation. If you've written for twelve years about space travel but have never seen a shuttle launch, go to Canaveral. If steam locomotives turn you on, take a trip with stops at train museums, or take a ride on the nearest tourist short line and see if you can talk to the crew and the hostler.

Don't confuse this with research. It's fine to travel to gather background for a project that you're thinking about writing. But an artist date, for an evening or for a week, is about seeking out things that excite you even before you know what to do with them.

On a short-term artist date, it's a good idea to go by yourself at least some of the time. This can be hard to justify if you have too little private time with your partner as it is, but going alone will let you pay full attention to what excites you and what *you* want to do. The artist's vacation may be even harder to pursue by yourself, but you can always take a vacation that incorporates some artist dates in it. That is, you and your loved ones may travel to Baltimore together, but you may send them off to another attraction while you spend the day at the B&O Railroad Museum.

Whether you abide by it or not is up to you, but my own rule is that reading doesn't count as an artist date, even if I'm reading something that feeds my heart. Reading, even if I'm reading far afield of my usual tastes or am reading for pure pleasure, is not ever a vacation for me. It's always an aspect of my work.

Sabbatical: Getting Away from Words

Like the religious observance of the Sabbath from which it gets its name, a sabbatical is a period of rest. Academics often get a sabbatical leave for a term or a year after they get tenure. Ministers and other religious leaders may take a sabbatical year away from the daily distractions of leading a congregation. In either case, the sabbatical is intended for reflection and education. It's not really time off from the job, but rather a period of concentrating on the more thoughtful and solitary aspects of academic or religious work.

Writing is already a thoughtful and solitary pursuit; a writer's sabbatical consists of an even deeper silence. It is a period in which the writer does not write, does not research, does not read, and does not oblige herself to think about writing.

I write every day, and I advise other writers to do the same. If I miss a day, then it can be hard to get started again. The more time that passes since I last wrote, the harder it is to get back to the keyboard. Even so, I think that an enforced period of not writing is sometimes exactly the sort of rest I need.

George R. R. Martin once observed that writing is the only job where you don't know you're getting a day off until you've taken it. If I've been pushing hard for a while and feel exhausted, if I'm no longer having fun, then I may find that I just don't get around to starting my writing day. I feel guilty when I get a day off like that. It feels much better, when I notice that I'm not having any fun, to declare a day of rest in advance.

A sabbatical of several weeks can be a reward for making a big push to get a novel in by its deadline, or for any other big writing accomplishment. If you write full time and can't afford the time off, consider the possibility that sabbatical time doesn't have to be time without work. It's just time away from your usual work. You can do some manual labor for a while, working your body while your mind rests.

At one time when I was feeling depressed, I didn't write for several weeks, but I sculpted little faces out of oven-bake plastic clay and made them into ornamental pins. That wasn't an intentional sabbatical, but I enjoyed it so much that I scheduled two weeks in the following year to do it on purpose. Making nonverbal art is a way for me to rest and recover yet be productive.

Coffee Break: Letting Go

Sometimes time off is just time off. And time off can make you more productive, especially if you're putting in a long stint of writing. Four fifty-minute periods of writing with ten-minute breaks in between may yield just as many words as four hours chained to the desk, and they'll certainly result in your feeling more enthusiastic about a fifth hour of work. And if you stop for thirty seconds in the middle of each of those writing periods to shake out your hands, stand up, and stretch, you may save yourself the later distraction of aching joints and muscles.

That doesn't necessarily mean, though, that you should set a timer to interrupt your work every fifty minutes. One of the things I love about writing is getting caught up in "flow"—being fully engaged in my work scene by scene, sentence by sentence, so that when I do finally break out of the spell, several hours have flown. Little breaks to rest body and mind are good for your productivity, but it's also good to be lost in the work. Like so much else, it's good to find a balance.

I feel entitled to take breaks. I try to remind myself to address any aches and pains that develop as I write. And sometimes I do set a timer to remind myself to stop and relax. But I also feel entitled to ignore the timer and keep writing when the spell is on and I don't want to break it.

Some of us are equipped with Internal Puritans whose job is to keep us working, working, working. Work is good, but a guilty relationship with work is not.

For a long time, I've had difficulty taking what most people would call a "real" vacation without a twinge of guilt. A writer's work is never done, and I can't easily set aside my ambitions for a week. Writers tend to carry their work with them wherever they go, even if it's only carried in their heads. There's no escaping this, but it should be possible to escape the *obligation* to work while away. That's hard for me. Because I've always fought the temptation to do nothing, the idea of intentionally "doing nothing" for days on end makes me anxious and, paradoxically, unproductive in the days leading up to the vacation. This is a problem I haven't yet resolved, but I think that the resolution may come in thinking of vacations as extended coffee breaks: something essential to maintaining my productivity the rest of the time. That may at last be a way to satisfy my own Internal Puritan.

Nap: *Really* Letting Go

There really is such a thing as a power nap. If my eyelids are drooping after lunch, then a half-hour snooze followed by half an hour of work will almost always be more productive than an hour of somnambular writing. A nap can also create some distance from the morning's work so that I can be more critical, more willing to see where I need to revise.

It's a shame, really, that I feel the need to justify taking a nap or any other sort of break. Lin-Chi, the Chinese Zen master, wrote, "When hungry, eat your rice; when tired, close your eyes. Fools may laugh at me, but wise men know what I mean." That should be justification enough.

But if it isn't, there is this: Taking a break feels good. As I said in the beginning, that alone is reason enough to moderate the drive to be writing all the time. Whether you take a sabbatical, a busman's holiday, a nap, or some other form of escape, getting away from it all can help you continue to feel that the writer's life is the life you want to live.

35

The Difficulty of Ending

When I first started writing stories, I had absolutely no difficulty with declaring them finished and putting them into the mail. After all, I was still a teenager and everything I did was perfect. I wrote as fast as I could move my hand across the page, typed up the manuscript (irritated that I could not type any faster), and shot it off to an editor. I had little doubt that an eager acceptance letter would appear in my mailbox the next week.

Many of us start out with tremendous ego and not much skill.

After years of rejection, after workshops and literature classes and extensive reading have taught me all the ways that a piece of writing can go wrong, I have more skill and at least a little less ego. I know that when I think excitedly, *Oh, this is perfect,* as I write, I am probably wrong. Fortunately, my impulse to rush things into the mail lingers in a weakened form. I don't immediately declare work finished and toss it into the mail, but I still have a healthy compulsion to kick my manuscripts out into the world.

Even so, I understand the two great challenges to ending a piece of writing: declaring it finished and sending it out. I'm not immune to the fears that make those acts challenging.

Declaring a manuscript finished means that you are giving up control. Any problems that are present in the finished version will be there for the editor to find. They may be the basis for rejection. And if the editor *buys* the manuscript, thinks it's perfect, and puts it right into production (a fond dream that is almost never realized), then with every subsequent step of production you'll have fewer and fewer opportunities to fix errors. You can't add a whole new chapter to the copyedited text. Your editor will disown you if you add whole sentences to the galley proofs. Declaring the work finished is the first step in being stuck with what you've done.

And what have you done? At the beginning of your project you may have feared that your writing revealed uncomfortable truths about you, truths you aren't aware of but which are made glaringly obvious in the manuscript. That fear is magnified here at the end. The manuscript that might embarrass you isn't hypothetical any longer—you can hold it in your hands.

Sending out the manuscript involves the same fears, only now the possibly terrible manuscript isn't in your hands, but an editor's.

Remember, though, that declaring the work finished and sending it out are the final steps in a long sequence from which other would-be writers have already washed out. Only a fraction of those who want to write begin a manuscript. A fraction of those write it all the way through to the end. Of those writers, only a few will say, "This book is ready for the world." And the ones who follow this declaration with a trip to the post office are a rare and courageous breed.

Be courageous.

Perhaps it will help to remember that the longer and more intimidating your manuscript, the less perfection is possible and the more interpretation will be a matter of the reader's nature. A whole school of literary criticism, reader response, is founded on the notion that every reader processes the text in a new way. Your control is limited. Endless fussing is no insurance against your readers' inventions. Readers will see things that you didn't intend, including perhaps things that embarrass you because they are real shortcomings in your thinking, shortcomings that you won't know about until some reader discovers them for you. Imperfection and exposure might make you anxious, but there is no perfect protection against them. You have to let go and let the reader read.

Works of art are not so much finished as abandoned. Perhaps poems can be perfect. A short-short story might even be perfectible, as effective and enjoyable for one reader as the next. But novels and other book-length narratives are great rambling things that always contain some flaws. For works of any length, there comes a point when your continued tinkering won't improve the whole, but will just trade one set of problems for another.

Reworking the same almost-perfect piece can become a trap. I have met writers who take the same novel manuscript from this teacher to that one, always revising according to a different expert's advice and never writing anything new. I sometimes wonder if their fear is not so much of ending as of beginning. They don't want to face a blank page with its infinite possibilities and infinite possible problems. The manuscript that they worry endlessly is at least finite. They manage their anxiety by staying stuck on the familiar.

The answer to the difficulty of ending may lie in beginning something new.

And writing something new can help with the depression that, for some of us, often follows putting a book manuscript into the mail. I may be in high spirits when I hand the manuscript to the postal clerk, but by the time I exit the post office, I am bereft.

A novelist who sends off the book is, ironically, being cast out of the garden. When I write a novel, I think about it every day. The characters are my companions and I inhabit their world. Once the manuscript is finished and in the mail, their constructed reality continues for them but I'm stuck here in mundane reality. The playground is closed. My friends are gone.

I've learned to deal with this in two ways. One is to try to be like Anthony Trollope. He wrote two thousand words a day, and if one novel ended when he was only five hundred words into the day's work, he would write "Chapter One" at the top of a fresh sheet and begin a new novel. It may be a short story or essay that I begin, rather than another novel, but I feel better about sending off my novel if I'm already in the midst of some new writing that absorbs my attention. If you can't be with the characters you love, invent some characters to be with.

My second way of dealing with an exile is the opposite of what I just recommended. I barely write at all for a few days. I spend most of my time straightening up my office, doing yard work, rediscovering what the vacuum cleaner does. (It reveals that the living room rug is green.)

A literary magazine, *The Fessenden Review,* once sent me a contributor's check bearing this motto: *Sic pilum jactum est.* Thus is the javelin thrown. I have always taken this as a classical and classy way of saying Just Do It. At no other time is this advice more appropriate than when the work is finished and you are hesitating on the brink of sending it out.

Hold the javelin. Lean back.

With your whole body, *throw*.

Chapter 1

1. Thom Hartmann, *Attention Deficit Disorder: A Different Perception* (Grass Valley, California: Underwood, 1997).
2. Edward M. Hallowell and John J. Ratey, *Driven to Distraction: Recognizing and Coping With Attention Deficit Disorder From Childhood Through Adulthood* (New York: Simon & Schuster, 1995), 73.
3. Bruce Holland Rogers, "With His Own Wings," *Elf Magic* (New York: DAW, 1997).

Chapter 3

1. Kenneth Atchity, *A Writer's Time* (New York: Norton, 1995), 7.

Chapter 4

1. Richard Scarry, *Richard Scarry's Pig Will and Pig Won't: A Book of Manners* (New York: Random House, 1990). In reexamining the book, I found to my dismay that Pig Won't *is* reformed in the end. "And do you know what? He isn't Pig Won't anymore. He's Pig Me Too. And everybody likes him." Whatever the story of Scarry's Pig Won't, my personal Pig Won't remains unreformed and unrepentant.
2. Dean Koontz, *Writing Popular Fiction* (Cincinnati: Writer's Digest, 1972), 189.

Chapter 6

1. George Plimpton, editor, *The Writer's Chapbook* (New York: Viking, 1989), 230; and Jon Winokur, *Writers on Writing* (Philadelphia: Running Press, 1986), 85.
2. Plimpton, *The Writer's Chapbook*, 66.
3. *Ibid.*, 60.
4. *Ibid.*, 62.
5. *Ibid.*, 230.
6. John Poppy, "The Rite Stuff," *Men's Health*, July–August 1994: 84.
7. The metaphor of the one-inch frame is from Anne Lamott, *Bird by Bird* (New York: Anchor, 1995). My own one-inch frame has a cracked pane of glass as a reminder not only of narrow focus, but of the uncertain vision I have of any draft.

Chapter 7

1. Joseph Campbell with Bill Moyers, *The Power of Myth* (New York: Doubleday, 1988), 7.
2. Proverbs 1:26.

Chapter 9

1. J. A. Hobson and R. W. McCarley, "The brain as a dream state generator: An activation-synthesis hypothesis of the dream process," *American Journal of Psychiatry* 134 (1977): 1335–1348; and J. Allan Hobson, *The Dreaming Brain* (New York: Basic Books, 1988).

Chapter 10

1. Naomi Epel, *Writers Dreaming* (New York: Carol Southern, 1993), 33; and Clive Barker, "The Age of Desire," *The Inhuman Condition* (New York: Pocket, 2001).
2. Epel, *Writers Dreaming*, 9.
3. *Ibid.*, 214.
4. *Ibid.*, 102.
5. *Ibid.*, 201.
6. *Ibid.*, 30.
7. Michael Swanwick, "Writing in My Sleep," a series of nine features running in consecutive issues, *New York Review of Science Fiction* 30–38 (1991).

Chapter 11

1. Sherwin B. Nuland, *How We Die* (New York: Knopf, 1994).
2. Ernest Becker, *The Denial of Death* (New York: Free Press, 1973).
3. *Ibid.*, 36.
4. *Ibid.*, 88.
5. *Ibid.*, 87.
6. R. C. Bald, *John Donne: A Life* (New York: Oxford University Press, 1970), 529.
7. Carlos Castaneda, *Journey to Ixtlan: The Lessons of Don Juan* (New York: Simon & Schuster, 1972), 55.
8. Sören Kierkegaard, *The Sickness Unto Death* and *Fear and Trembling*, translated by Walter Lowrie (New York: Anchor, 1954), 175.
9. *Ibid.*, 174.
10. Becker, *The Denial of Death*, 173.

Chapter 12

1. Kevin Byrne, "Office Too Quiet? Try a Laugh Track," *Christian Science Monitor*, 26 October 1999.
2. Matt Braun, *How to Write Western Novels* (Cincinnati: Writer's Digest, 1988), 117.
3. Plimpton, *The Writer's Chapbook*, 65.
4. Winokur, *Writers on Writing*, 81.
5. Janet Asimov and Isaac Asimov, *How to Enjoy Writing: A Book of Aid and Comfort* (New York: Walker, 1987).

6. Winokur, *Writers on Writing*, 81.

7. Michael Armstrong, "One Skookum Little Office," *Bulletin of the Science Fiction and Fantasy Writers of America* 141 (spring 1999).

8. Annie Dillard, *The Writing Life* (New York: Harper & Row, 1989), 26.

9. Plimpton, *The Writer's Chapbook*, 52.

10. *Ibid.*, 61.

11. *Ibid.*, 61.

12. *Ibid.*, 50.

13. *Ibid.*, 63.

Chapter 14

1. Peter Elbow, "Metaphors for Priming the Pump," *Writing With Power* (New York: Oxford, 1981).

Chapter 15

1. Robert M. Pirsig, *Zen and the Art of Motorcycle Maintenance* (New York: William Morrow, 1999), 413.

2. Bill Henderson and André Bernard, *Pushcart's Complete Rotten Reviews and Rejections* (Wainscott, New York: Pushcart, 1998), 182.

3. *Ibid.*, 192.

4. *Ibid.*, 219.

5. *Ibid.*, 190, 259.

6. *Ibid.*, 229, 264, 227, 226.

7. *Ibid.*, 253.

Chapter 17

1. Plimpton, *The Writer's Chapbook*, 159.

2. *Ibid.*, 161.

3. Winokur, *Writers on Writing*, 117.

4. Plimpton, *The Writer's Chapbook*, 157.

5. James Patrick Kelly, "Brief Encounters: The Magazine Review," *New York Review of Science Fiction* 80 (1995): 17.

6. James Charlton, editor, *The Writer's Quotation Book* (New York: Penguin, 1981), 61.

7. Winokur, *Writers on Writing*, 120.

Chapter 18

1. N. C. Andreasen, "Creativity and mental illness: Prevalence rates in writers and their first-degree relatives," *American Journal of Psychiatry* 144 (1987): 1288-1292.

2. R. L. Richards, D. K. Kinney, I. Lunde, and M. Benet, "Creativity in manic-depressives, cyclothymes, and their normal first-degree relatives: A preliminary report," *Journal of Abnormal Psychology* 97 (1988): 281-288.

3. L. B. Alloy and L. Y. Abramson, "Judgement of contingency in depressed and non-depressed students: Sadder but wiser?" *Journal of Experimental Psychology* 108 (1979): 441–485; and J. S. Albright and M. C. Henderson, "How real is depressive realism? A question of scales and standards," *Cognitive Therapy & Research* 19 (1995): 589–609. Recent studies have called into question the validity of depressive realism, including D. Dunning and A. L. Story, "Depression, realism, and the overconfidence effect: Are the sadder wiser when predicting future actions and events?" *Journal of Personality & Social Psychology* 61 (1991): 521–532; and J. Kistner, M. Balthazor, S. Risi, and C. David, "Adolescents' perceptions of peer acceptance: Is dysphoria associated with greater realism?" *Journal of Social & Clinical Psychology* 20 (2001): 66–81.
4. Mark D. Litt, "Self-efficacy and perceived control: Cognitive mediators of pain tolerance," *Journal of Personality & Social Psychology* 54 (1988): 149–160.

Chapter 19

1. D. G. Dutton and A. P. Aron, "Some evidence for heightened sexual attraction under conditions of high anxiety," *Journal of Personality & Social Psychology* 30 (1974): 510–517.
2. S. Schachter and J. Singer, "Cognitive, social, and physiological determinants of emotional state," *Psychological Review* 69 (1962): 379–399.
3. J. M. Olson and M. Ross, "False feedback about placebo effectiveness: Consequences for the misattribution of speech anxiety," *Journal of Experimental Social Psychology* 24 (1988): 275–291.

Chapter 20

1. S. I. Hayakawa, *Symbol, Status, and Personality* (New York: Harcourt, 1963), 37.

Chapter 21

1. Hayakawa, *Symbol, Status, and Personality,* 122.
2. *Ibid.,* 131–132.
3. Gillian Kendall, "Protection," *The Sun* 268 (April 1998).
4. Julia Cameron, *The Artist's Way* (New York: Tarcher, 1992), 3.

Chapter 22

1. Barbara Sher with Annie Gottlieb, *Wishcraft: How to Get What You Really Want* (New York: Ballantine, 1983), 91.

Chapter 24

1. Alison Clement, "Trudy Deere Goes to Heaven," *The Sun* 267 (March 1998). The story was an excerpt from Clement's novel, *Pretty Is as Pretty Does* (San Francisco: MacAdam/Cage, 2001).

Chapter 25

1. Paul Theroux, *Sir Vidia's Shadow: A Friendship across Five Continents* (New York: Houghton Mifflin, 1998).

Chapter 27

1. Leonard Bishop, *Dare to Be a Great Writer* (Cincinnati: Writer's Digest, 1988), 223.
2. Terry Gross radio interview of Donald Hall, *Fresh Air* (WHYY-FM Philadelphia), 25 April 1996.
3. Sophy Burnham, *For Writers Only* (New York: Ballantine, 1996), 55.

Chapter 31

1. Timothy Ray Miller, *How to Want What You Have: Discovering the Magic and Grandeur of Ordinary Existence* (New York: Avon, 1996).

Chapter 32

1. Rabbi Zusya is a historical figure (d. 1800), but his remark occurs as a Hasidic folktale with many variants.
2. Bovine Smoke Society (Peteso, Randy Fox, Thalia Ragsdale, Stephen Merritt, Cynthia Merritt, Jim Goad, and Alan M. Clark), *The Pain Doctors of Suture Self General* (Eugene, Oregon: Blue Moon, 1995).

Chapter 34

1. Richard Hugo, "The Triggering Town," *The Triggering Town* (New York: Norton, 1982).
2. The term *Artist Date* is from Cameron, *The Artist's Way*, 18.

Atchity, Kenneth. *A Writer's Time,* rev. ed. New York: Norton, 1995. Filled with useful, sometimes counterintuitive advice about story, publishing, Hollywood, and getting words on the page.

Bender, Sheila, and Christi Killien. *Writing in a New Convertible With the Top Down,* rev. ed. Hillsboro, Oregon: Blue Heron, 1997. A breezy exchange of letters between two writers who are keen observers of their own writing process.

Bradbury, Ray. *Zen in the Art of Writing.* Santa Barbara, California: Capra, 1989. Charming essays about being authentic and productive.

Brande, Dorothea. *Becoming a Writer.* Los Angeles: Tarcher, 1981. A reprint of the 1934 edition that remains thoroughly useful as a guide to overcoming inertia and fear.

Burnham, Sophy. *For Writers Only.* New York: Ballantine, 1994. Alternates pages of writers' quotations with the author's account of her own process, struggles, and path to mastery.

Cameron, Julia. *The Artist's Way.* Los Angeles: Tarcher, 1992. This volume in Tarcher's Inner Workbook series is useful to individual readers, but it has been enormously successful as a guide for groups of writers and other artists who seek to rediscover their creative fire.

Cornyn-Selby, Alyce P. *Procrastinator's Success Kit.* Portland, Oregon: Beynch Press, 1986. A useful workbook for exploring the psychological payoffs of procrastination.

Dillard, Annie. *The Writing Life.* New York: Harper, 1989. Dillard writes beautifully and engagingly about her work habits, her thought processes, and about the lifelong path of being a writer.

Epel, Naomi. *Writers Dreaming.* New York: Carol Southern, 1993. Interviews with twenty-six writers, including Stephen King, Amy Tan, and Maurice Sendak, about what they dream at night and how as writers they use those dreams.

Friedman, Bonnie. *Writing Past Dark.* New York: HarperCollins, 1993. Eight essays on meeting envy, fear, and even success along the writing path.

Goldberg, Natalie. *Writing Down the Bones.* Boston: Shambala, 1986. Perhaps the best-known book on writing-as-process and an excellent guide to cultivating spontaneity.

———. *Wild Mind.* New York: Bantam, 1990. More on writing-as-process, this time with writing exercises at the end of chapters, making them easier to find.

Henderson, Bill, and André Bernard. *Pushcart's Complete Rotten Reviews & Rejections.* Wainscott, New York: Pushcart, 1998. A compilation of awful things said about the work of writers who went on to prove the critics wrong. This book is an excellent antidote to rejection letters and other disappointments.

Johnstone, Keith. *Impro: Improvisation and the Theatre*. London: Faber and Faber, 1979. Although intended for actors, the chapters on spontaneity and narrative skills are useful to writers as well.

Keyes, Ralph. *The Courage to Write*. New York: Henry Holt, 1995. A comprehensive dissection of what writers fear, with varied and helpful prescriptions for soothing authorial anxieties.

Lamott, Anne. *Bird by Bird*. New York: Anchor, 1995. A very funny autobiographical account of one writer's fears, disappointments, and successes, with excellent advice on meeting such challenges.

Lerner, Betsy. *The Forest for the Trees*. New York: Riverhead, 2000. An editor-turned-agent's perspective on negotiating the psychological and practical pitfalls of writing.

Levoy, Gregg. *Callings: Finding and Following an Authentic Life*. New York: Harmony, 1997. An excellent guide to following one's true vocation. Because the author's own calling is as a writer and speaker, his personal examples are particularly illuminating for writers.

——. *This Business of Writing*. Cincinnati: Writer's Digest Books, 1992. A realistic and indispensable guide to many aspects of the freelance life, from setting the right goals to building a career.

MacShane, Frank. *The Life of Raymond Chandler*. New York: Dutton, 1976. A fascinating biography of a writer whose first serious efforts at fiction came when he was fifty-two years old.

Maisel, Eric. *A Life in the Arts*. New York: Tarcher, 1994. Maisel is a therapist who specializes in helping creative and performing artists. This expanded edition of *Staying Sane in the Arts* includes new exercises to help artists get out of their own way.

——. *Fearless Creating*. New York: Tarcher, 1995. A step-by-step workbook and guidebook through the obstacles that keep some artists from fulfilling their ambitions to create.

Sher, Barbara. *Wishcraft: How to Get What You Really Want*. New York: Ballantine, 1979. A practical, inspiring, and widely beloved guide to determining what you want in life and finding a realistic path to that goal.

Simon, Rachel. *The Writer's Survival Guide*. Cincinnati: Story Press, 1997. Wide-ranging advice about emotion, logistics, and community in the writing life.

Sinetar, Marsha. *Do What You Love and the Money Will Follow*. New York: Dell, 1989. Serves as an antidote to the advice that you shouldn't quit your day job.

——. *Work as a Spiritual Path*. Boulder, Colorado: Sounds True, 1992. An audiotape presentation about achieving the inner success that can lead to outer accomplishment.

Ueland, Brenda. *If You Want to Write*. Saint Paul, Minnesota: Graywolf, 1987. This reissue of a 1938 book is chatty and dated, but that somehow adds to its charm as Ueland exhorts writers to write with joyful abandon.